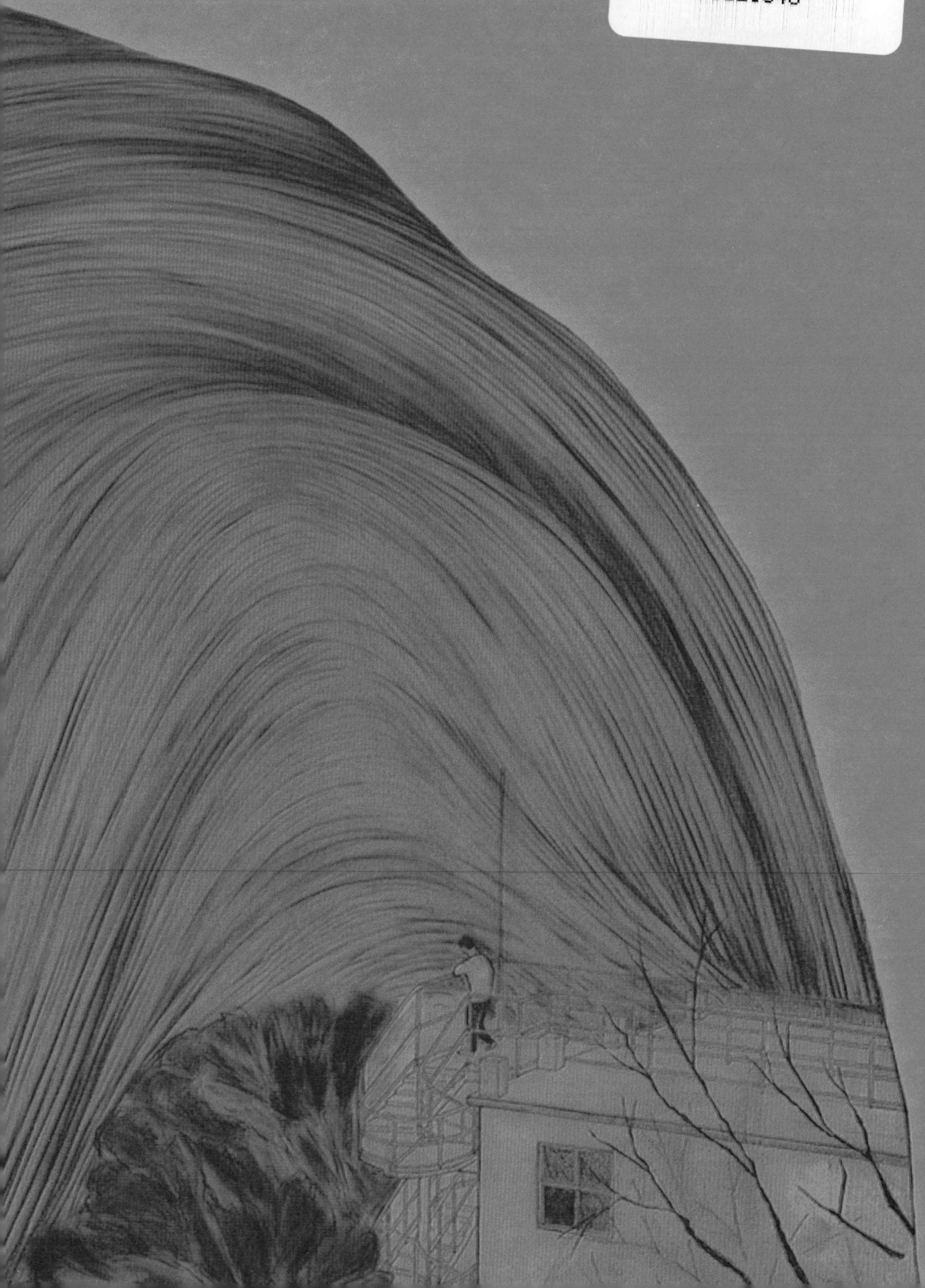

# The Library

*The Library*

© Chihoi, 2013

Introduction © Christian Gasser, 2013
Introduction translated from the French by Helge Dascher

Translations by Chihoi, edited by Andy Brown

#1 in the Conundrum International Imprint
Edited by Andy Brown
First Edition

Printed in Singapore by TWP

Chihoi would like to thank Son, Tak, Kongkee, Chi-Leung and Mom. Thanks to Dawei Charitable Foundation for the studio space all these years, and Andy of Conundrum Press for realizing this book

The publisher would like to thank Daniel at Les Éditions Atrabile

Some of these stories were published previously:
Summer and Father in *Still Life* (Wheatear Publishing, Chinese with English subtitles), 2003
Sorry, Canine, and The Sea in *À l'Horizon* (Atrabile, French), 2008
I'm with my Saint in *Lustfully Yours* (Hoolahoop Gallery, Chinese and English), 2009
The Library in *Canicola* (Italian), 2012
Borrowed Books appears here for the first time

Conundrum Press
Greenwich, Nova Scotia, Canada
www.conundrumpress.com

Conundrum Press acknowledges the financial support of the Canada Council for the Arts toward its publishing activities.

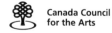

Canada Council    Conseil des Arts
for the Arts      du Canada

# The Library

## Chihoi

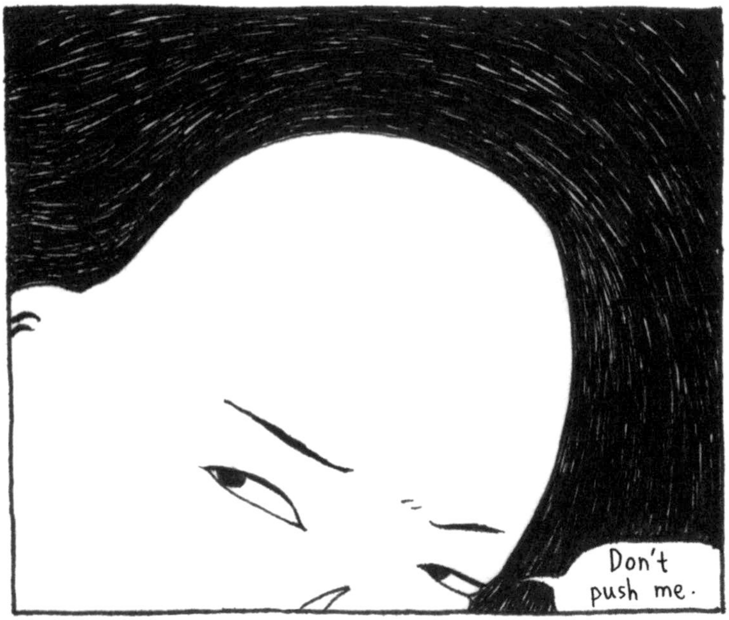
Don't push me.

# CHIHOI
# POET OF SILENCE

CHRISTIAN GASSER

*Translation by Helge Dascher*

When you first meet Chihoi Lee, he comes across as a polite, shy and somewhat frail young man who likes to think twice before he talks—until he catches you off guard with a sarcastic remark that seems at odds with his soft-spoken manner.

That was our impression of Chihoi after his first visit to Fumetto, the international comics festival in Lucerne, Switzerland, which celebrated Hong Kong comics with a major exhibition in 2000. Chihoi had brought along a few photocopied, self-published books and sketchbooks. The drawings were strikingly fine, simple, modest and natural, and the stories were equally refined, spare and poetic.

Since then, Chihoi has returned regularly to Europe. He travels from festival to festival, and wherever he goes, he strikes up friendships with European authors who share his sensibilities. He always has new books in his backpack—both his own and those of other Hong Kong artists. He shows them around and swaps them for alternative European comics that he brings back to Hong Kong to share with his friends.

It wasn't long before his comics began appearing in magazines and independent anthologies in France (*COMIX 2000, Stereoscomic*), Switzerland (*Strapazin, Bile Noire*), Italy (*Canicola*), Germany (*Orang*), Canada (*Spoutnik*) and elsewhere. Thanks to Chihoi, ties between the Hong Kong and European comics scenes have grown closer. Yet Chihoi himself has hardly changed over the years: he still looks like a boy, an eternal teenager with an enduring and contagious curiosity and enthusiasm.

Hong Kong is a fascinating, complex and contradictory city. It is China and the Commonwealth, Chinese culture and western capitalism. It's a vast market, a place of exchange for goods, people, ideas and cultures. It's a bulimic metropolis with a rapacious, frenetic appetite for consumption. Hong Kong is the crossroads of two continents, a hybrid space. Especially culturally.

Cut off from China after the establishment of the People's Republic of China in 1949, the British colony of Hong Kong went on to develop its own popular culture. We're most familiar with its movies—from Bruce Lee to John Woo to Wong Kar-Wai—but a similar evolution has marked its comics as well. While the leaders of the People's Republic used comics as educational and propaganda tools, artists in Hong Kong mixed Chinese manhua traditions with American and Japanese influences. They invented a tough and direct style that was suited to their stories about kung-fu, gangsters and sex. These comics, which had a certain charm when they first appeared in the 60s, peaked commercially in the late 70s. But when computers emerged as the dominant production tool, they became increasingly anonymous and uniform, and less interesting as well.

Born in 1977, Chihoi grew up with little exposure to comics. For one thing, comics were a luxury his parents could hardly afford. As well, an alliance of teachers, parents and media launched a virulent campaign in the 80s that denounced comics as fostering laziness and illiteracy. As a teen, Chihoi was drawn to French literature and European cinema. Bored by his Nutritional Sciences classes, he began sketching drafts of stories in the margins of his notebooks. In 1996, he stumbled across a comic by Lai Tat Tat Wing in the quarterly publication *Cockroach*. It was a shock, and Chihoi immediately recognized comics as his medium. A year later, just 20 years old, the self-taught artist published his first story in the second issue of *Cockroach*.

The Cockroach group, created in the mid 90s by Craig Au Yeung, was a free association of Hong Kong comics artists. They had one thing in common: they were all operating outside the mainstream. Craig Au Yeung, a globetrotter involved in countless projects, is known in Hong Kong not only as a comics artist, but also as a journalist and food critic, a radio host, a Scandinavian design importer and more. With tongue in cheek, he liked to explain the group's name by describing comics artists as the cockroaches of culture: little critters people "adore" but can never fully exterminate. Thanks to Craig's travels and especially to the artists' personal artwork and surprising stories, which were often suffused with a dark, surrealistic sarcasm, the nightmares of the Hong Kong cockroaches invaded Europe, comics festivals, specialty shops and magazines like *Strapazin*. It was a real discovery, and it was only natural for a few of the artists—including Craig, Chihoi and Hok Tak Yeung—to be included in *COMIX 2000*, the landmark anthology produced by the French publisher L'Association.

It's interesting to consider that Hong Kong's alternative artists draw on the same influences as their mainstream counterparts—manhua, manga and western comics—but take them in entirely different directions. Hong Kong's independent comics scene bridges east and west. The artists have absorbed the various influences and assimilated them into something new that escapes easy definition. This openness and diversity are also due to the fact that none of the artists can live on comics alone. All are involved in other trades: they are illustrators, graphic designers or website creators; they develop games and dolls; they create storyboards for movies; and, given the cost of living in Hong Kong, they don't refuse advertising contracts, either. These experiences enrich their approaches to narrative and their artwork. They also make the small world of independent comics in Hong Kong a rich, fertile and varied environment. So far, we've discovered only Lai Tat Tat Wing, Hok Tak Yeung and Chihoi—but Hong Kong has other surprises in store for us.

When Cockroach came to an end, Craig Au Yeung took a break from comics for a few years, and Chihoi emerged as his natural successor. He published a number of anthologies, including *Yummy Dragon* (two volumes in 2000 and 2001), to keep the scene from breaking up.

Chihoi is that rare breed of artist whose focus extends beyond his own work and personal career, and who puts as much energy into the work of others as his own. He knows that strength lies in numbers, and he stays in touch with authors, festivals and magazines the world over, promotes collaboration and exchange, organizes exhibitions and more. His commitment has made him a vital link between the independent scenes in Europe and Hong Kong.

When Craig returned to comics in 2005, he and Chihoi got together with Hok Tak Yeung, Sihak and Eric So to found the group Springrolllll. The concept is in the name, with its five "l"s representing each of its five members: spring rolls (the Chinese word has erotic connotations) are a popular snack around the world that you can fill any way you like and enjoy raw, boiled or fried. Which is how the five see their comics.

The Springrolllll authors tell stories of life in the gigantic, fast-paced and ever-changing city of Hong Kong, keeping a sharp eye on its transition from British rule to control by the Chinese motherland. They offer a close-up view of a chaotic, overpopulated, lively, noisy, tender and brutal metropolis. It's a personal and always surprising vision, with a corrosive humour that is sometimes macabre and often surrealistic and poetic.

Chihoi is an anomaly in the Hong Kong scene. He's neither a virtuoso like Hok Tak Yeung, nor a trenchant social commentator like Craig Au Yeung. When you talk about Hong Kong's current situation with Chihoi, his answers are clear but also cautious and ambivalent. He is grateful, he says, for the privilege of living in times as eventful and rich as these, but he is also apprehensive about the future: on the one hand, he worries that Hong Kong may lose its freedom under the authority of totalitarian China, and on the other he is critical of the excesses of unbridled capitalism to which the residents of Hong Kong sacrifice their quality of life. But he never thinks about leaving Hong Kong. Now more than ever, he says, it's critical to stay and be active. After a moment of silence, he adds that despite the current situation, he feels no obligation to talk about politics in his work. He is interested in inner lives. His own. And ours.

Chihoi is the poet of the everyday, the poet of small things, small gestures, silences. He is also the poet of the unseen, bringing the spirit of the dead or of a lost love back to life without surprising us. Chihoi tells stories about love and life, about heartache and death, with a finesse that makes ghosts and spirits seem real. They're sad stories, but Chihoi is a poet—he's not trying to bring us down, and he never gives in to easy sentimentality. He offers his stories with a melancholy smile, and lights them up with a faint but warm glow. His stories are disarmingly simple. He tells them with few words and a spare line, and he punctuates them, like his conversation, with pauses—moments of doubt and reflection that let readers enter into his work and grasp its meanings.

We need those moments because his stories aren't as simple as they first seem. Like life, they're open and complex and full of little contradictions, and they resonate long after you've turned the last page. That's because Chihoi is a poet and his stories ring true. Real inspiration comes from within, says Chihoi. That's why art is universal. And that's why Chihoi's comics have the ability to touch us all.

*Christian Gasser is, among other things, a writer, a journalist, the editor of* Strapazin *and the creator of numerous radio dramas and documentaries. His most recent book,* Blam! Blam! Und Du bist tot! (Bang! Bang! You're Dead!), *is a collection of short stories inspired by comics. He lives in Lucerne, Switzerland.*

# Summer

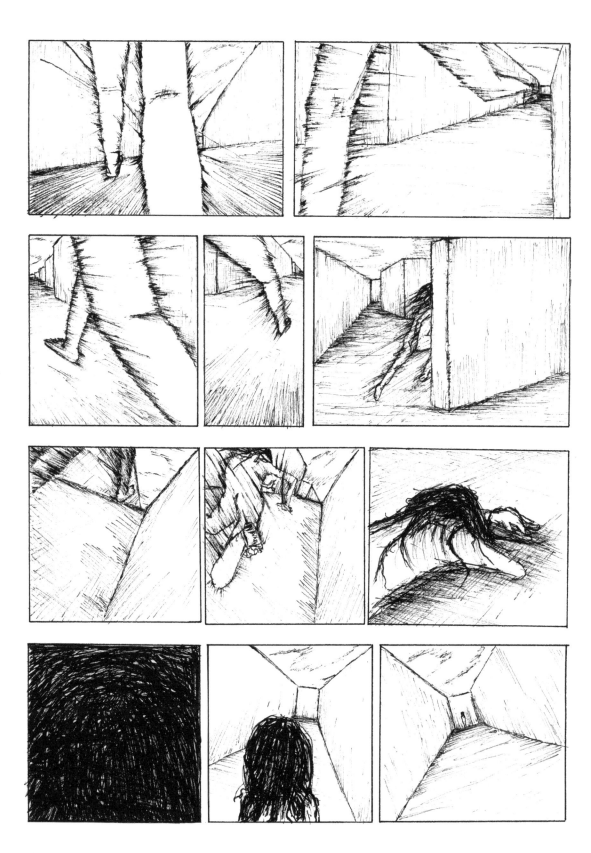

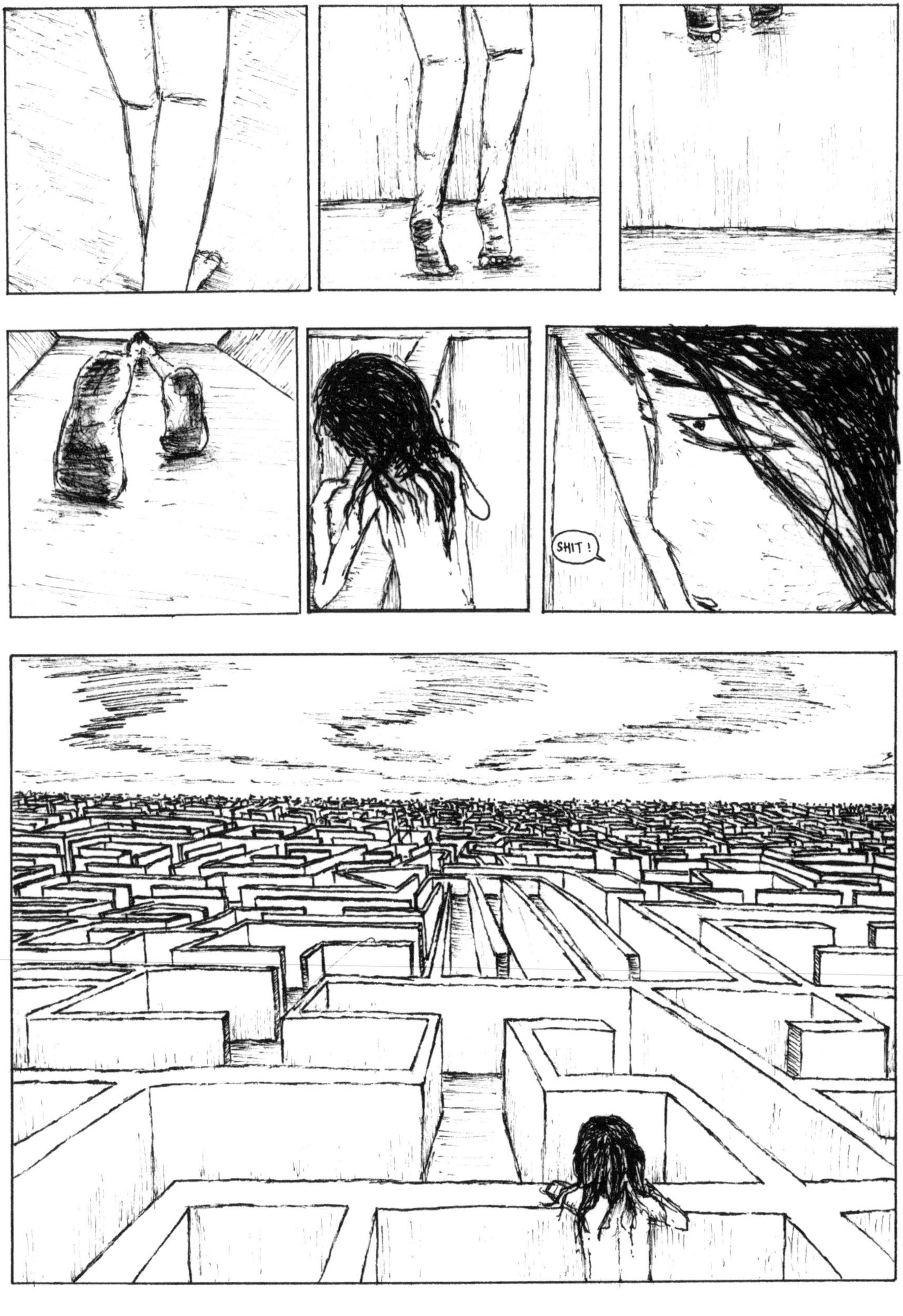
SHIT!

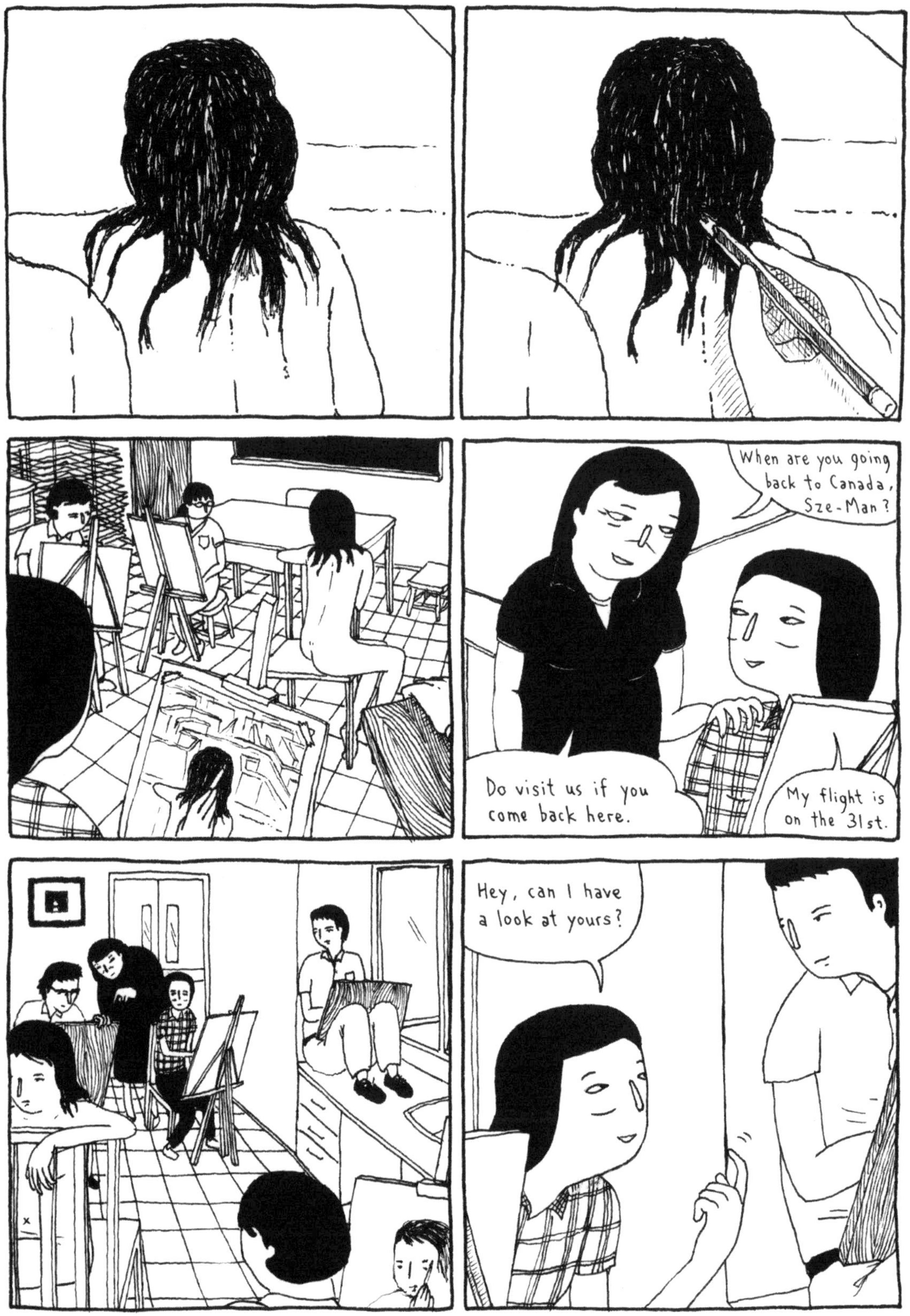
When are you going back to Canada, Sze-Man?
Do visit us if you come back here.
My flight is on the 31st.
Hey, can I have a look at yours?

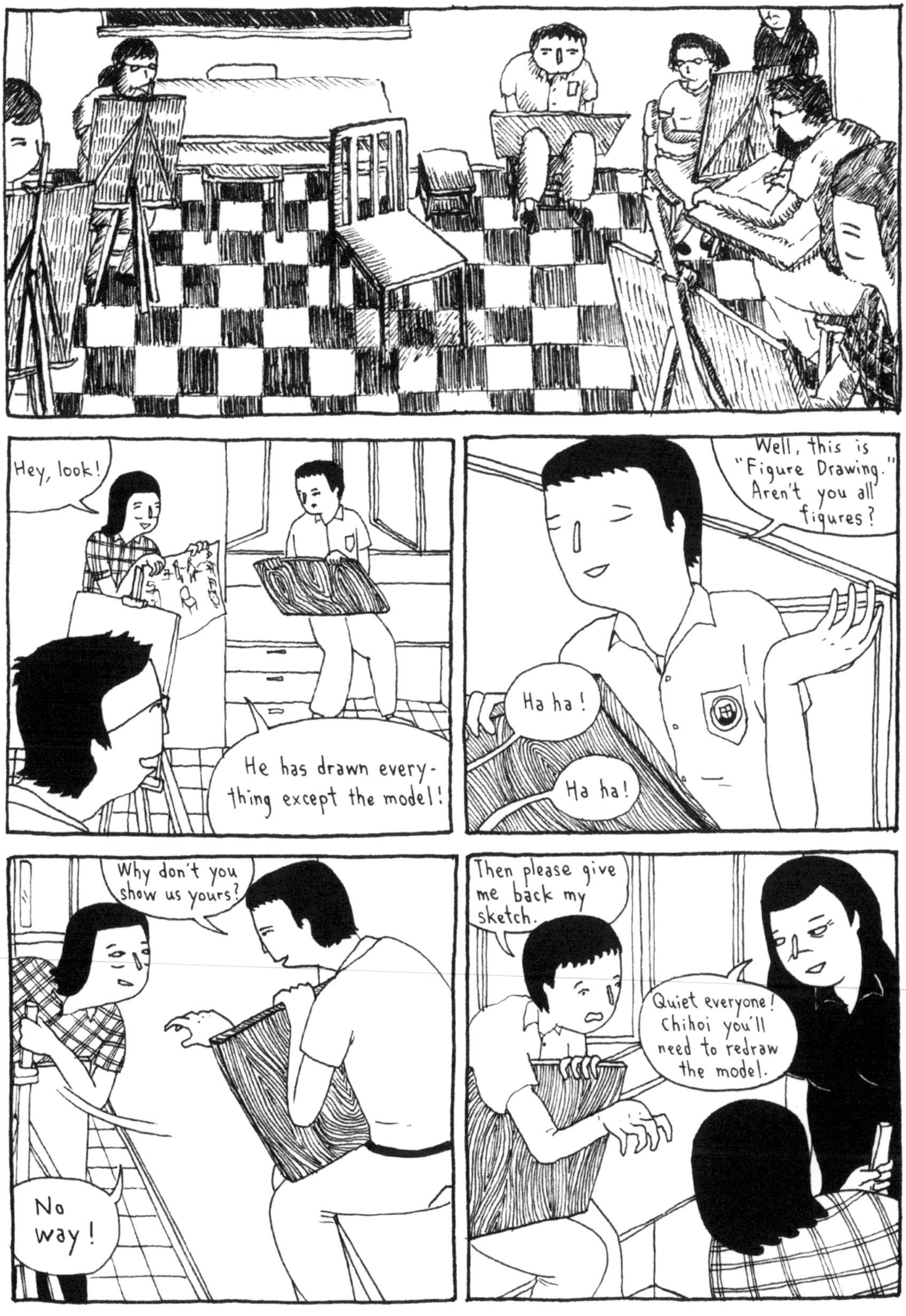
Hey, look!
He has drawn every-thing except the model!
Well, this is "Figure Drawing." Aren't you all figures?
Ha ha!
Ha ha!
Why don't you show us yours?
No way!
Then please give me back my sketch.
Quiet everyone! Chihoi you'll need to redraw the model.

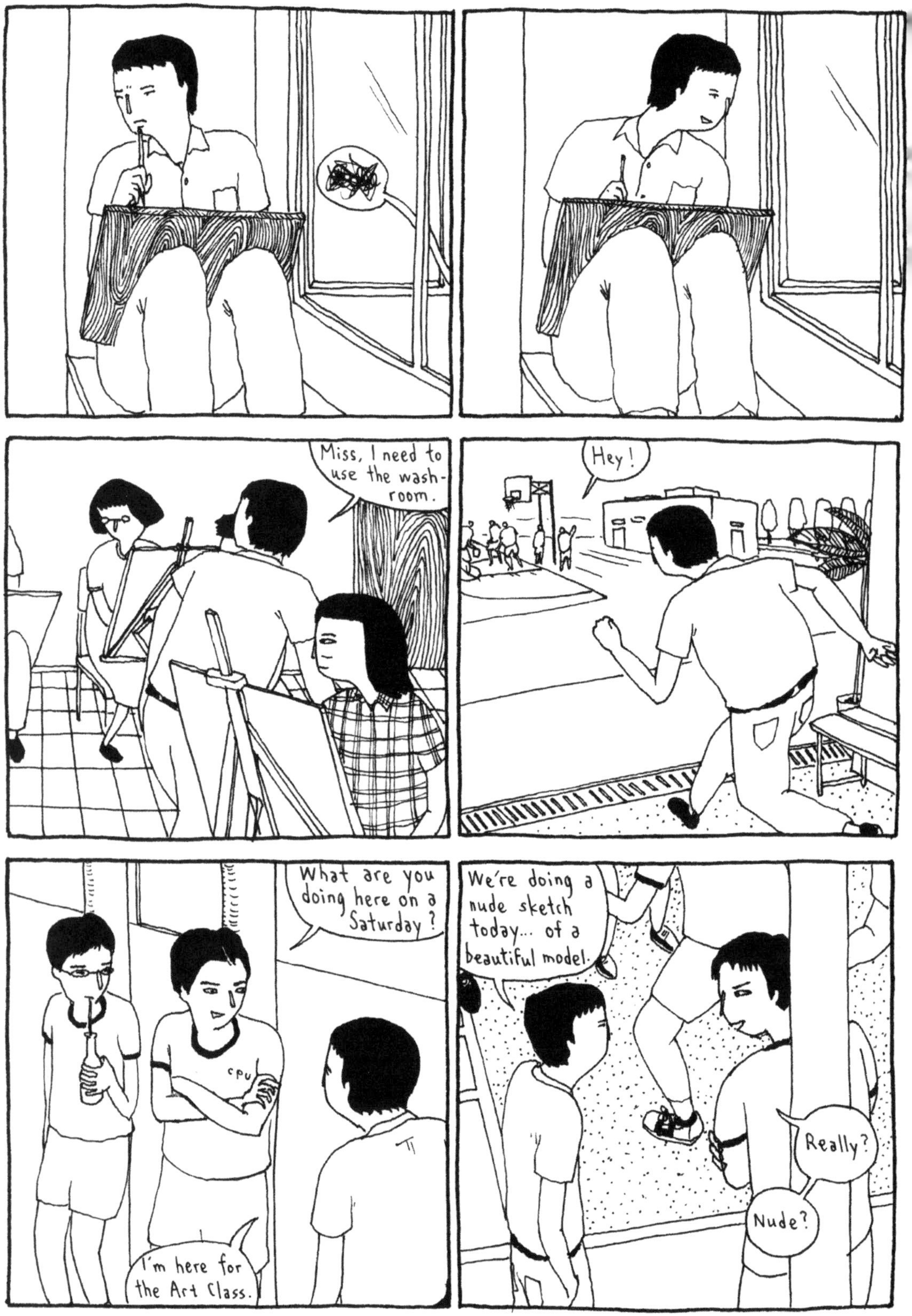
Miss, I need to use the wash-room.
Hey!
What are you doing here on a Saturday?
I'm here for the Art Class.
We're doing a nude sketch today... of a beautiful model.
Really?
Nude?

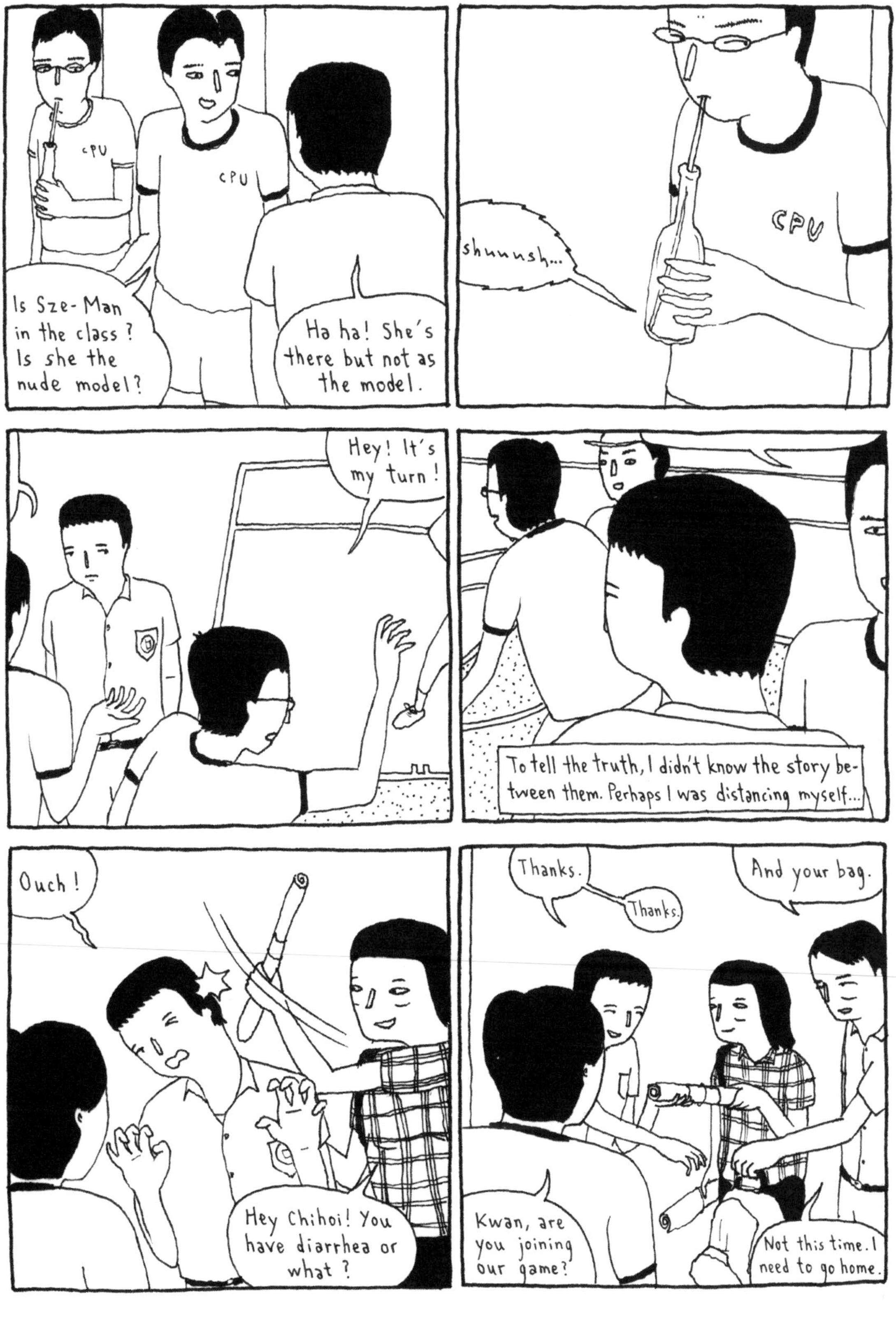
CPU
CPU
Is Sze-Man in the class? Is she the nude model?
Ha ha! She's there but not as the model.
CPU
shuuush...
Hey! It's my turn!
To tell the truth, I didn't know the story between them. Perhaps I was distancing myself...
Ouch!
Hey Chihoi! You have diarrhea or what?
Thanks.
Thanks.
And your bag.
Kwan, are you joining our game?
Not this time. I need to go home.

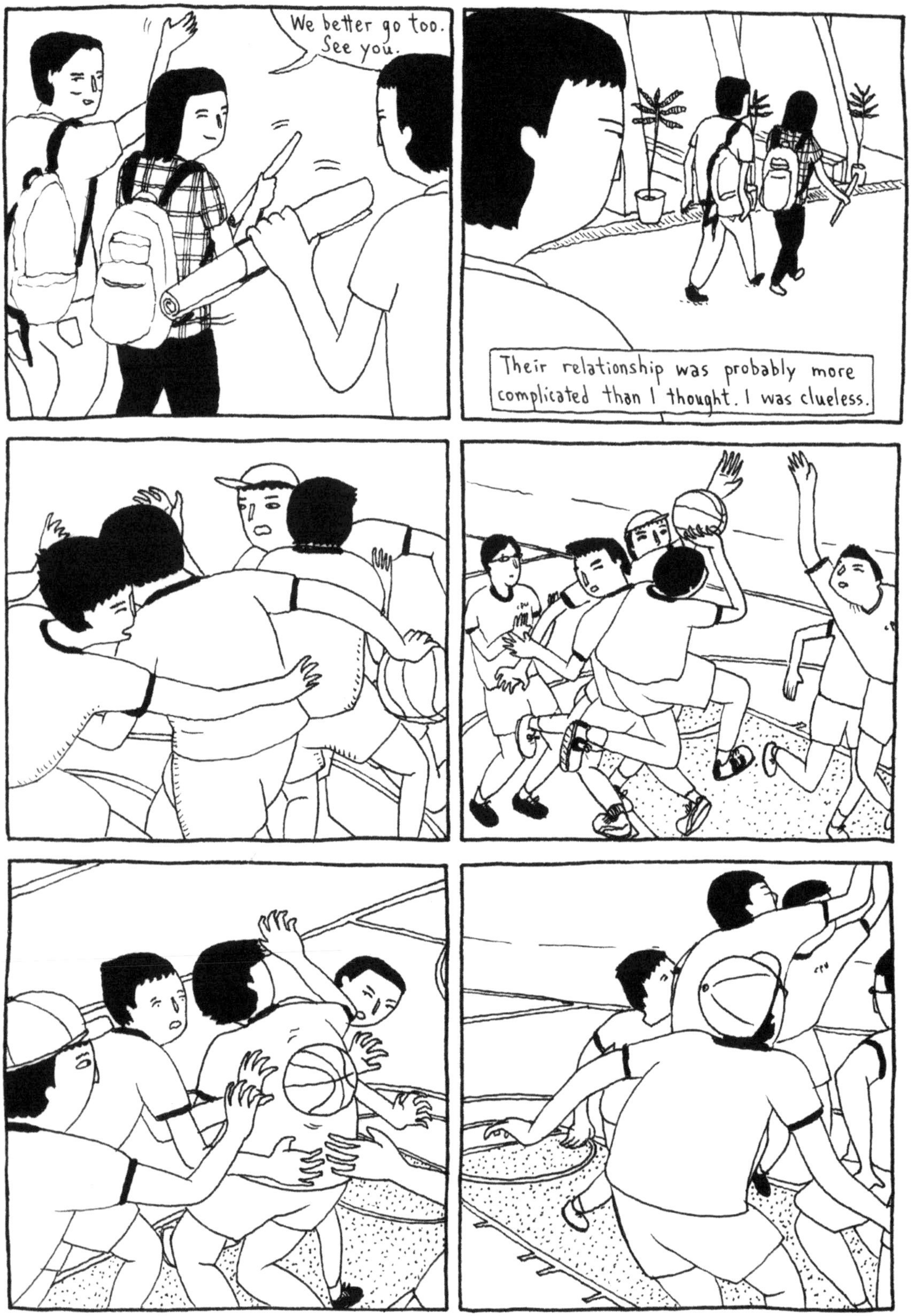
We better go too. See you.
Their relationship was probably more complicated than I thought. I was clueless.

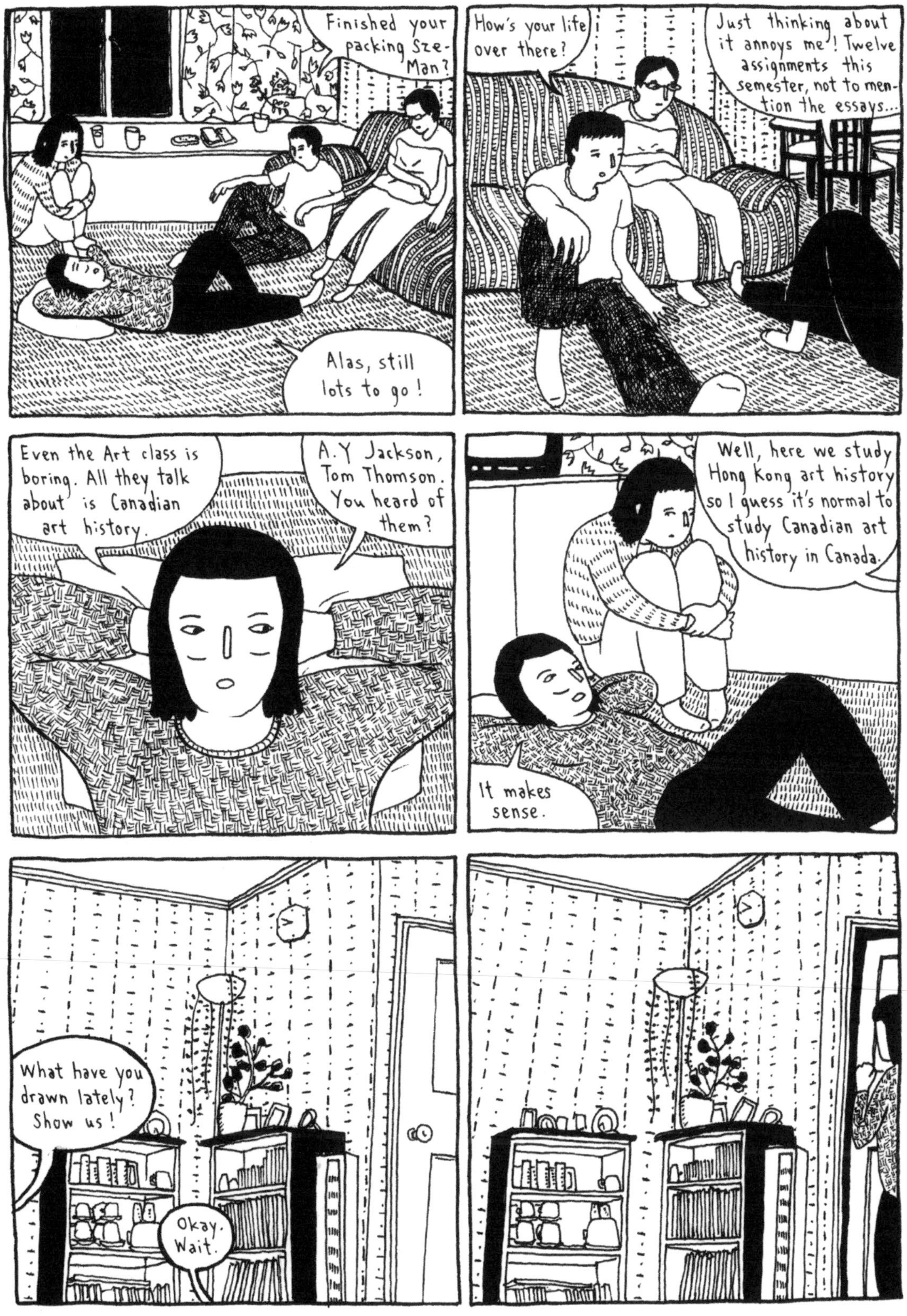
Finished your packing Sze-Man?
Alas, still lots to go!
How's your life over there?
Just thinking about it annoys me! Twelve assignments this semester, not to mention the essays...
Even the Art class is boring. All they talk about is Canadian art history.
A.Y Jackson, Tom Thomson. You heard of them?
Well, here we study Hong Kong art history so I guess it's normal to study Canadian art history in Canada.
It makes sense.
What have you drawn lately? Show us!
Okay. Wait.

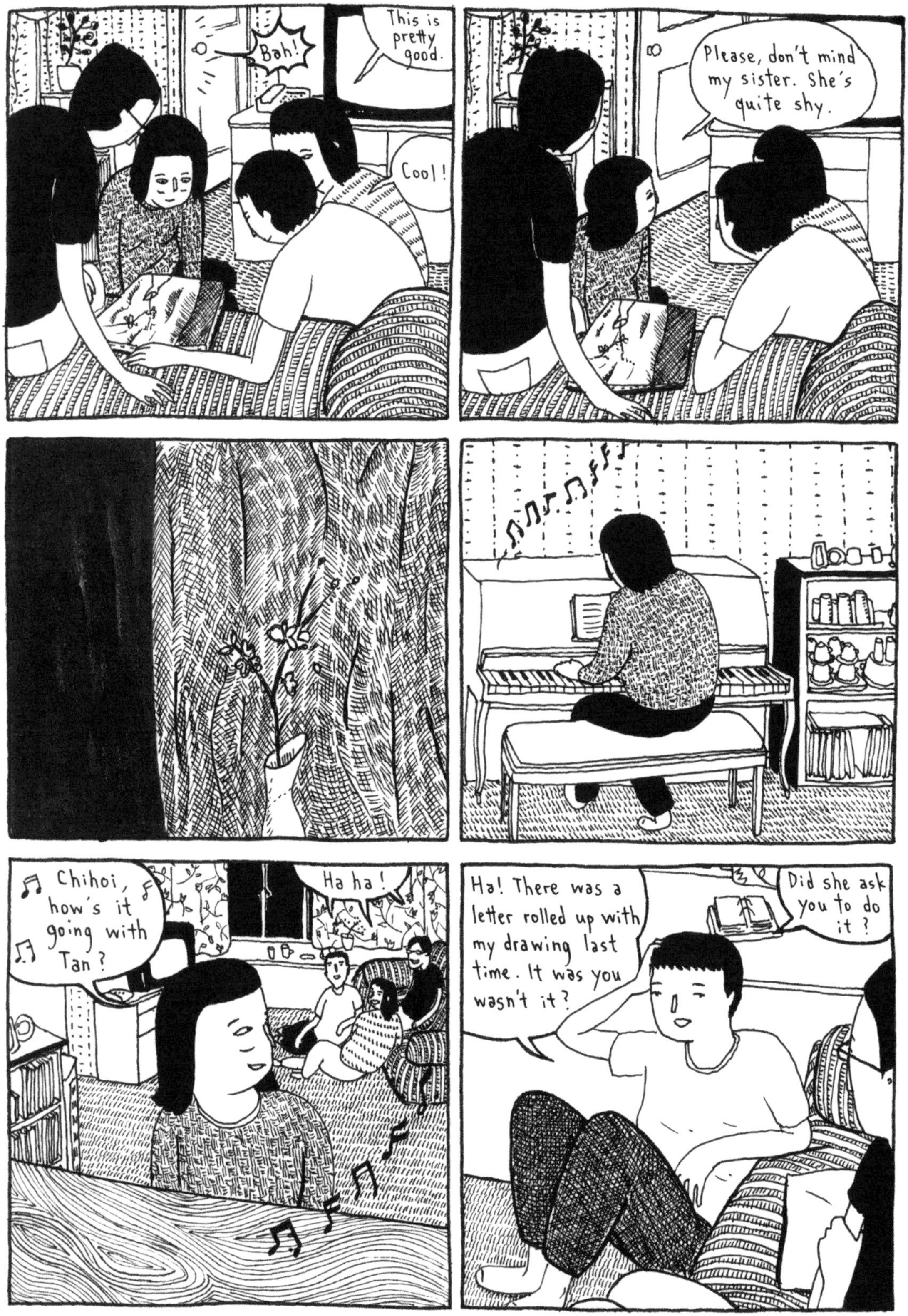
Bah!
This is pretty good.
Cool!
Please, don't mind my sister. She's quite shy.
Chihoi, how's it going with Tan?
Ha ha!
Ha! There was a letter rolled up with my drawing last time. It was you wasn't it?
Did she ask you to do it?

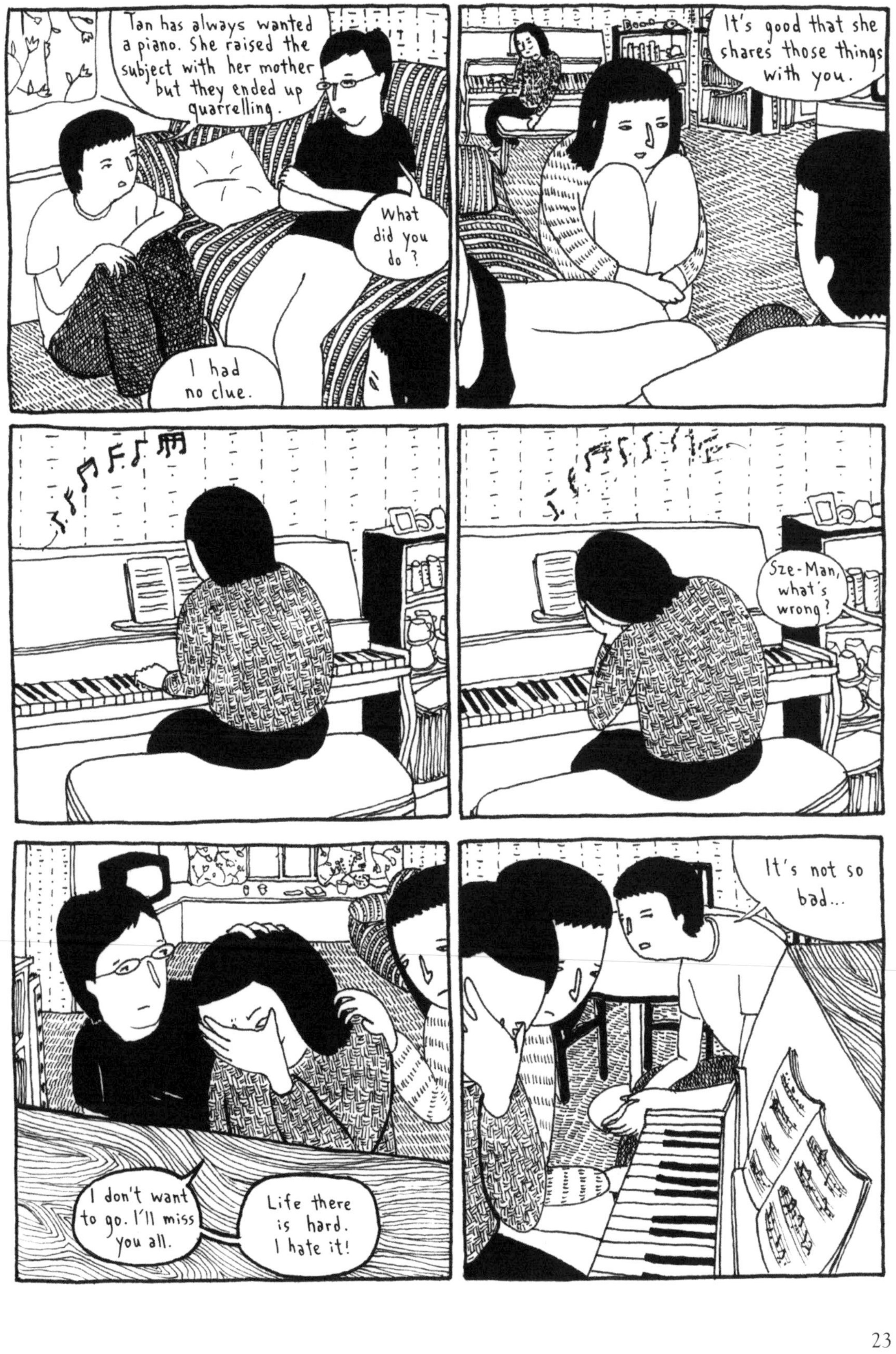
Tan has always wanted a piano. She raised the subject with her mother but they ended up quarrelling.
What did you do?
I had no clue.
It's good that she shares those things with you.
Sze-Man, what's wrong?
I don't want to go. I'll miss you all.
Life there is hard. I hate it!
It's not so bad...

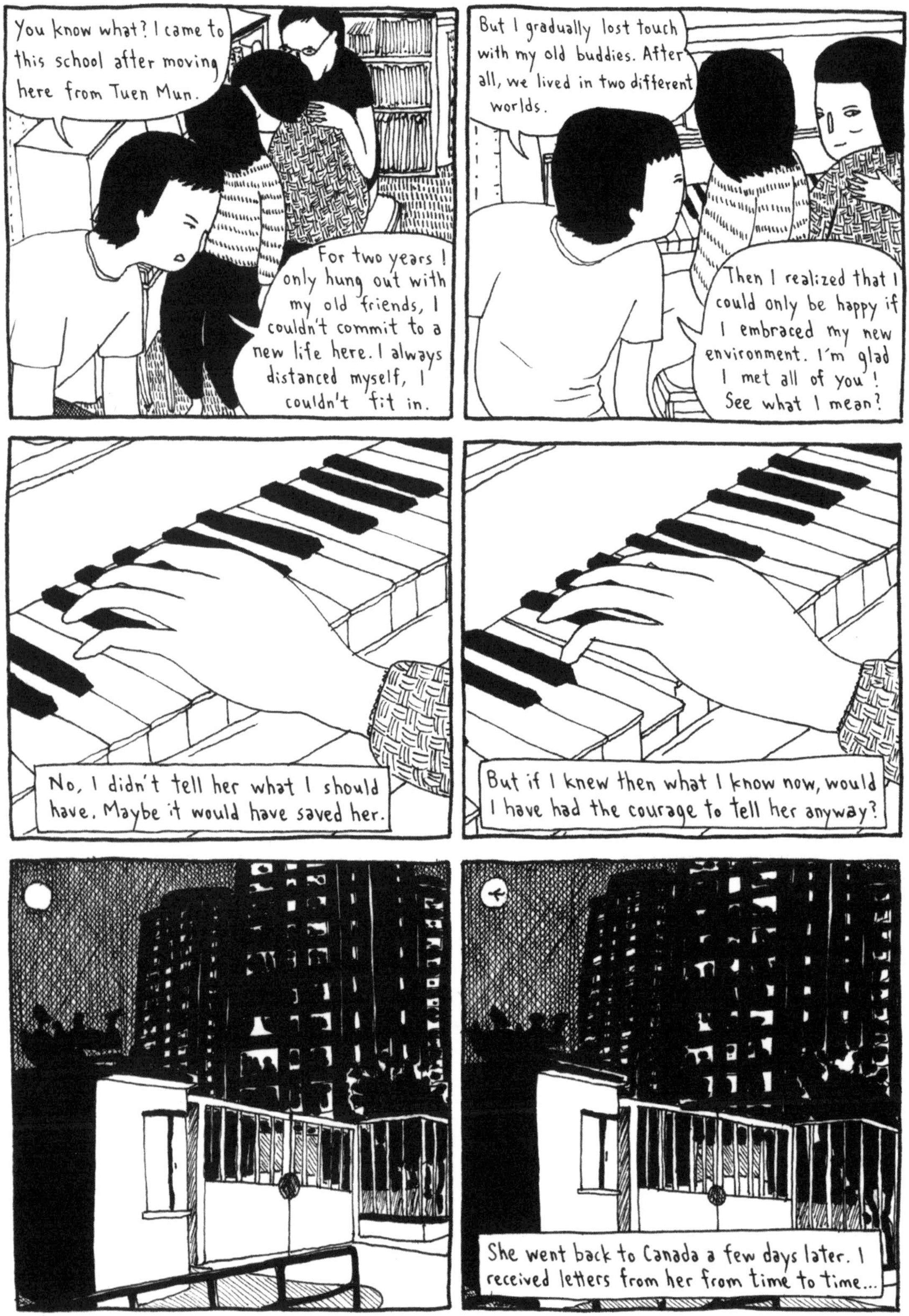

You know what? I came to this school after moving here from Tuen Mun.
For two years I only hung out with my old friends, I couldn't commit to a new life here. I always distanced myself, I couldn't fit in.
But I gradually lost touch with my old buddies. After all, we lived in two different worlds.
Then I realized that I could only be happy if I embraced my new environment. I'm glad I met all of you! See what I mean?
No, I didn't tell her what I should have. Maybe it would have saved her.
But if I knew then what I know now, would I have had the courage to tell her anyway?
She went back to Canada a few days later. I received letters from her from time to time...

Today I successfully made my first decent meal. Rice (freshly steamed from the cooker), stir-fried celery with chicken, pork chops with baked beans and sausages. Um, yummy. But I'm going to make leftovers — I can't spend too much time on cooking, since I am preparing for exams.

And there are the assignments to hand in after the exams. It bugs me when I think of it. I am writing an essay on William Wordsworth and I will need to read his poem in class, but I know nothing about him. What am I going to do?

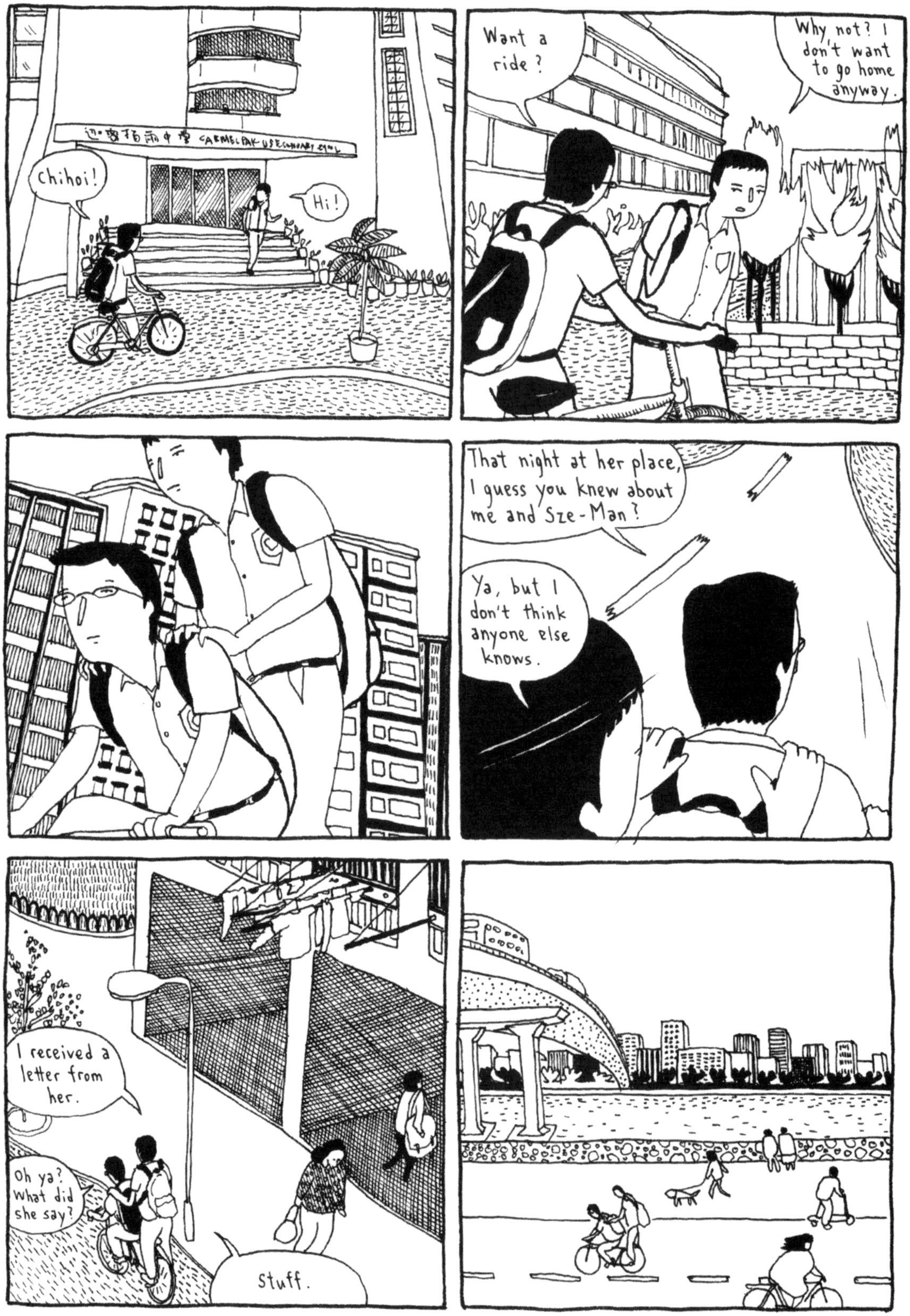
Chihoi!
Hi!
Want a ride?
Why not? I don't want to go home anyway.
That night at her place, I guess you knew about me and Sze-Man?
Ya, but I don't think anyone else knows.
I received a letter from her.
Oh ya? what did she say?
Stuff.

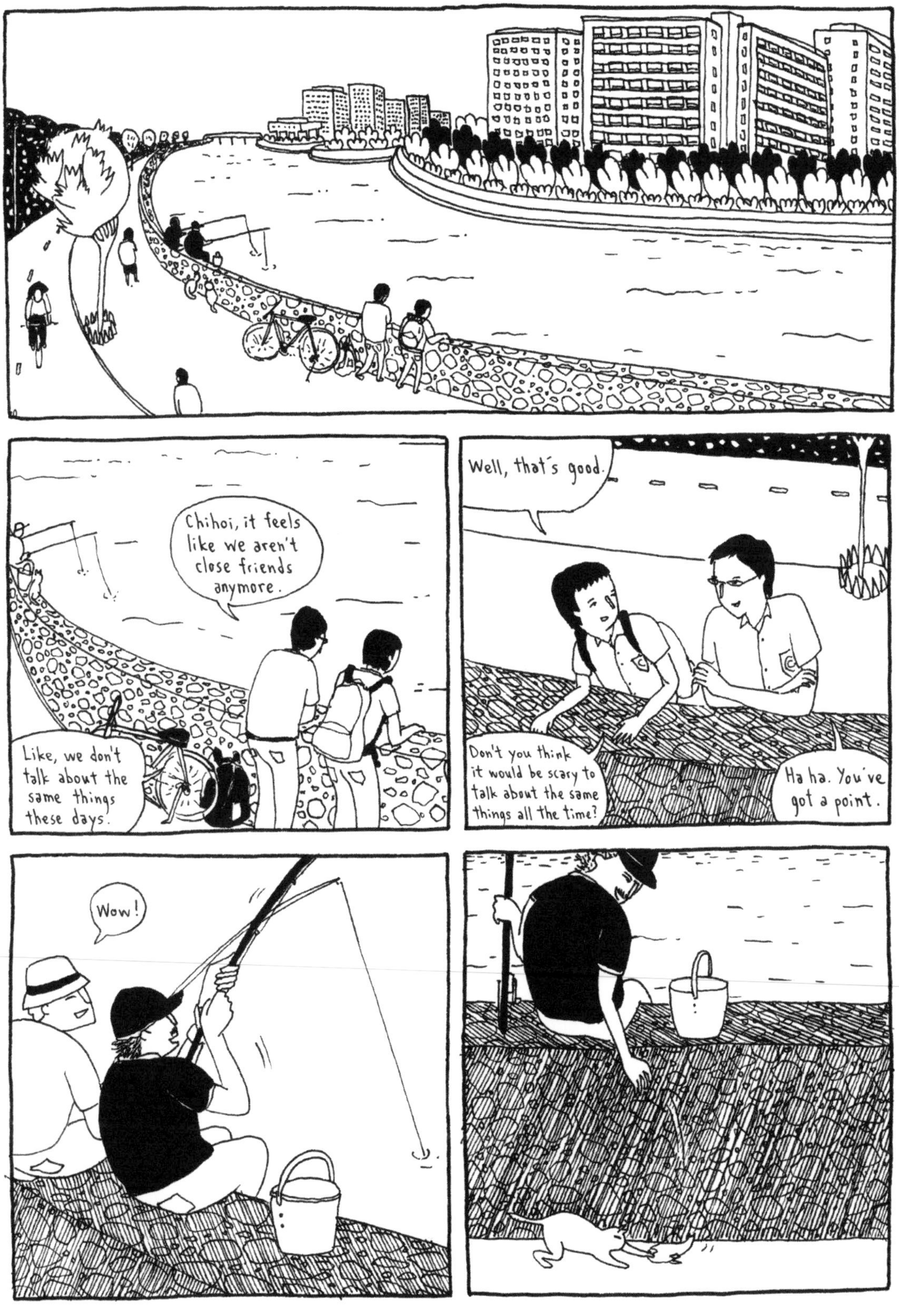
Chihoi, it feels like we aren't close friends anymore.
Like, we don't talk about the same things these days.
Well, that's good.
Don't you think it would be scary to talk about the same things all the time?
Ha ha. You've got a point.
Wow!

My cousin hasn't been home for dinner lately. I make dinner for myself. I feel comfortable, happy and free, rather than lonely. Everyday after school I cook, I eat, I shower, and then I go back to my own room and do my own things. The place might be small but I feel at home. I don't need to see people and other people can't see me.

I'm performing on Monday night. I'm very nervous about it. I feel like I'm representing Hong Kong, performing in front of foreigners. It was more than six months since I last practised. I've been practising it now for seven weeks, but it still doesn't sound right and it worries me. I'm afraid that I can only strike the keys accurately, without emotionally relating to the piece. There is only sound, no involvement. Impossible! Impossible!

♪ Happy
Birthday to ♪ ♫
you...

Happy Birthday ♪
to you...

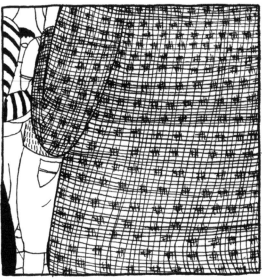

Happy Birthday, Tan!

Oh, thanks!

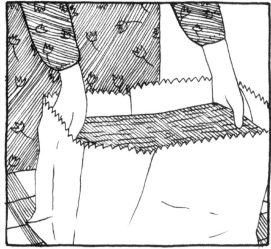

Wow! This is wonderful!

Hope you don't mind that it's out of tune.

Say cheese!

1... 2 ...3...

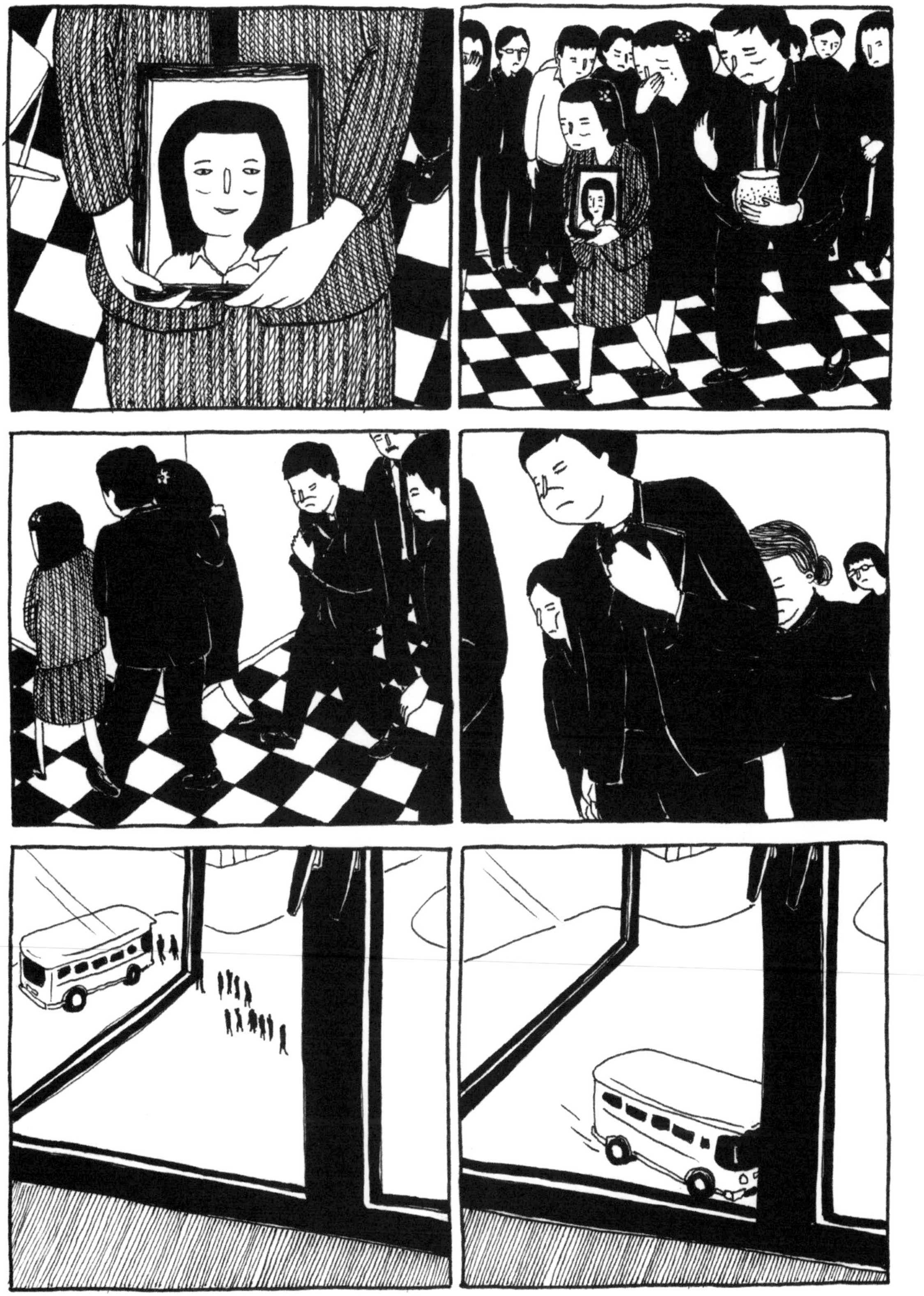

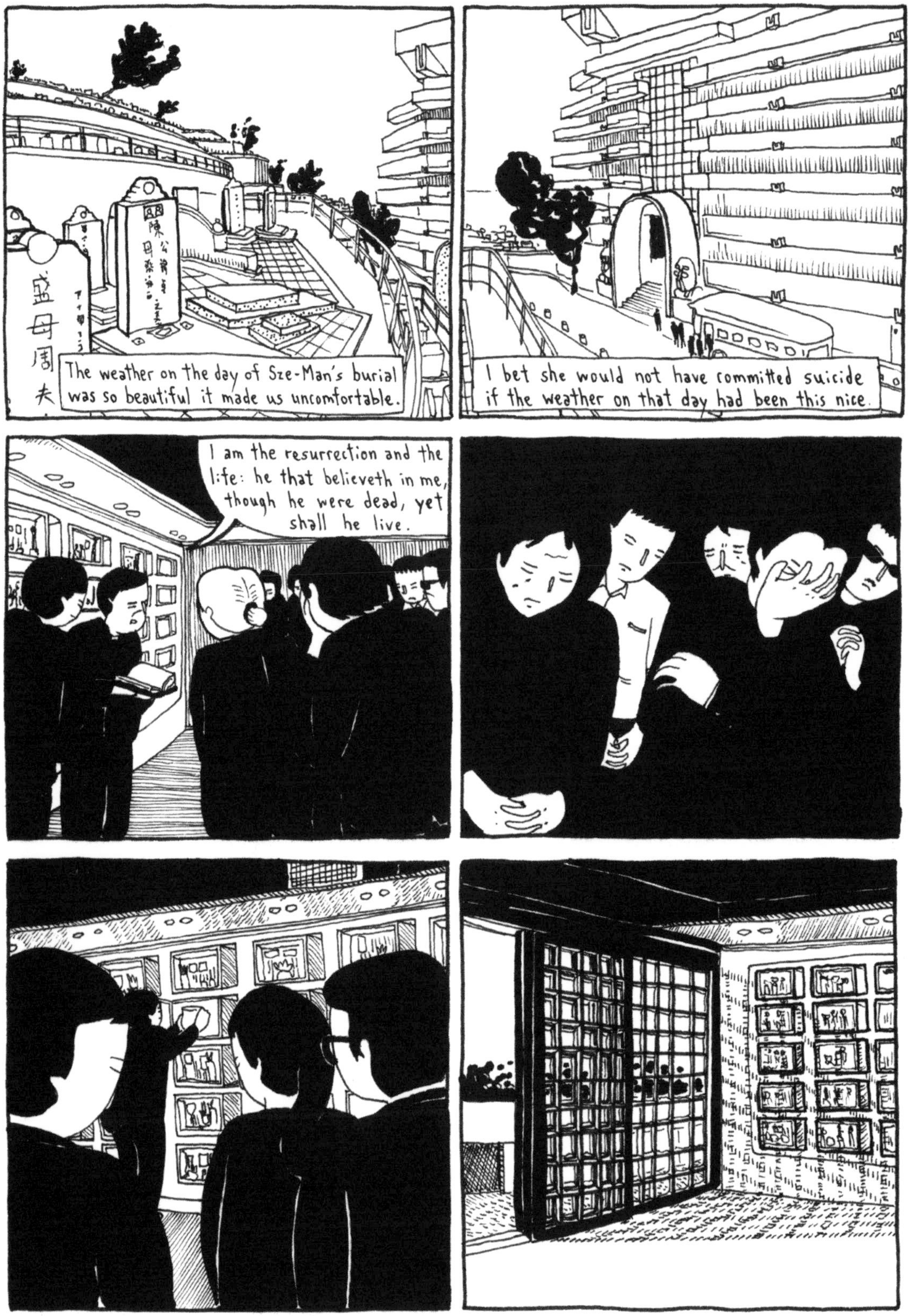

The weather on the day of Sze-Man's burial was so beautiful it made us uncomfortable.
I bet she would not have committed suicide if the weather on that day had been this nice.
I am the resurrection and the life: he that believeth in me, though he were dead, yet shall he live.

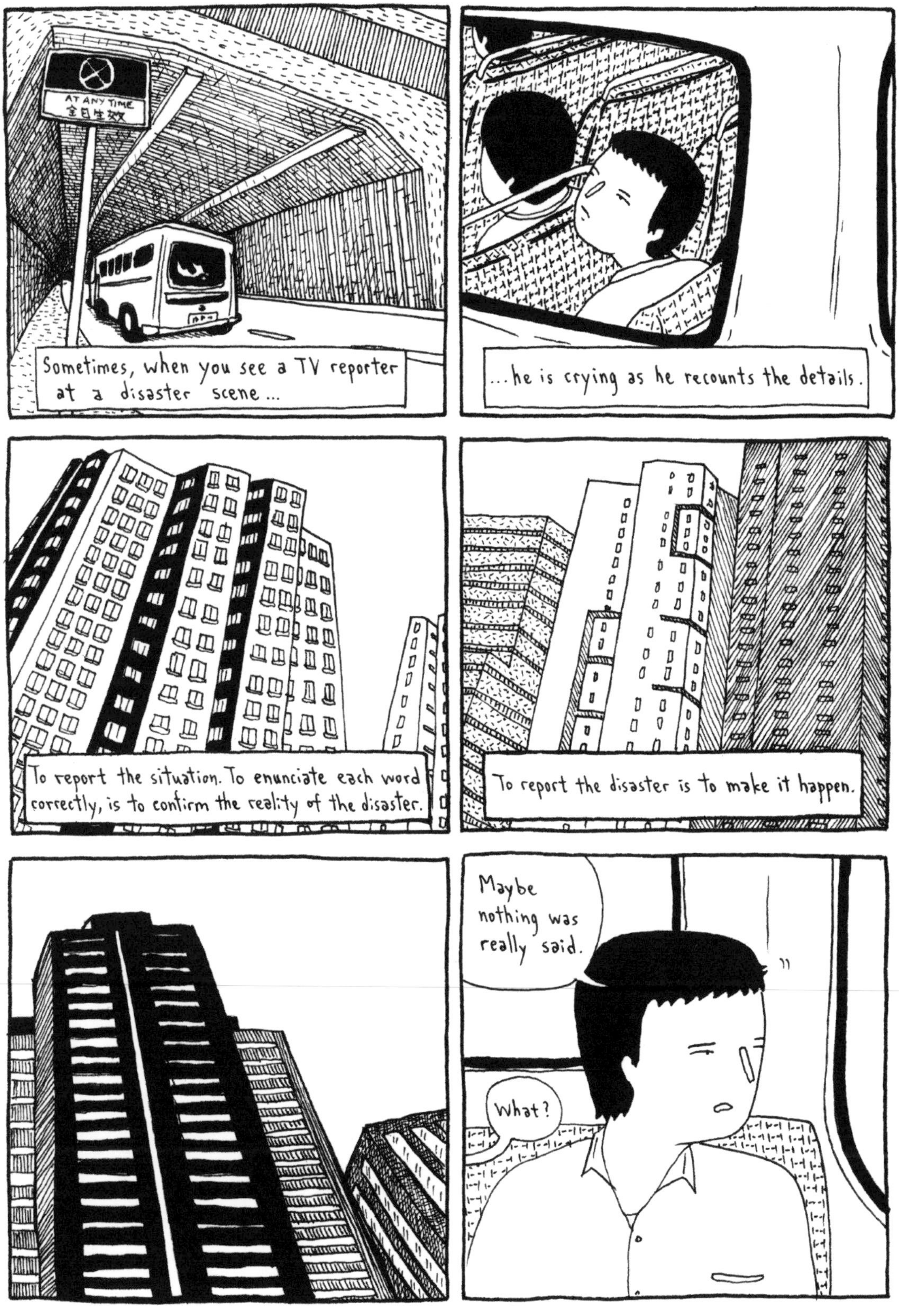
AT ANY TIME
全日生效
Sometimes, when you see a TV reporter at a disaster scene...
...he is crying as he recounts the details.
To report the situation. To enunciate each word correctly, is to confirm the reality of the disaster.
To report the disaster is to make it happen.
Maybe nothing was really said.
What?

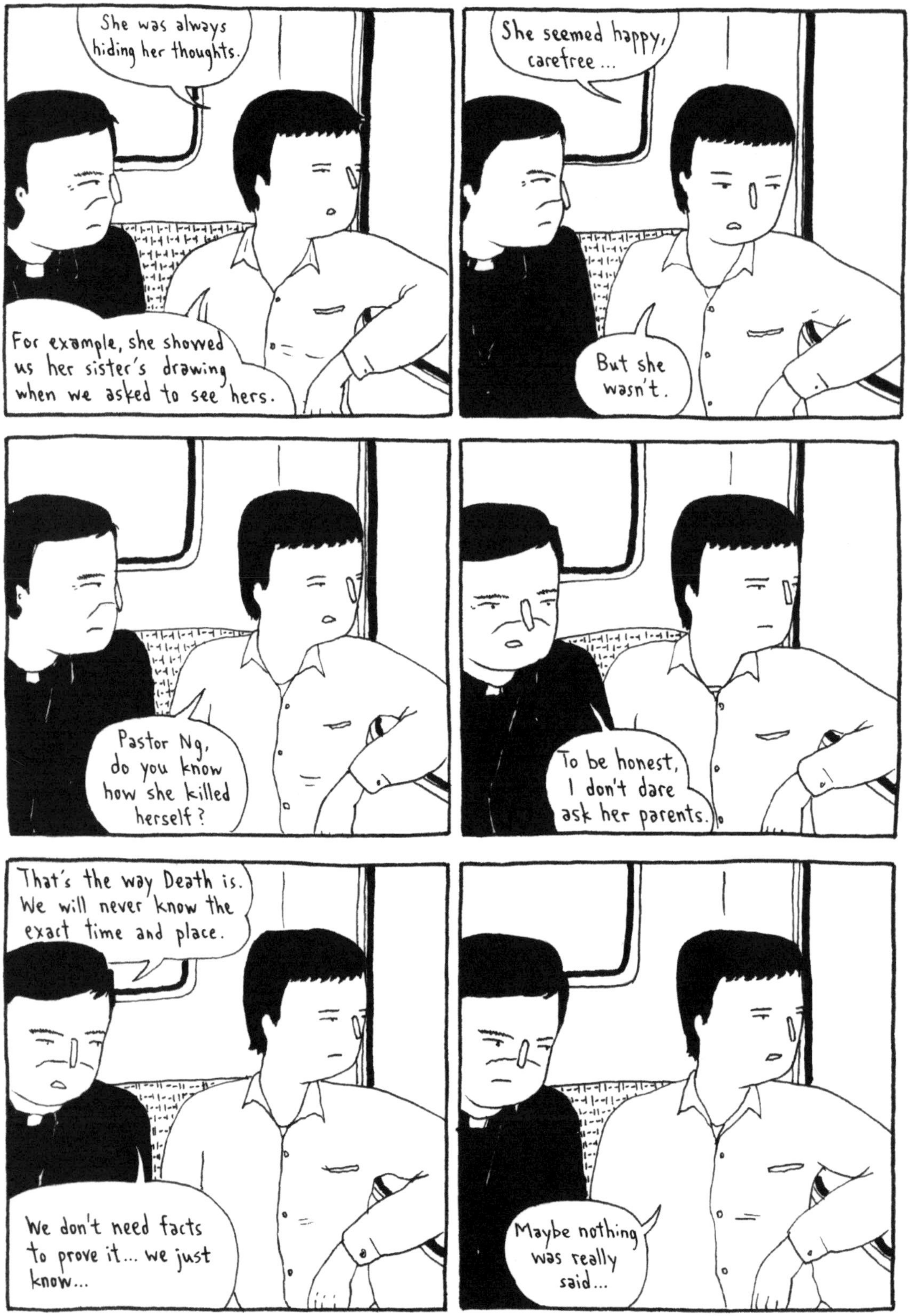
She was always hiding her thoughts.
For example, she showed us her sister's drawing when we asked to see hers.
She seemed happy, carefree ...
But she wasn't.
Pastor Ng, do you know how she killed herself?
To be honest, I don't dare ask her parents.
That's the way Death is. We will never know the exact time and place.
We don't need facts to prove it... we just know...
Maybe nothing was really said...

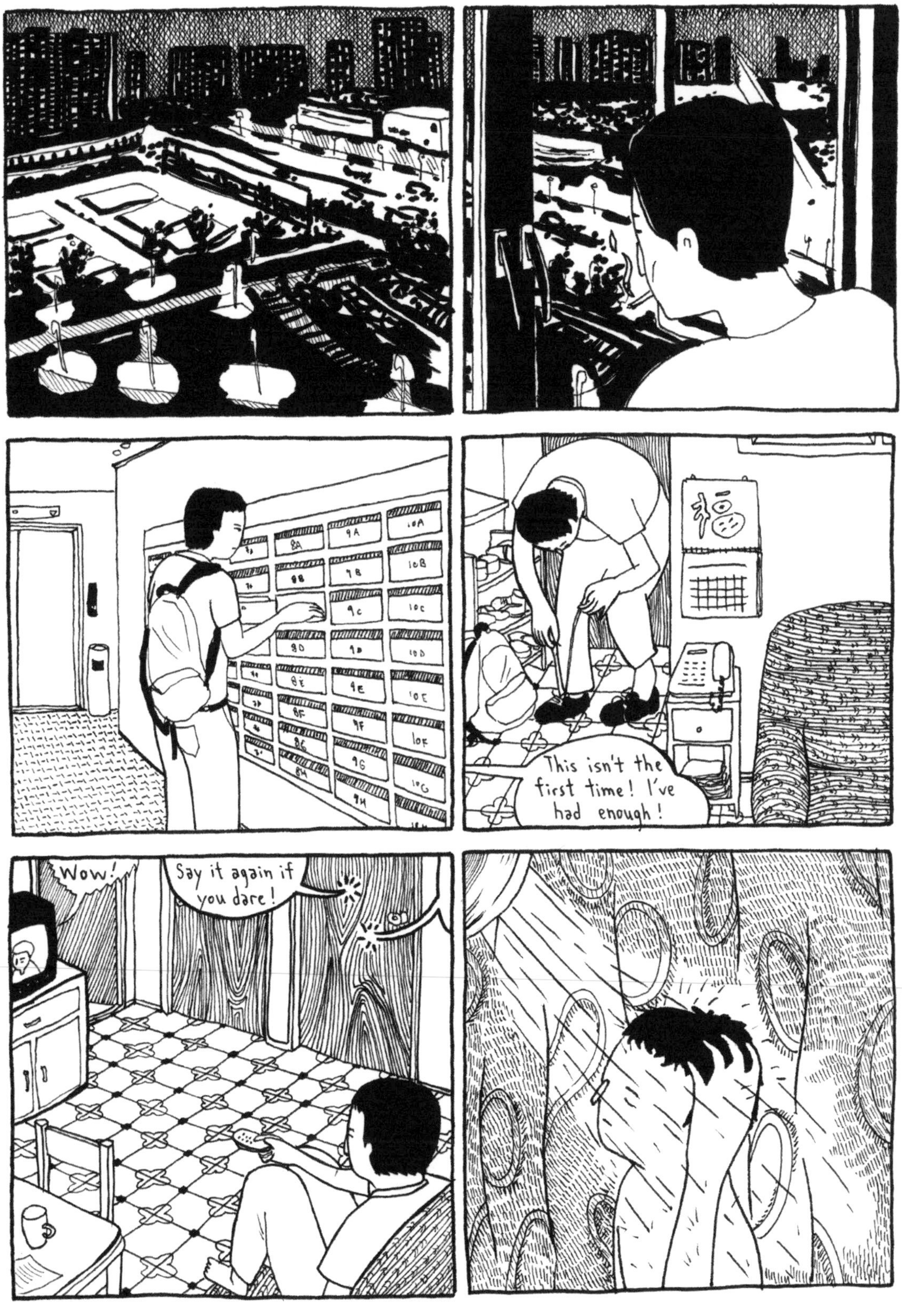
This isn't the first time! I've had enough!
Wow!
Say it again if you dare!

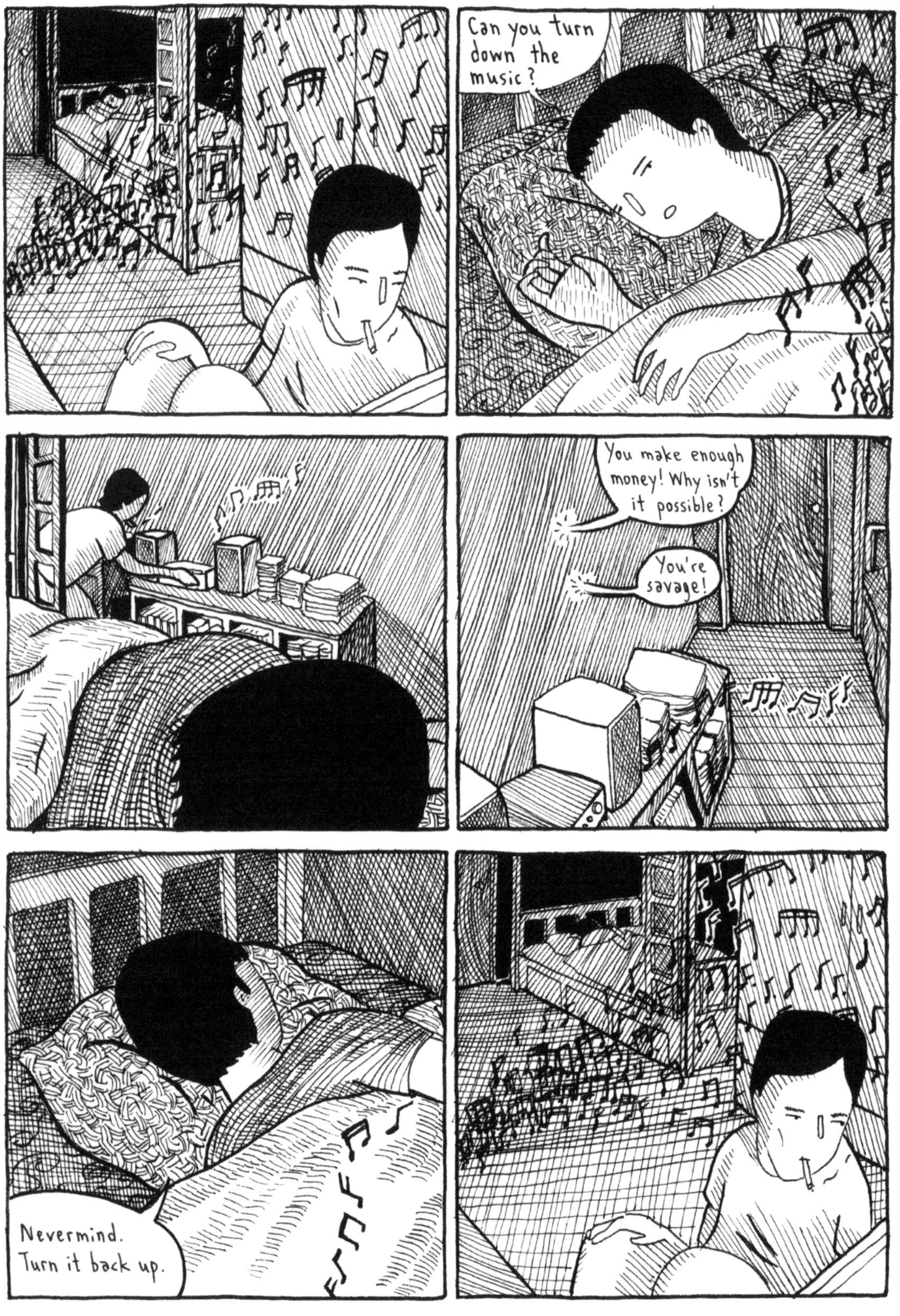
Can you turn down the music?
You make enough money! Why isn't it possible?
You're savage!
Nevermind. Turn it back up.

It was already midnight when I got home. After I settled down I started to cry. My head was aching so I took a couple of Tylenol. They were all asleep. I couldn't cry out loud, so I listened to my own weeping. I turned on the lamp and saw my ugly face in the mirror. I miss my family. I miss him. I miss you all. If I were an only child I would be able to stay in Hong Kong. If I were an only child I could go back home anytime I wanted. If I were an only child I could do anything I wanted and no one would say a word. If I were an only child.... But this is out of the question.

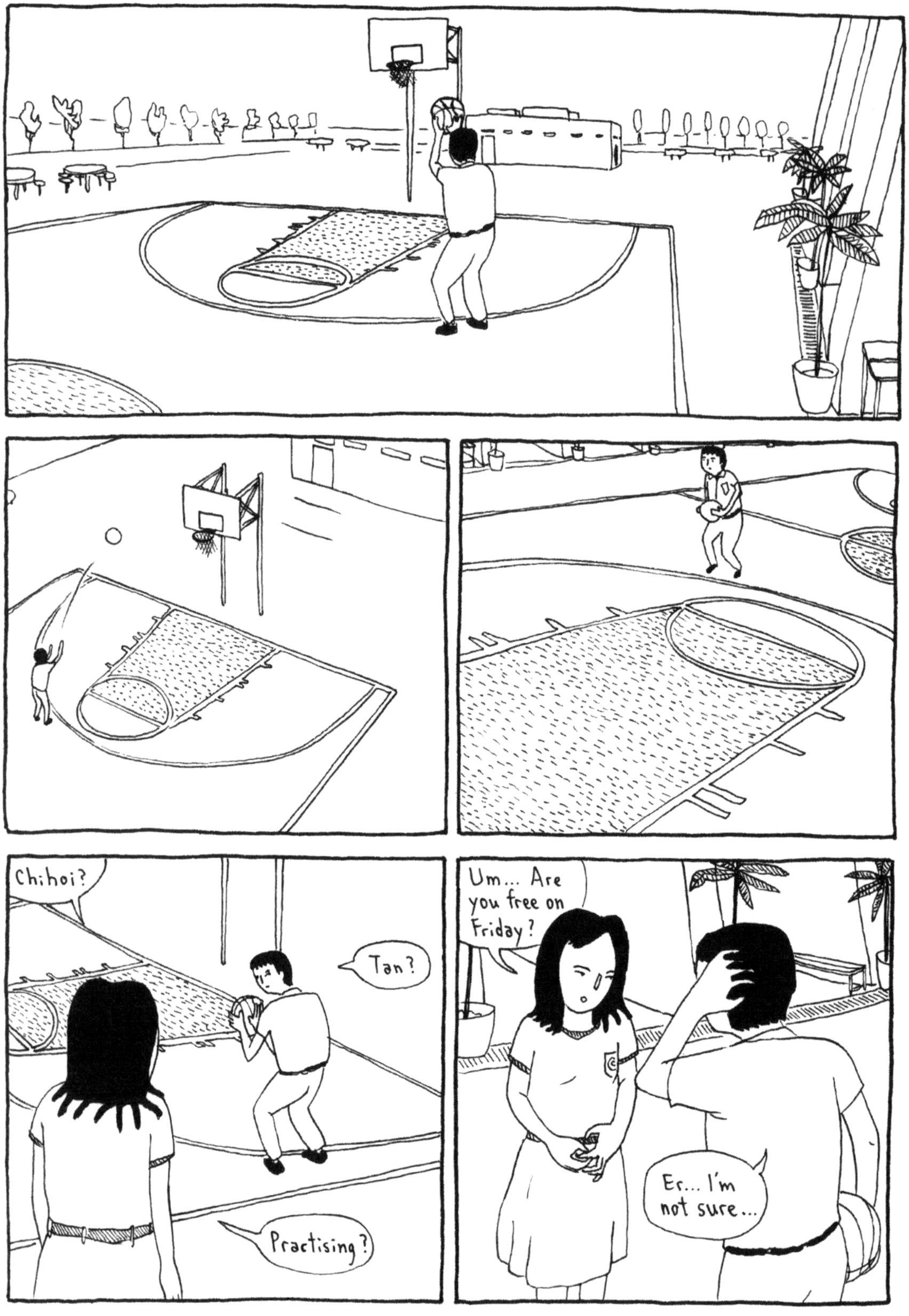
Chihoi?
Tan?
Practising?
Um... Are you free on Friday?
Er... I'm not sure...

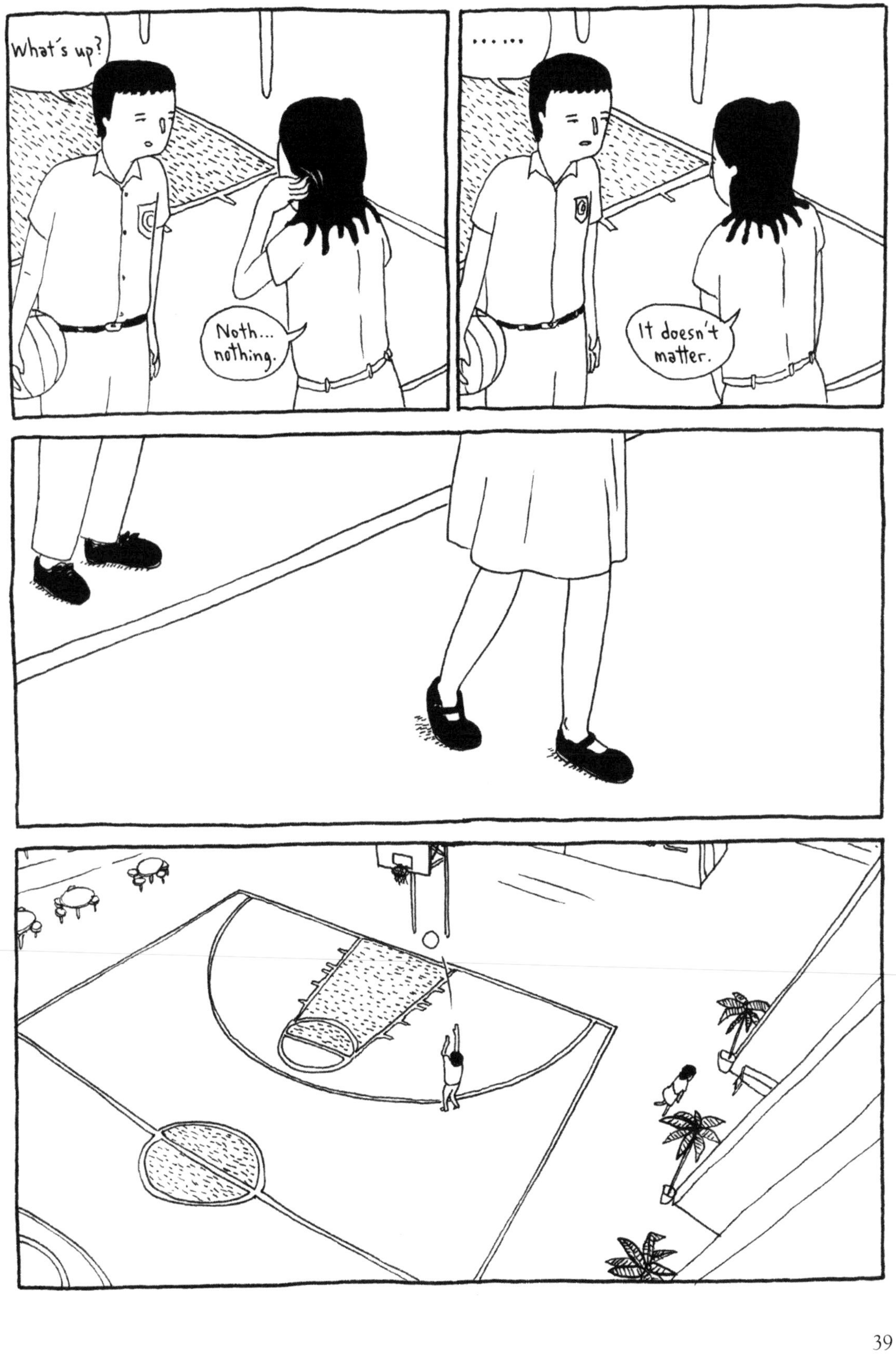
What's up?
Noth... nothing.
......
It doesn't matter.

# Father

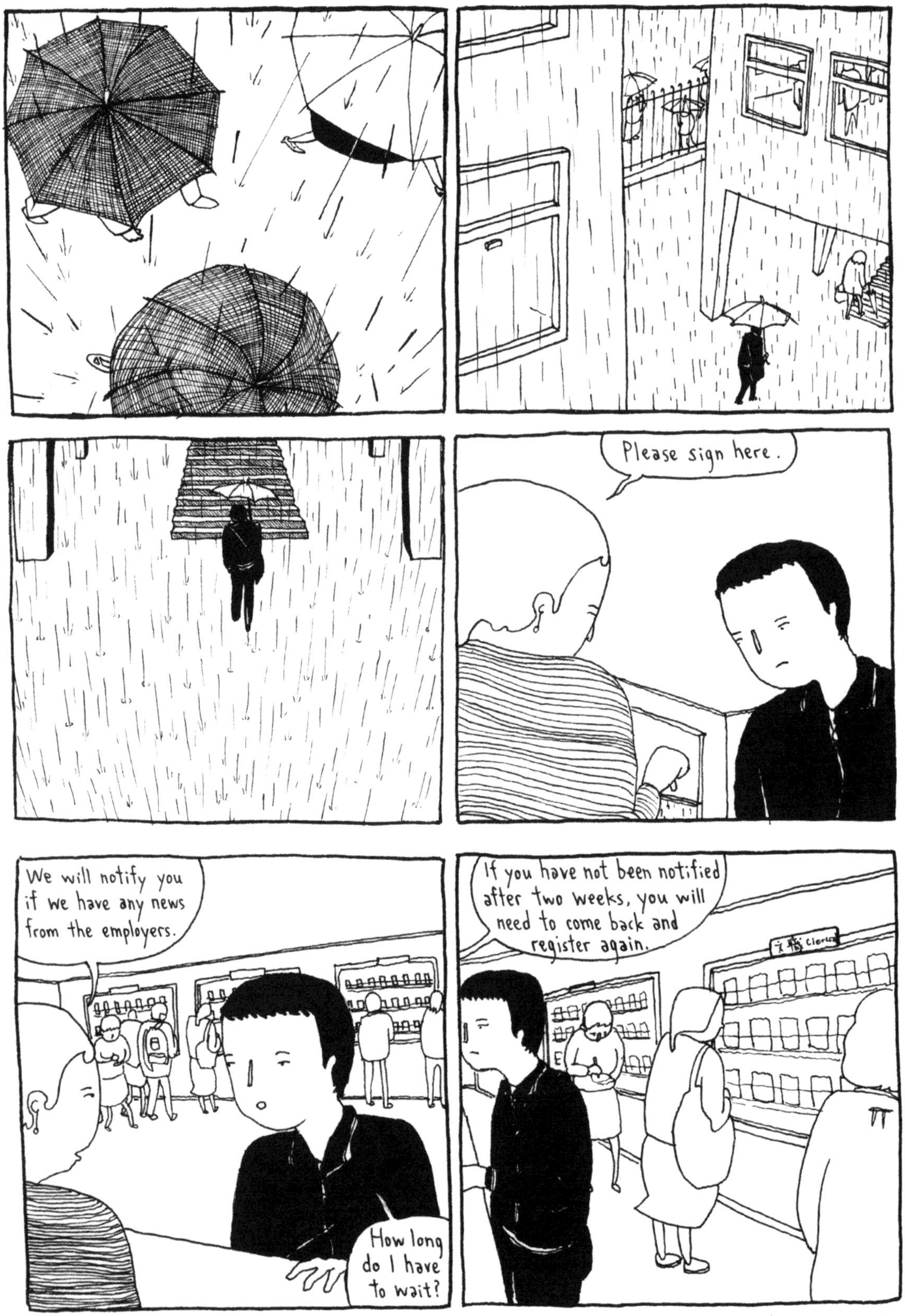
Please sign here.
We will notify you if we have any news from the employers.
How long do I have to wait?
If you have not been notified after two weeks, you will need to come back and register again.

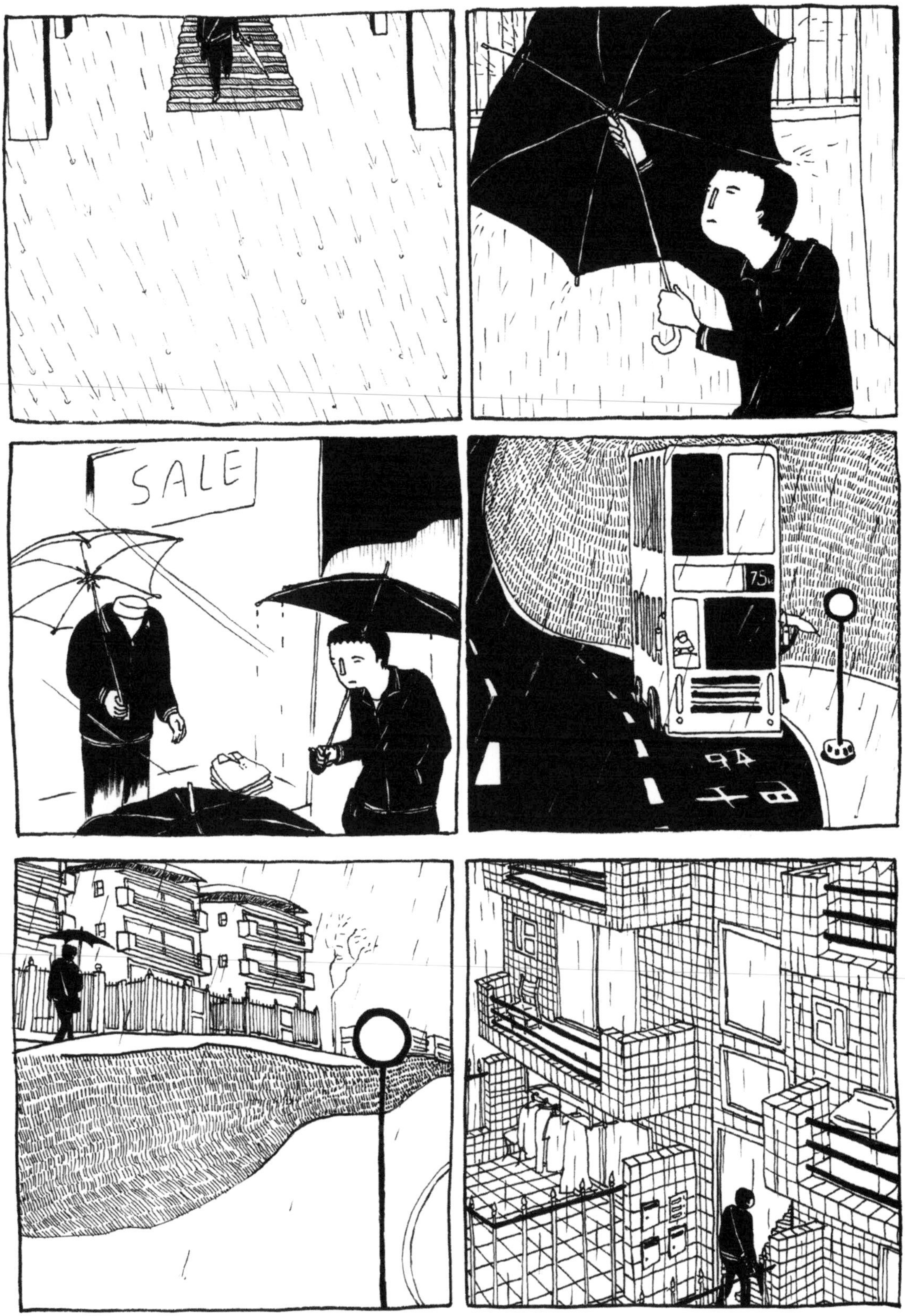
SALE
75

Father was dead by the time I came home.

Father?

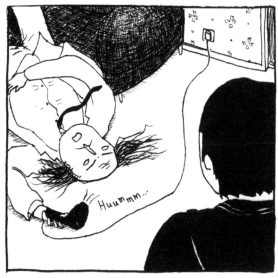

Huuumm...

Huuumm...

What should I do?

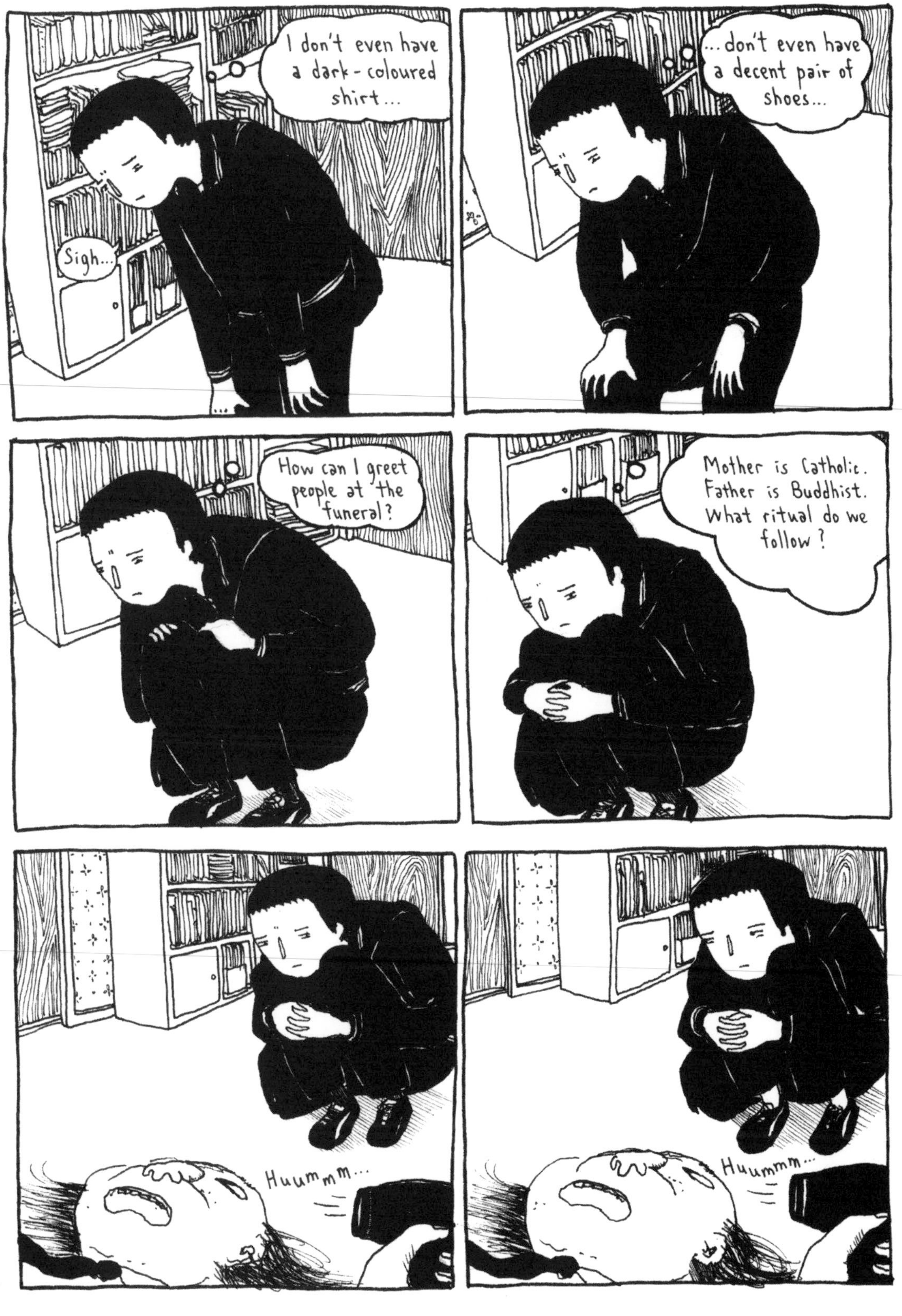
I don't even have a dark-coloured shirt...
Sigh...
...don't even have a decent pair of shoes...
How can I greet people at the funeral?
Mother is Catholic. Father is Buddhist. What ritual do we follow?
Huummm...
Huummm...

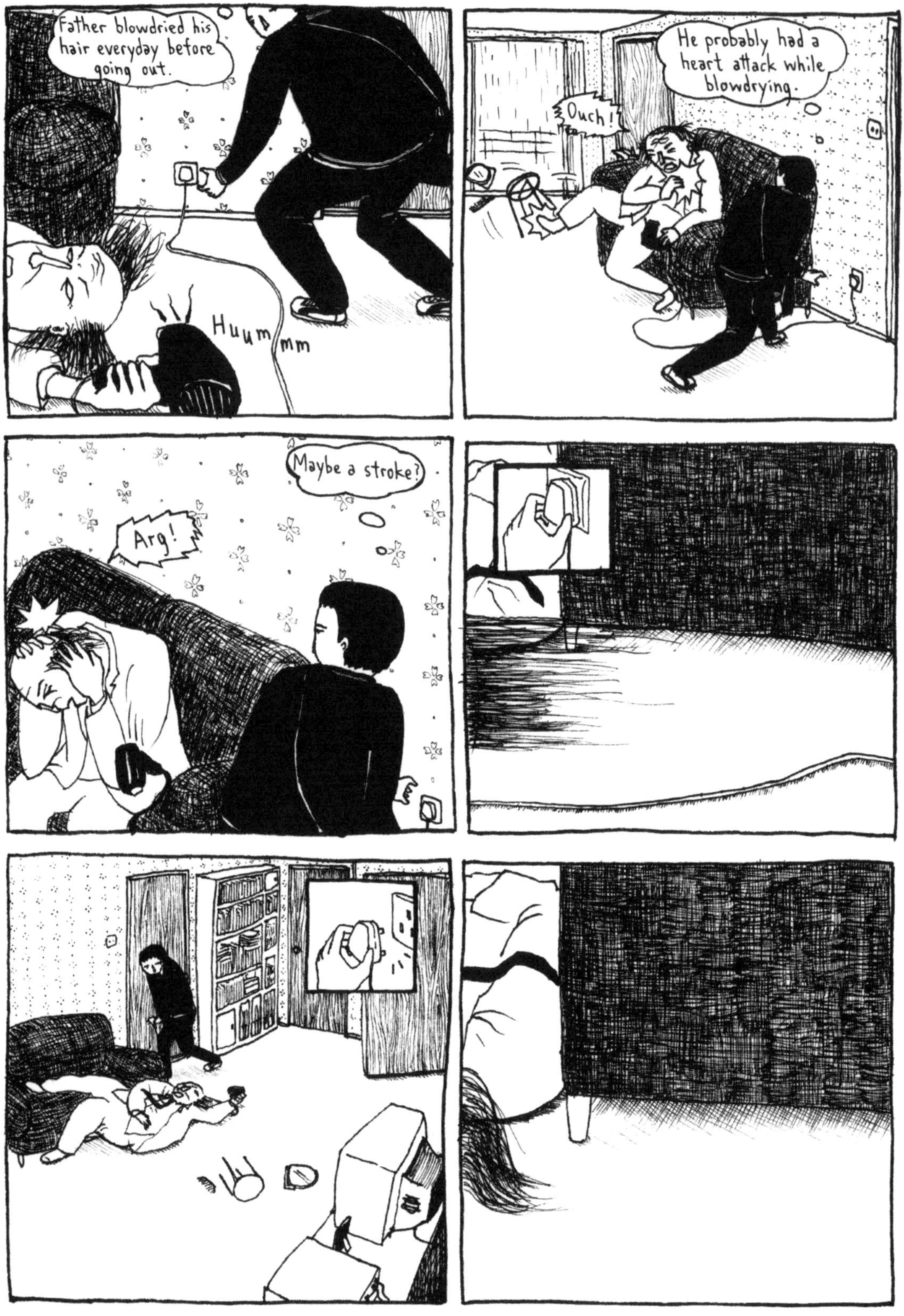
Father blowdried his hair everyday before going out.
Huummm
He probably had a heart attack while blowdrying.
Ouch!
Maybe a stroke?
Arg!

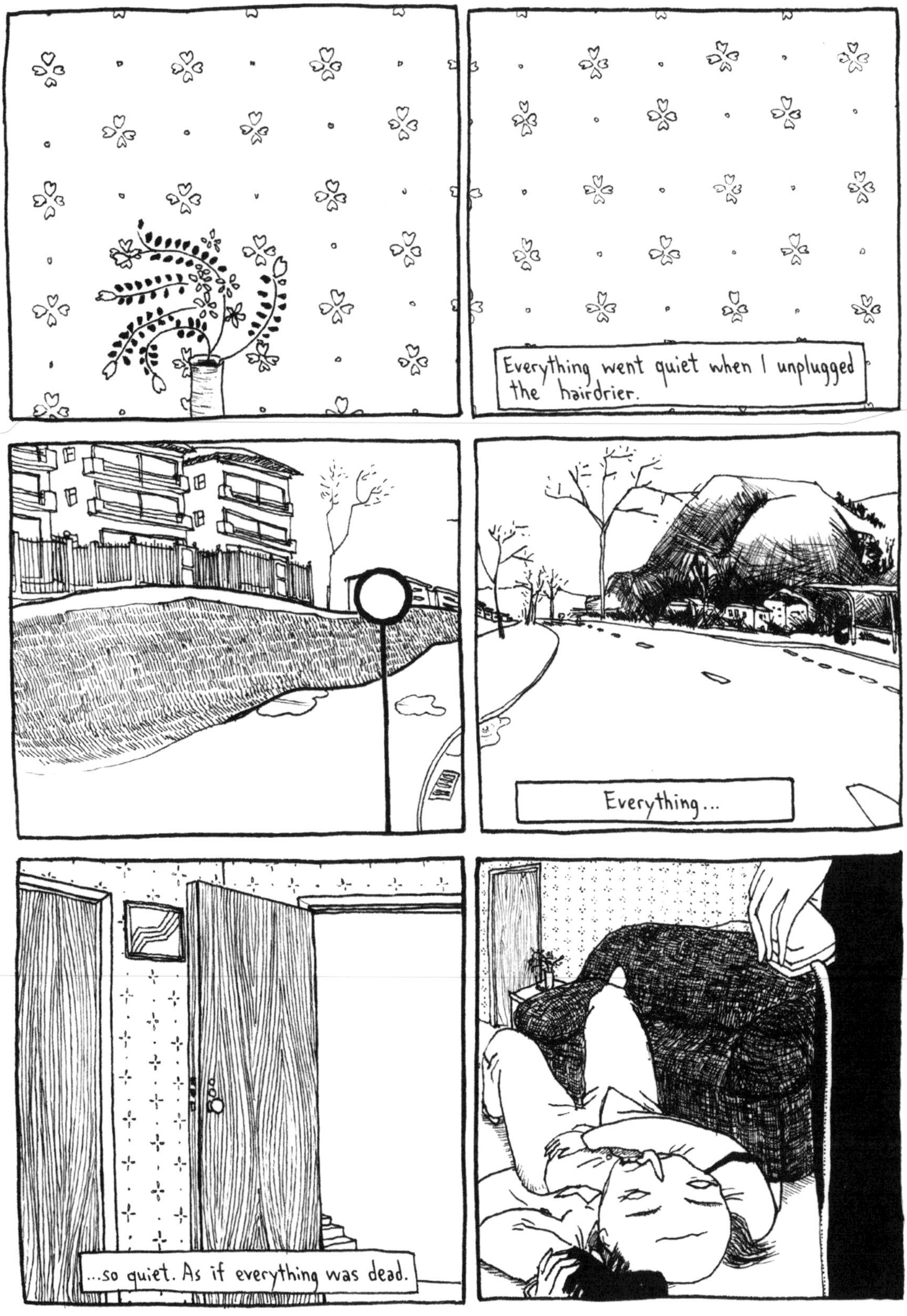
Everything went quiet when I unplugged the hairdrier.
Everything...
...so quiet. As if everything was dead.

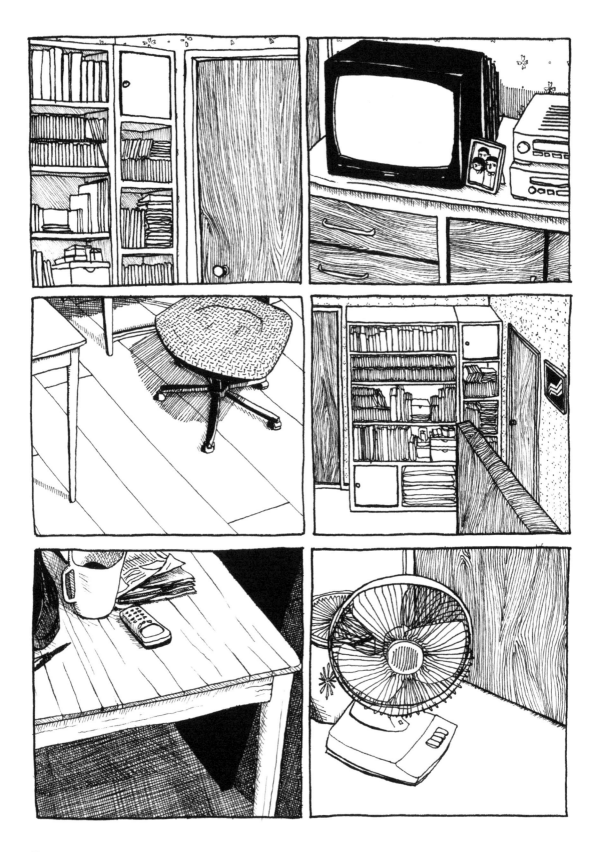

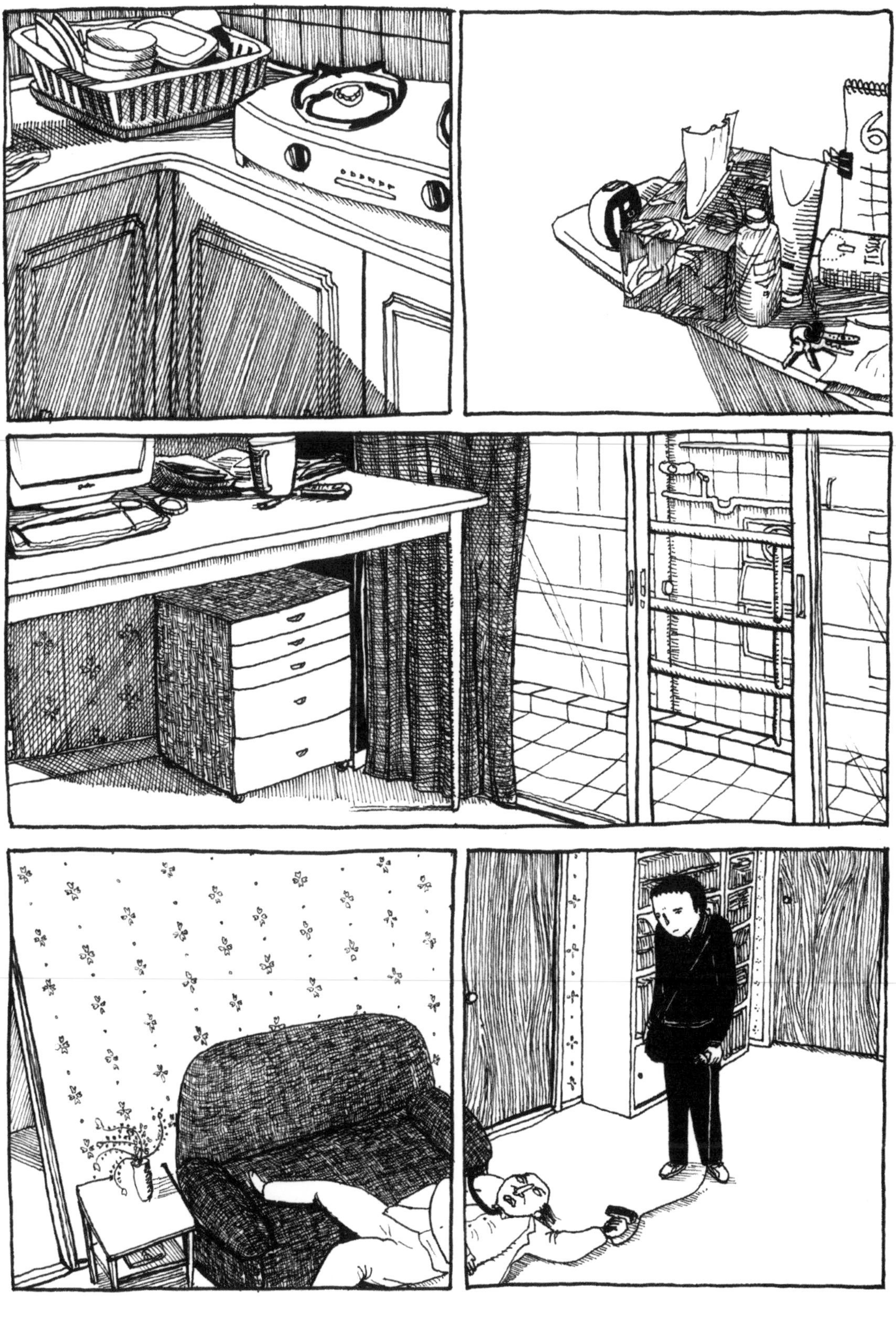

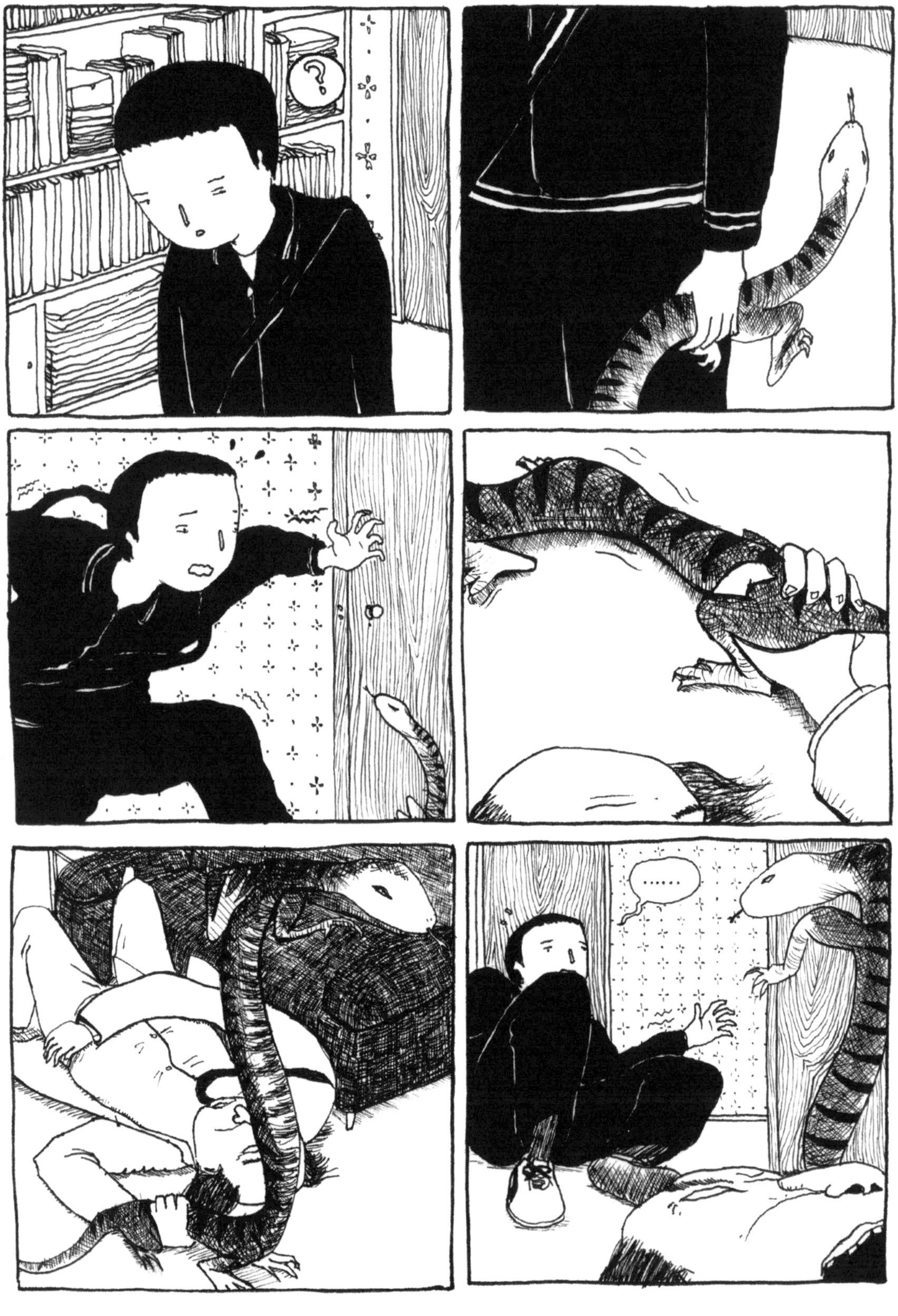
?
……

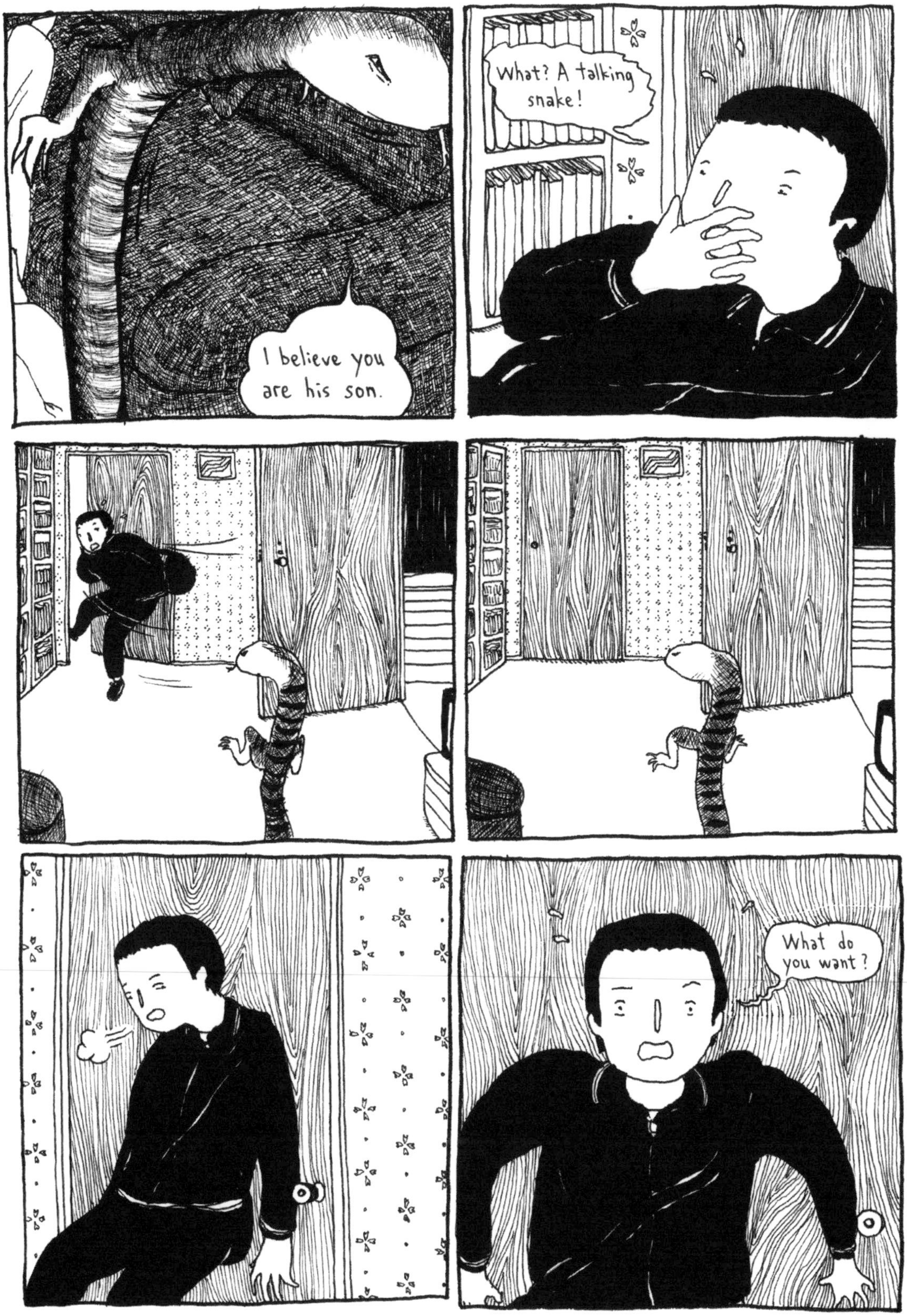
I believe you are his son.
What? A talking snake!
What do you want?

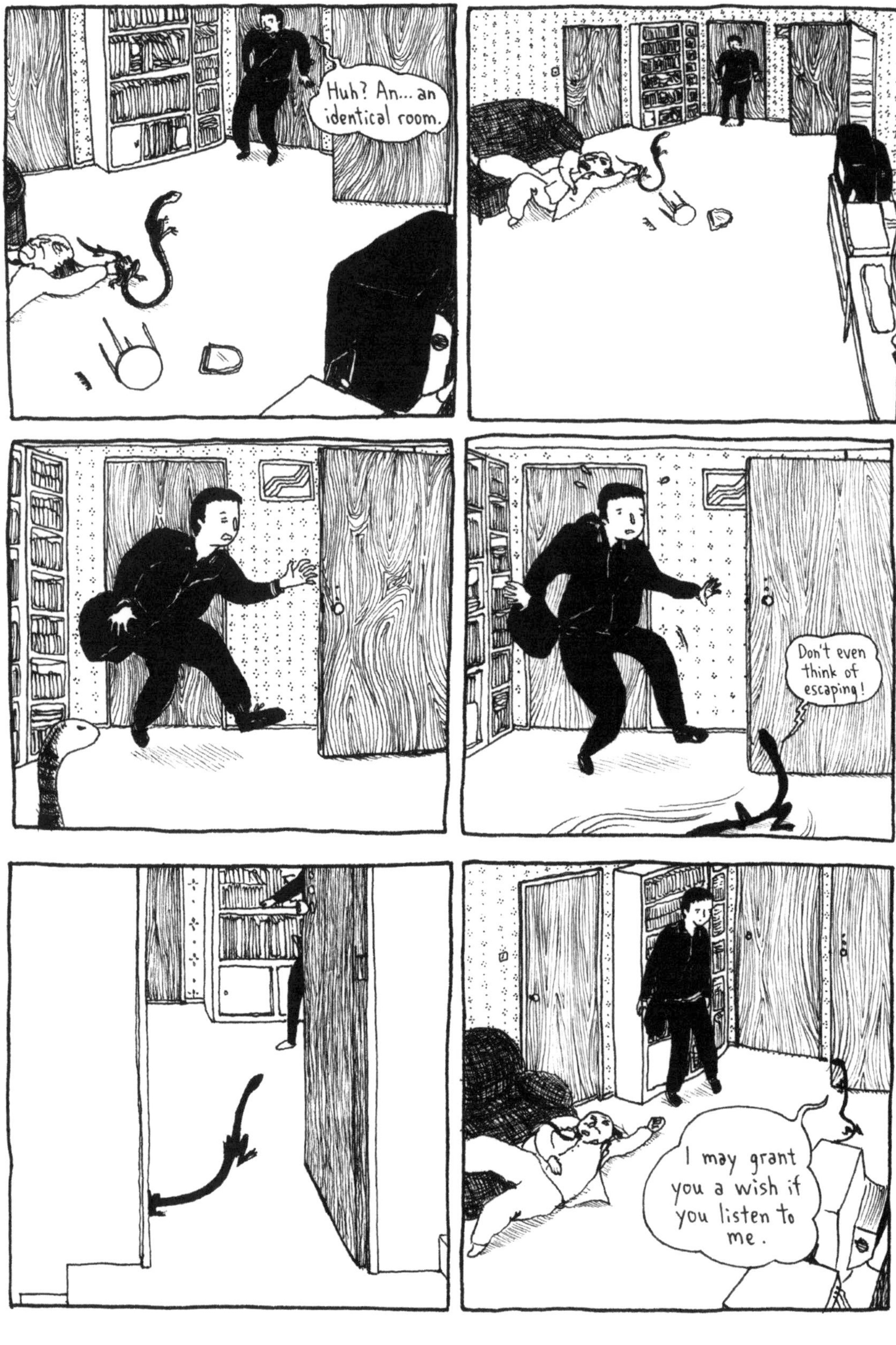
Huh? An... an identical room.
Don't even think of escaping!
I may grant you a wish if you listen to me.

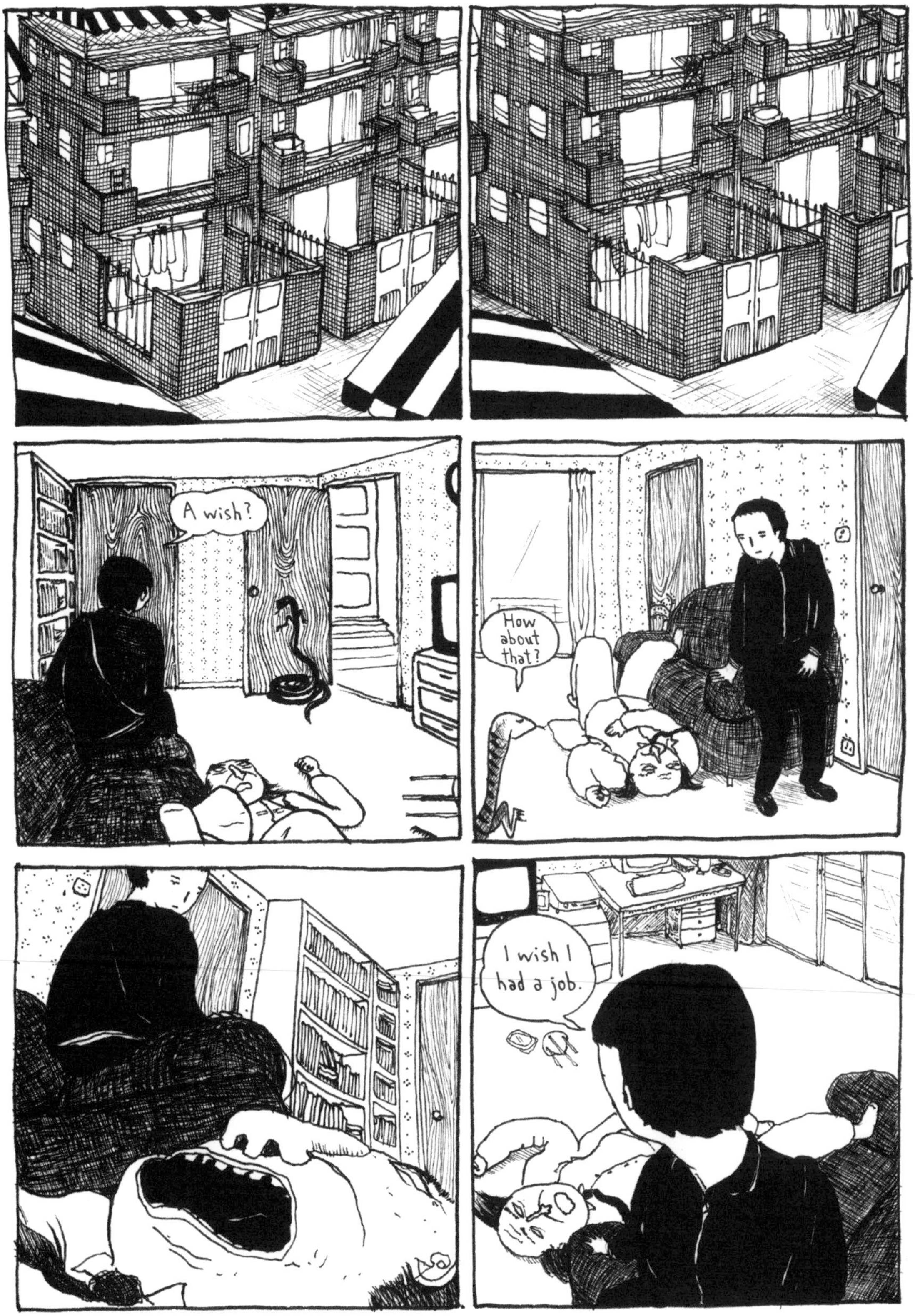
A wish?
How about that?
I wish I had a job.

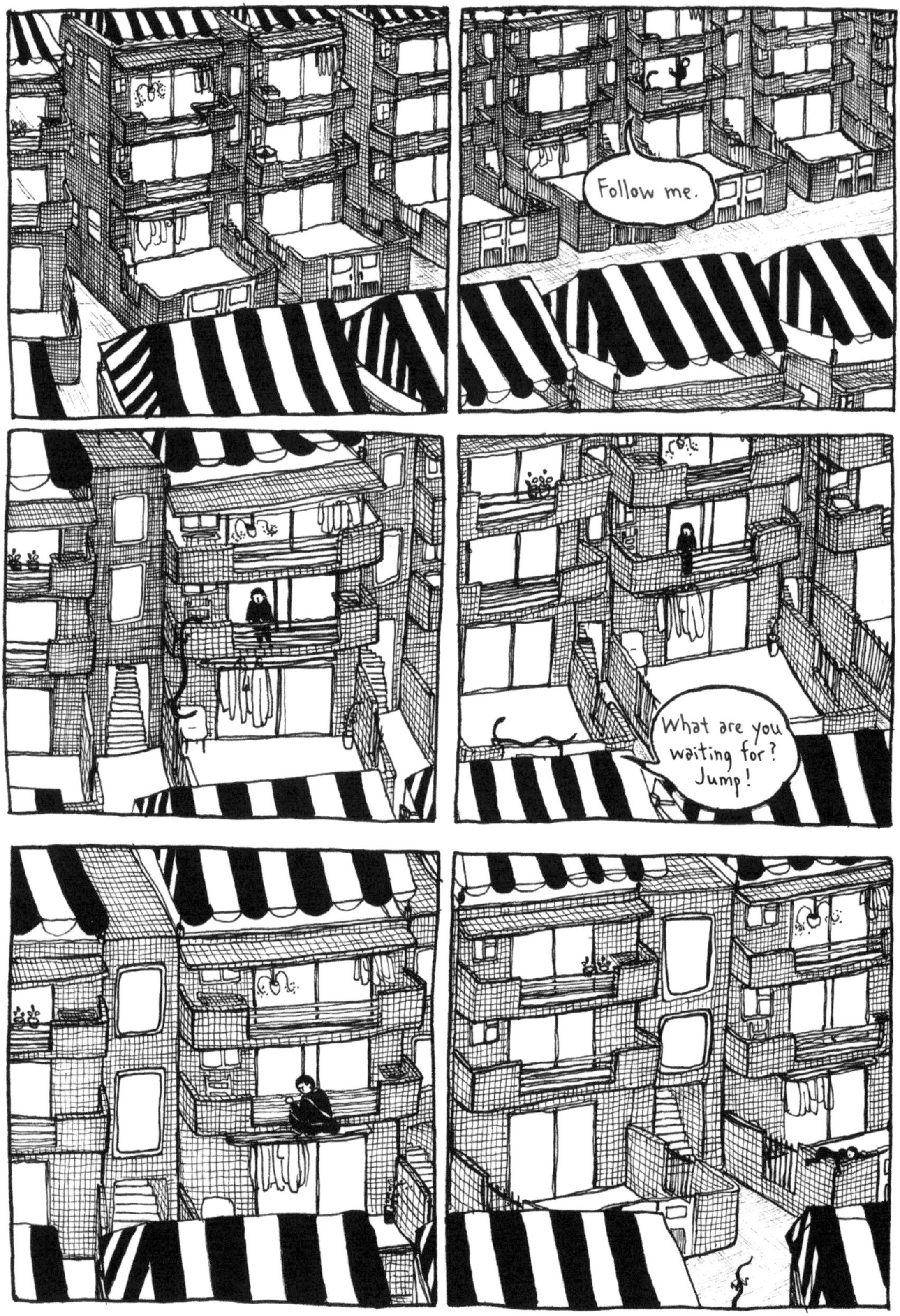
Follow me.
What are you waiting for? Jump!

Strange... I've never noticed this place before.
What are you waiting for? Come on up!

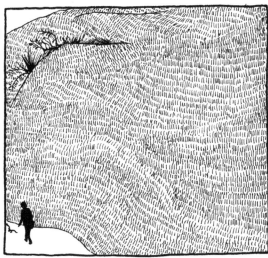

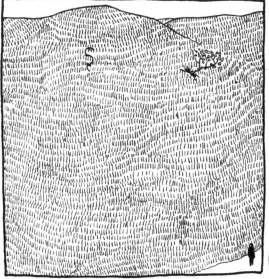

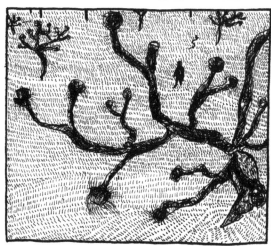

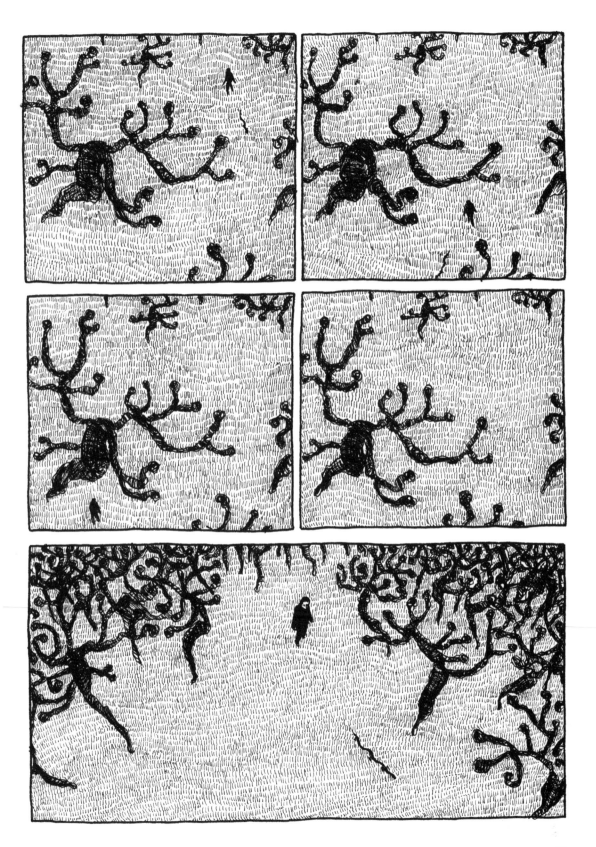

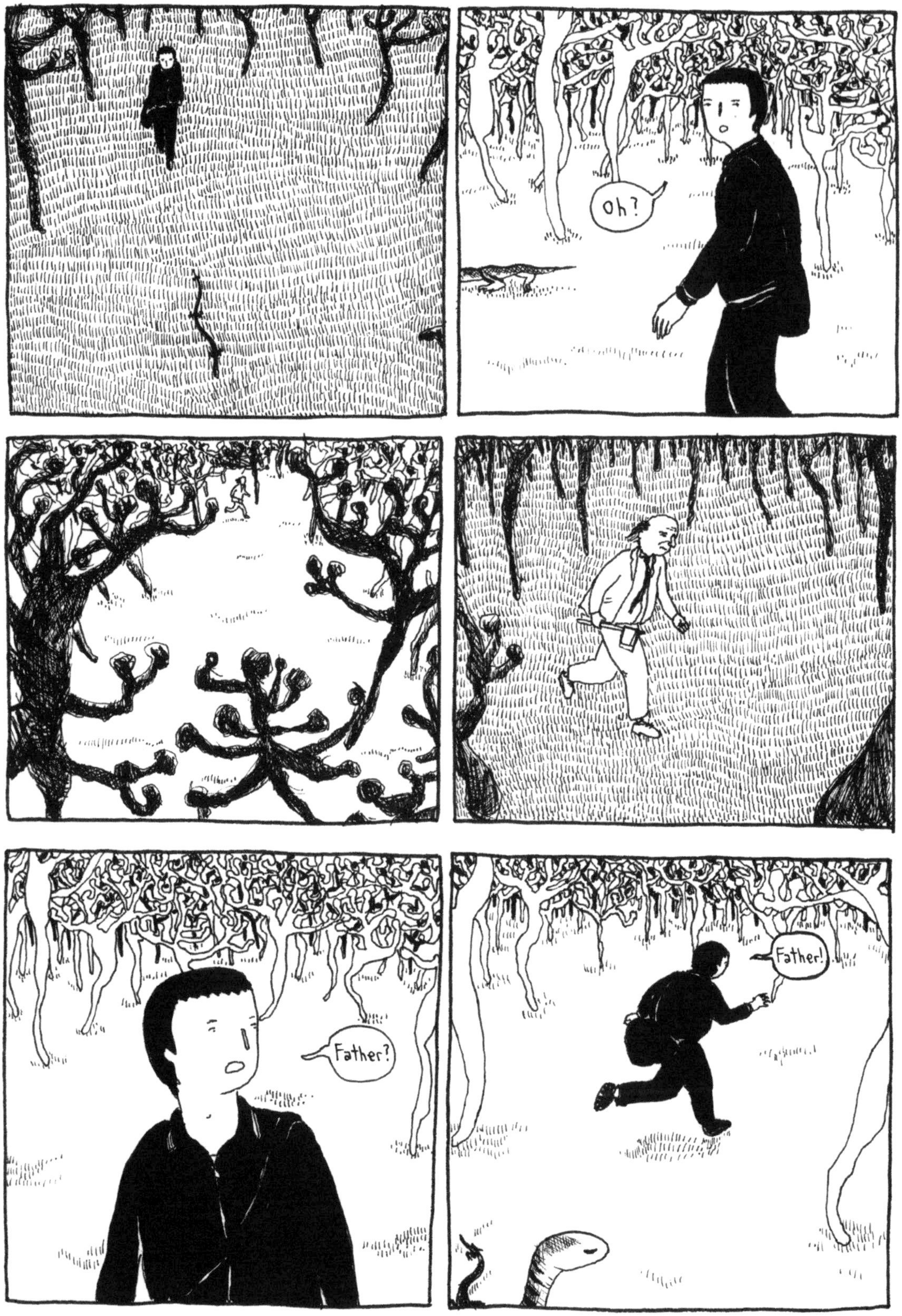
Oh?
Father?
Father!

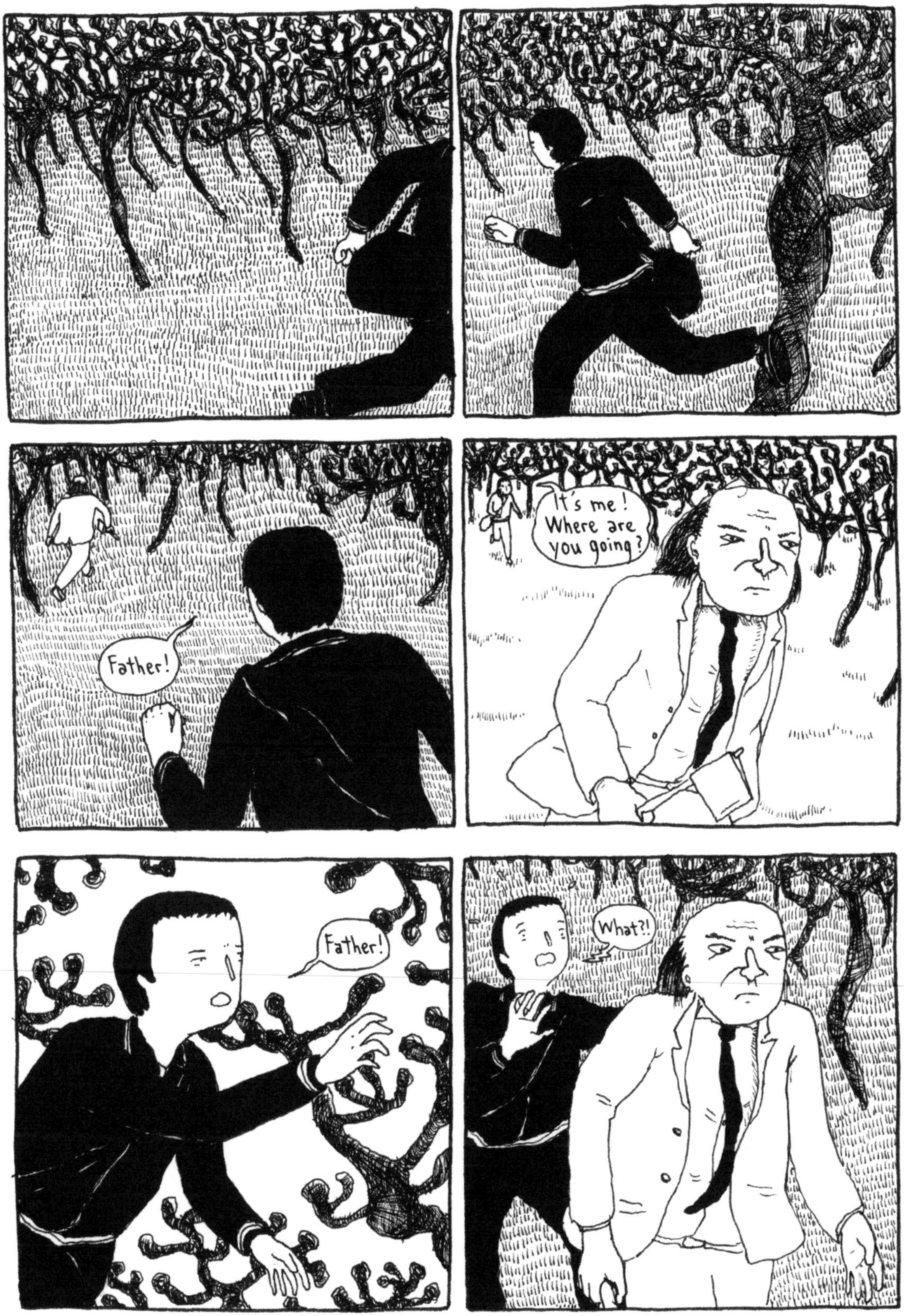
Father!
It's me! Where are you going?
Father!
What?!

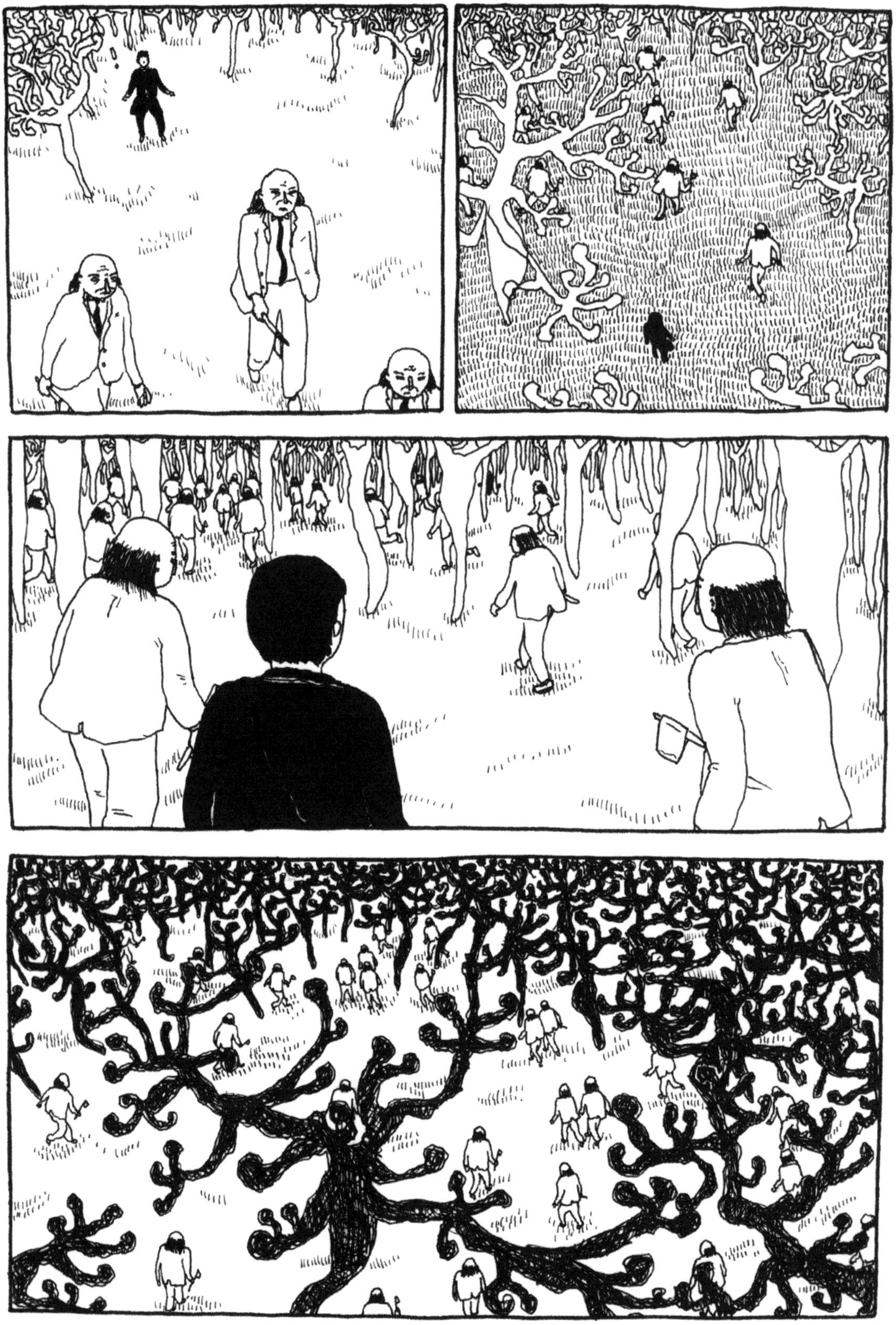
!

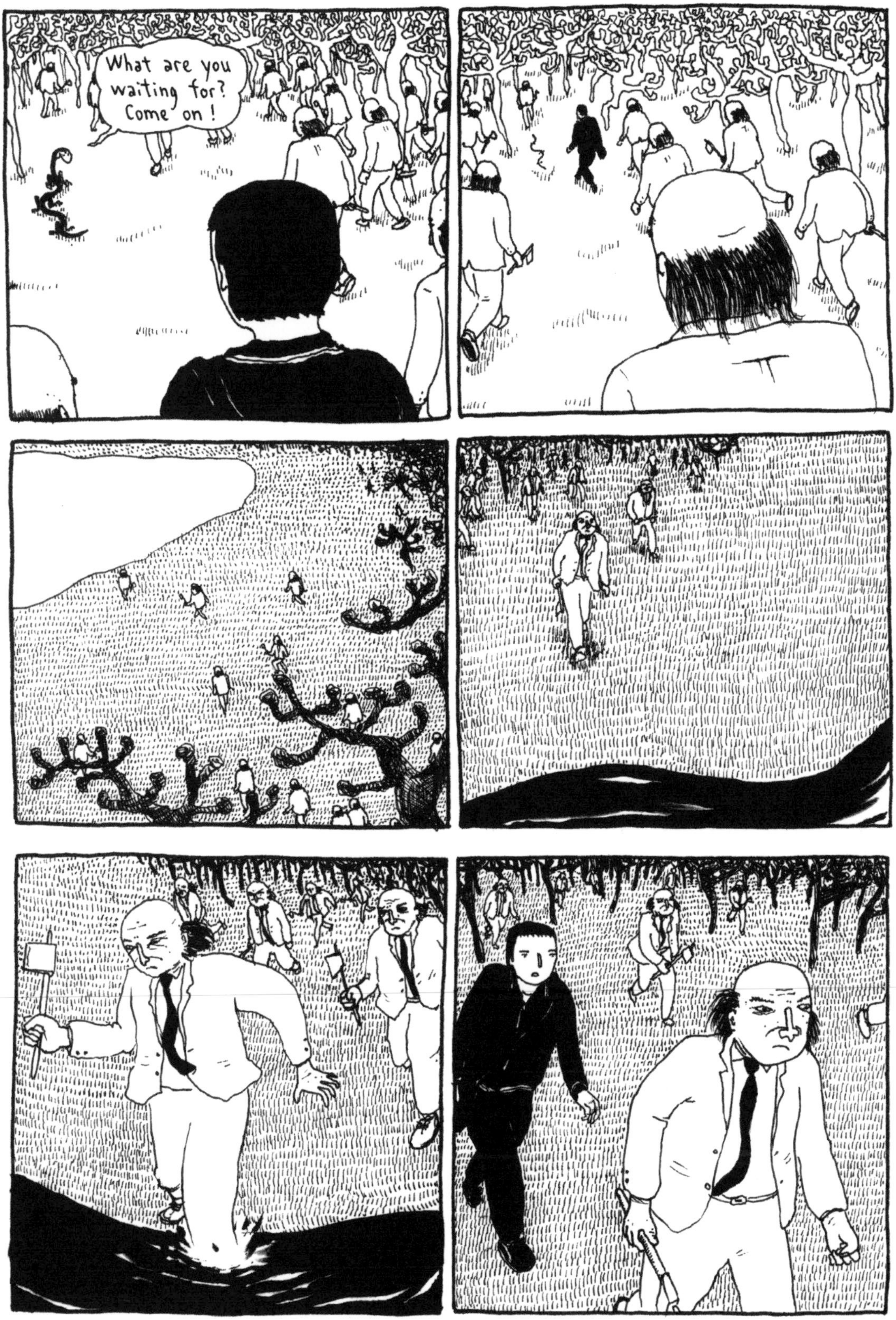
What are you waiting for? Come on!

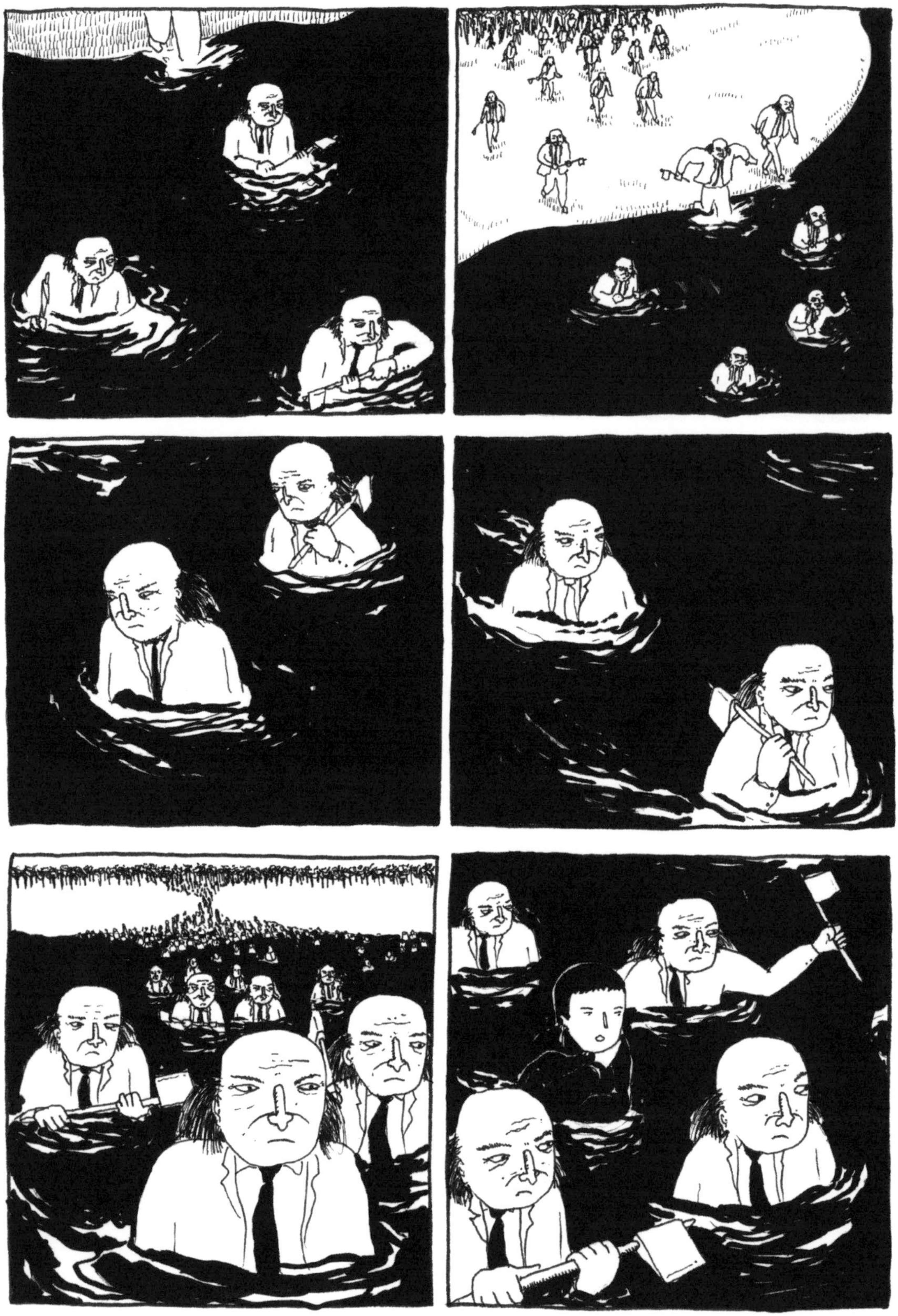

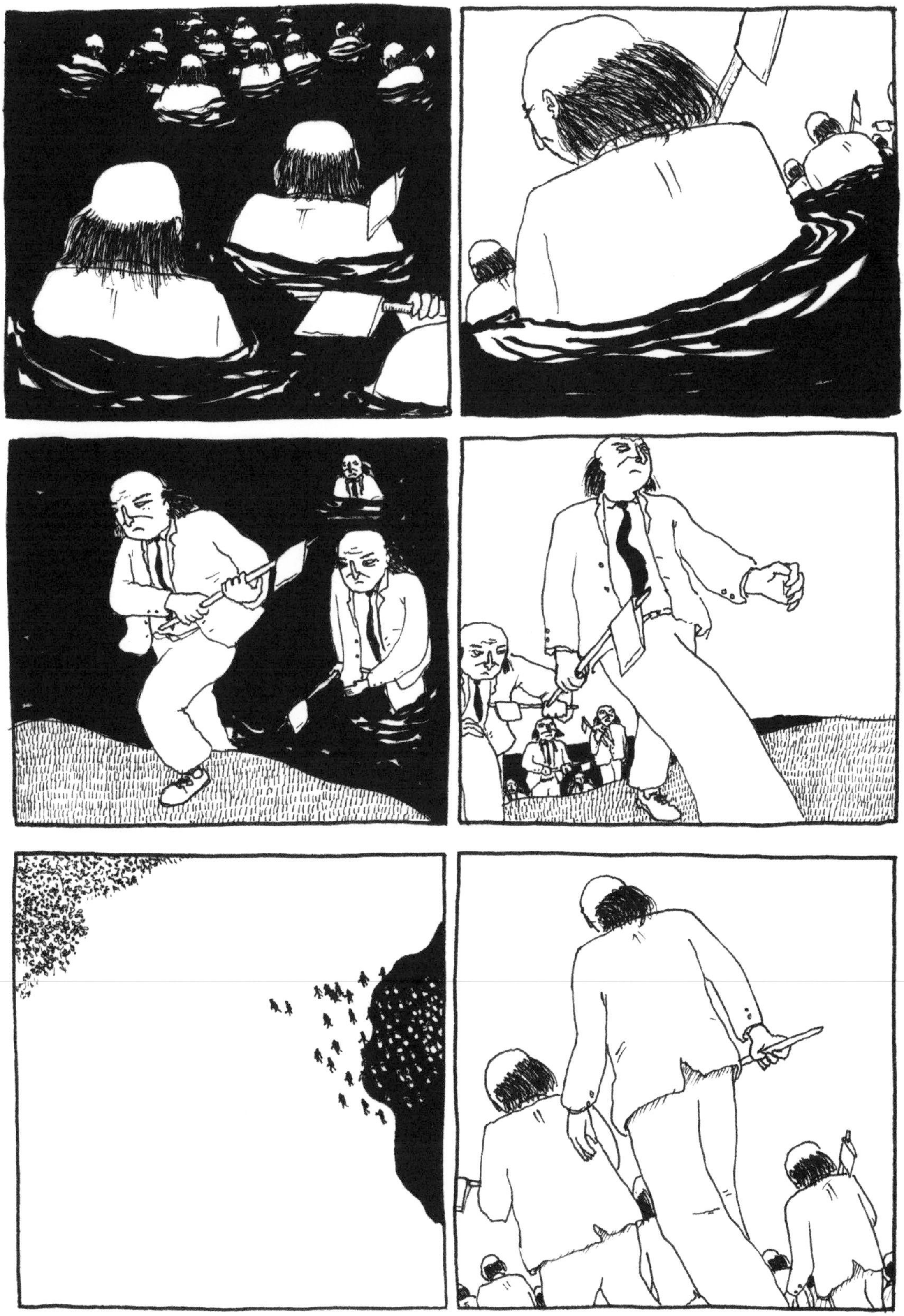

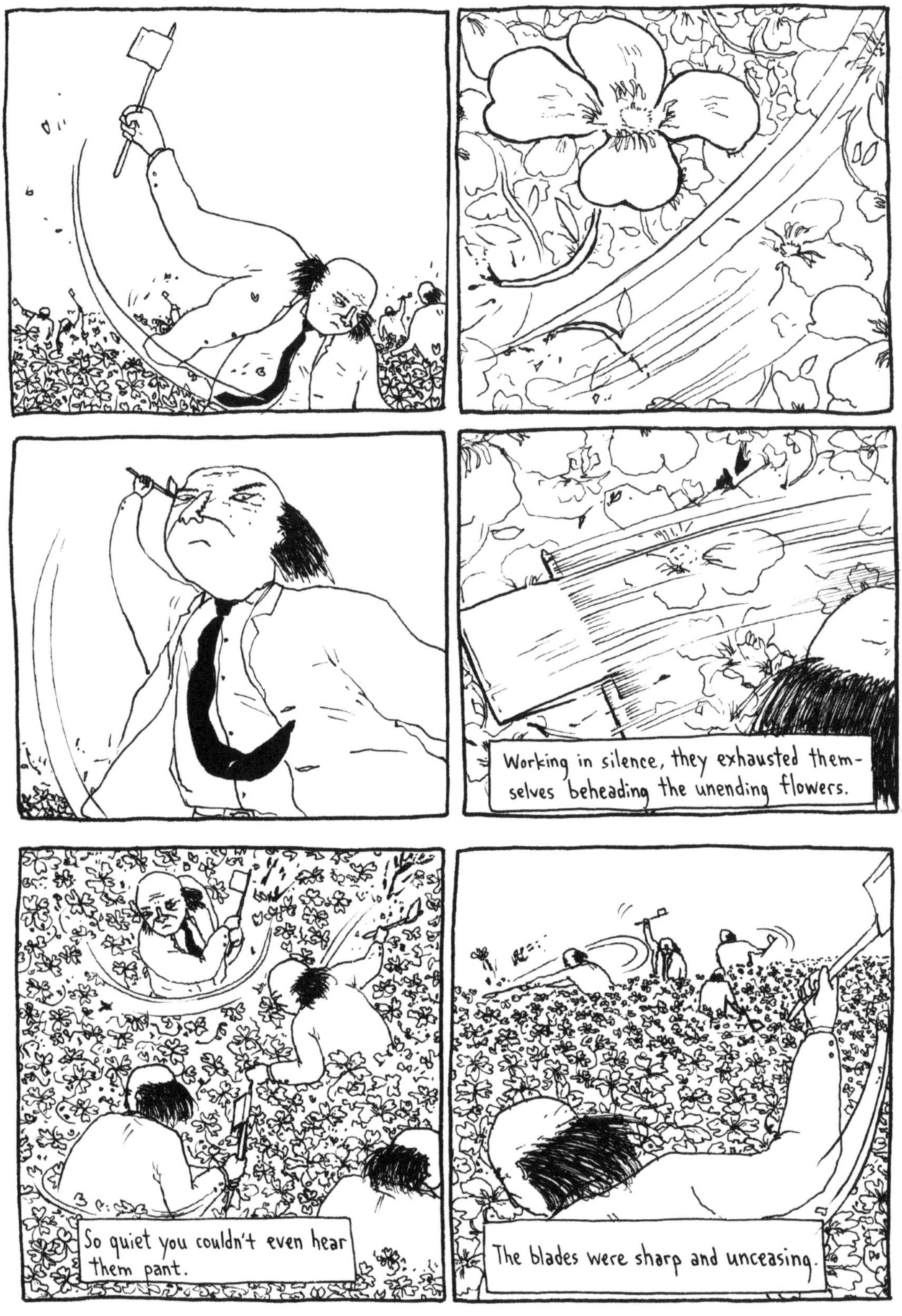
Working in silence, they exhausted them-
selves beheading the unending flowers.
So quiet you couldn't even hear
them pant.
The blades were sharp and unceasing.

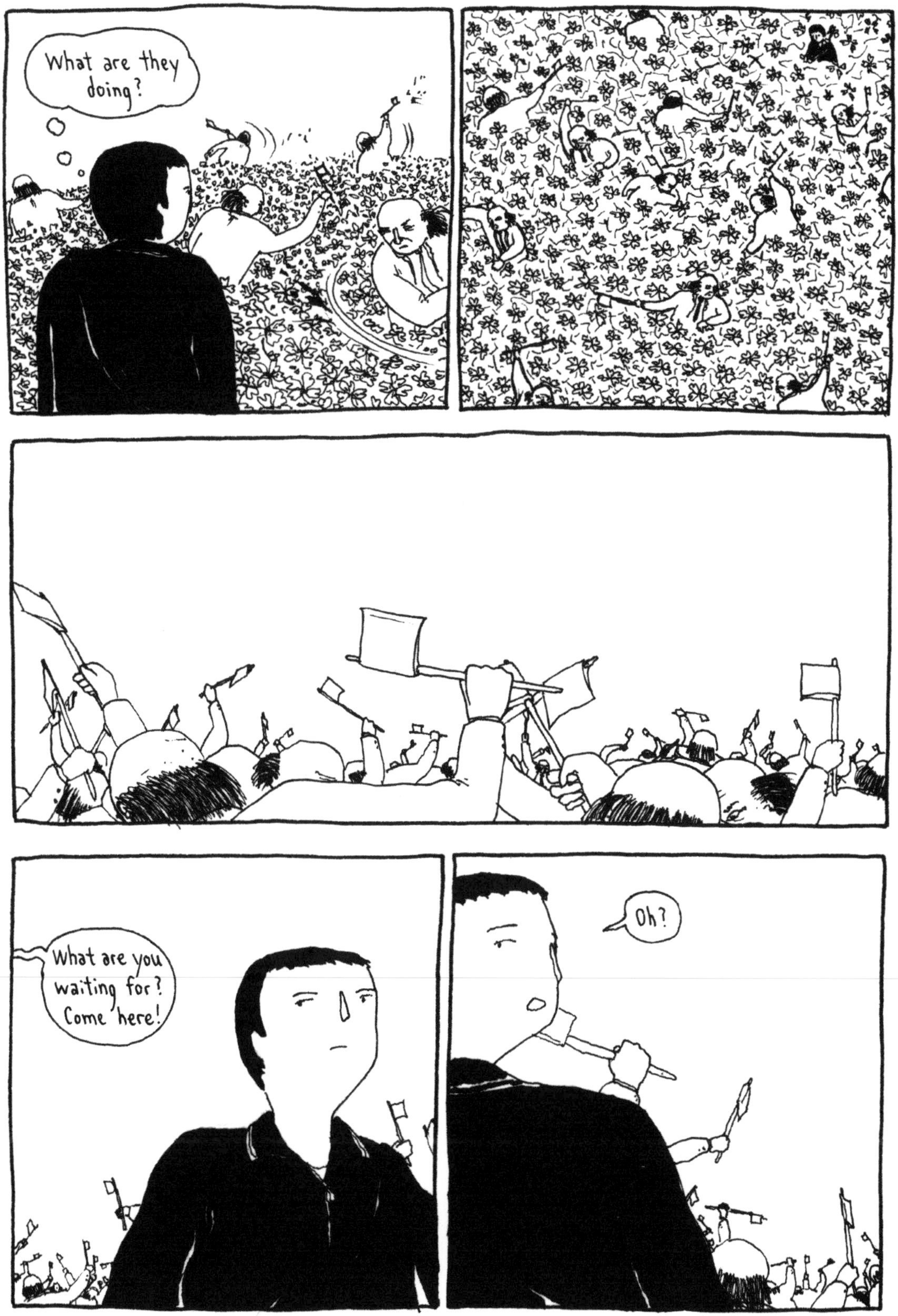
What are they doing?
What are you waiting for? Come here!
Oh?

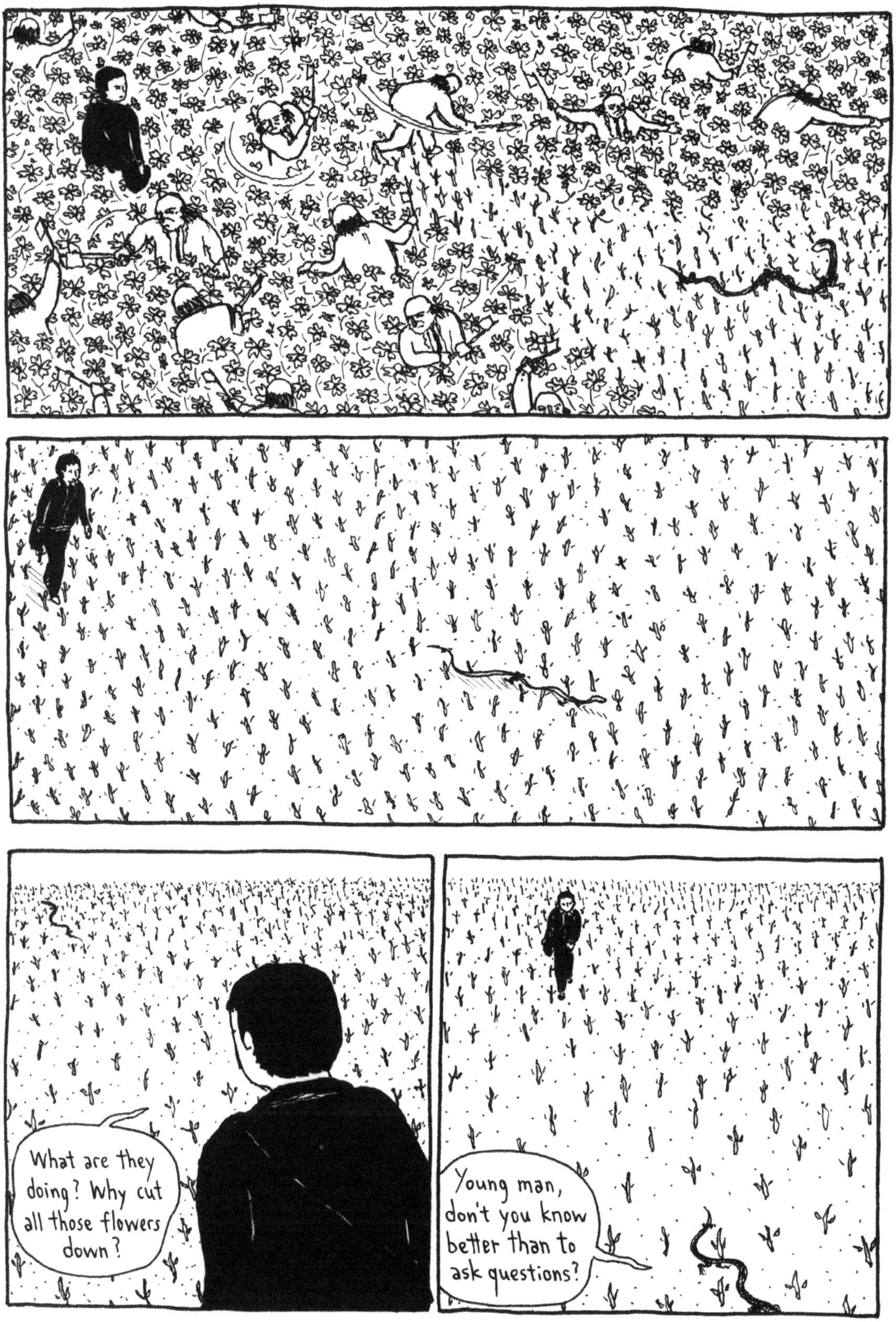
What are they doing? Why cut all those flowers down?
Young man, don't you know better than to ask questions?

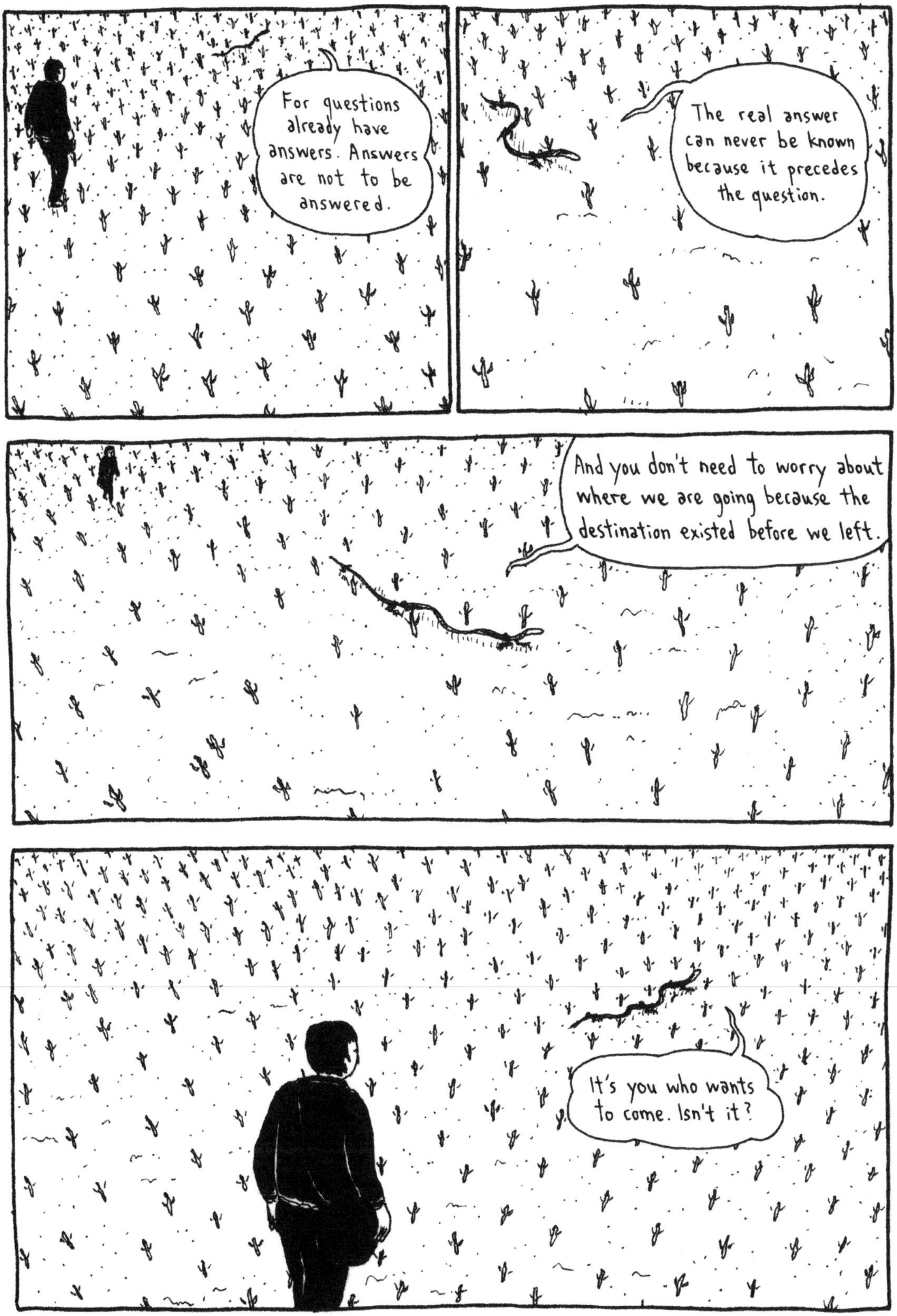
For questions already have answers. Answers are not to be answered.
The real answer can never be known because it precedes the question.
And you don't need to worry about where we are going because the destination existed before we left.
It's you who wants to come. Isn't it?

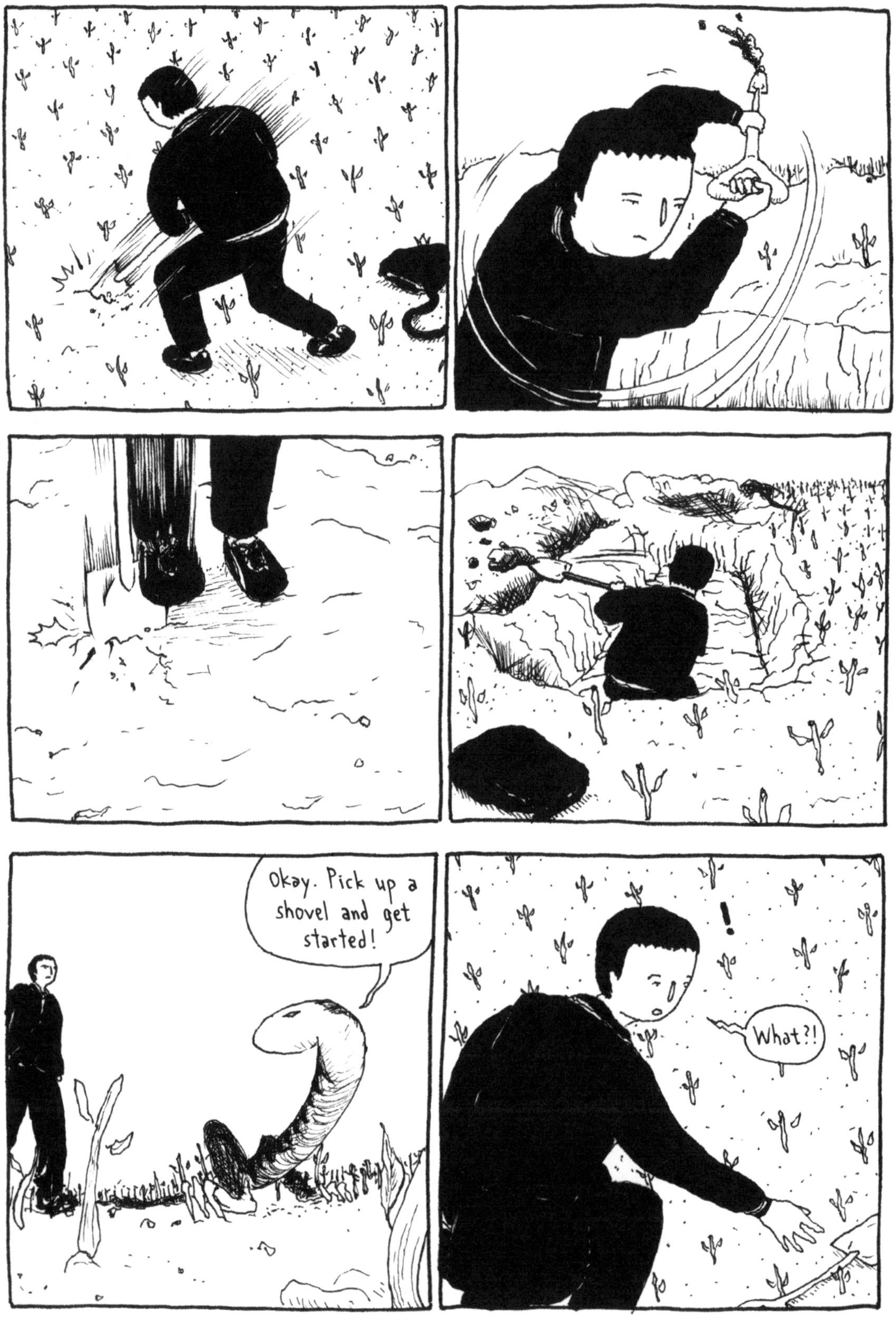
Okay. Pick up a shovel and get started!
!
What?!

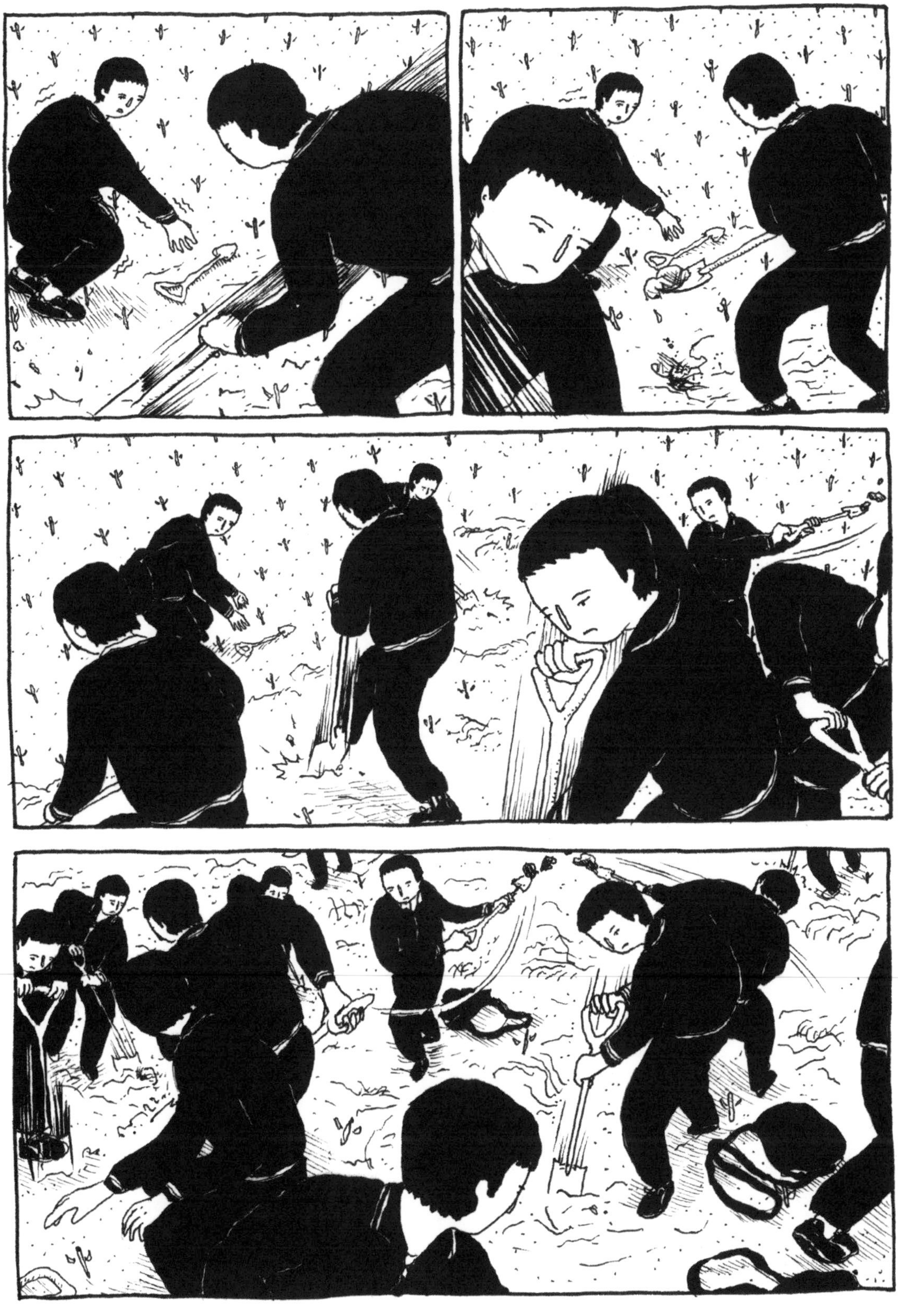

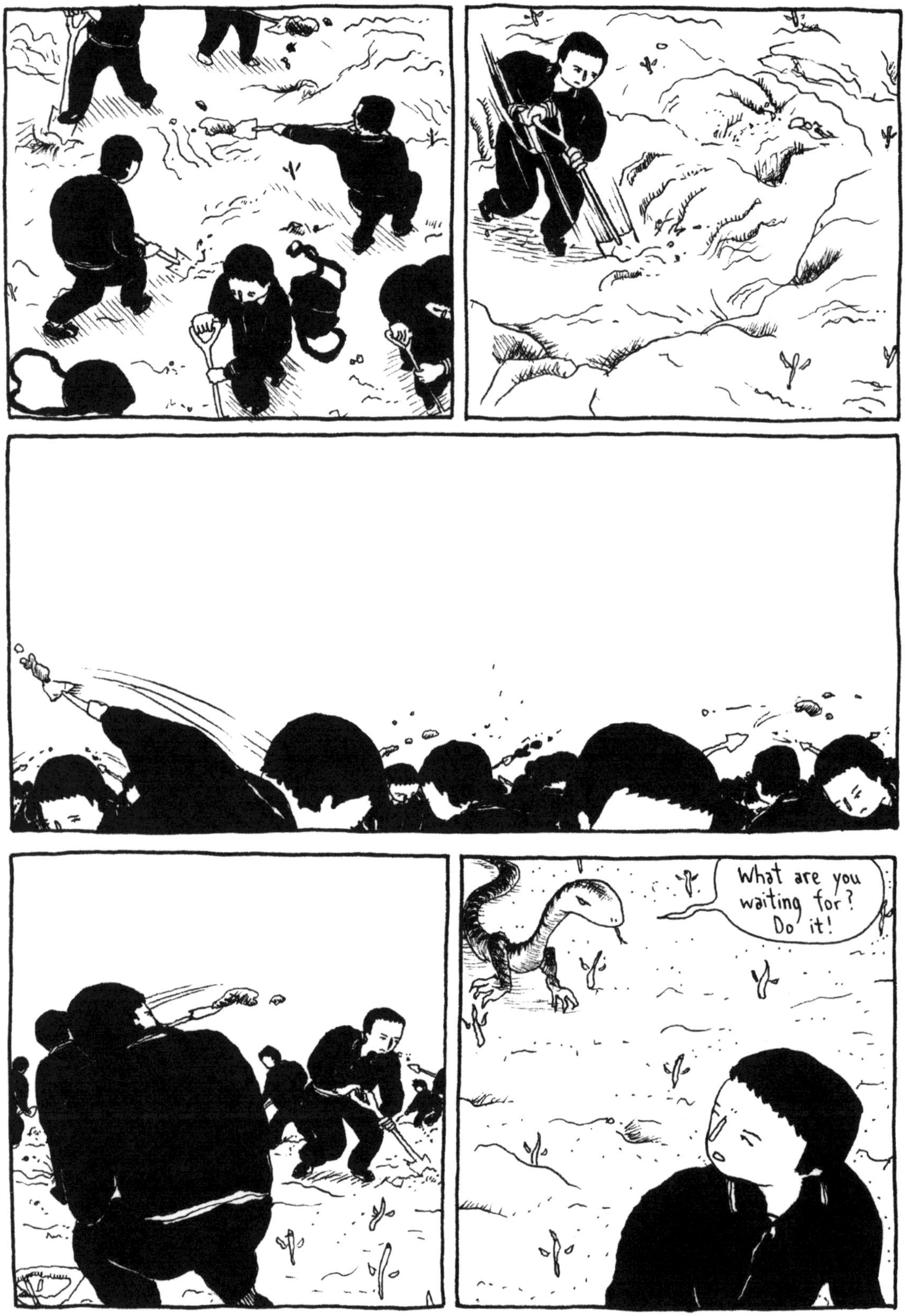
What are you waiting for? Do it!

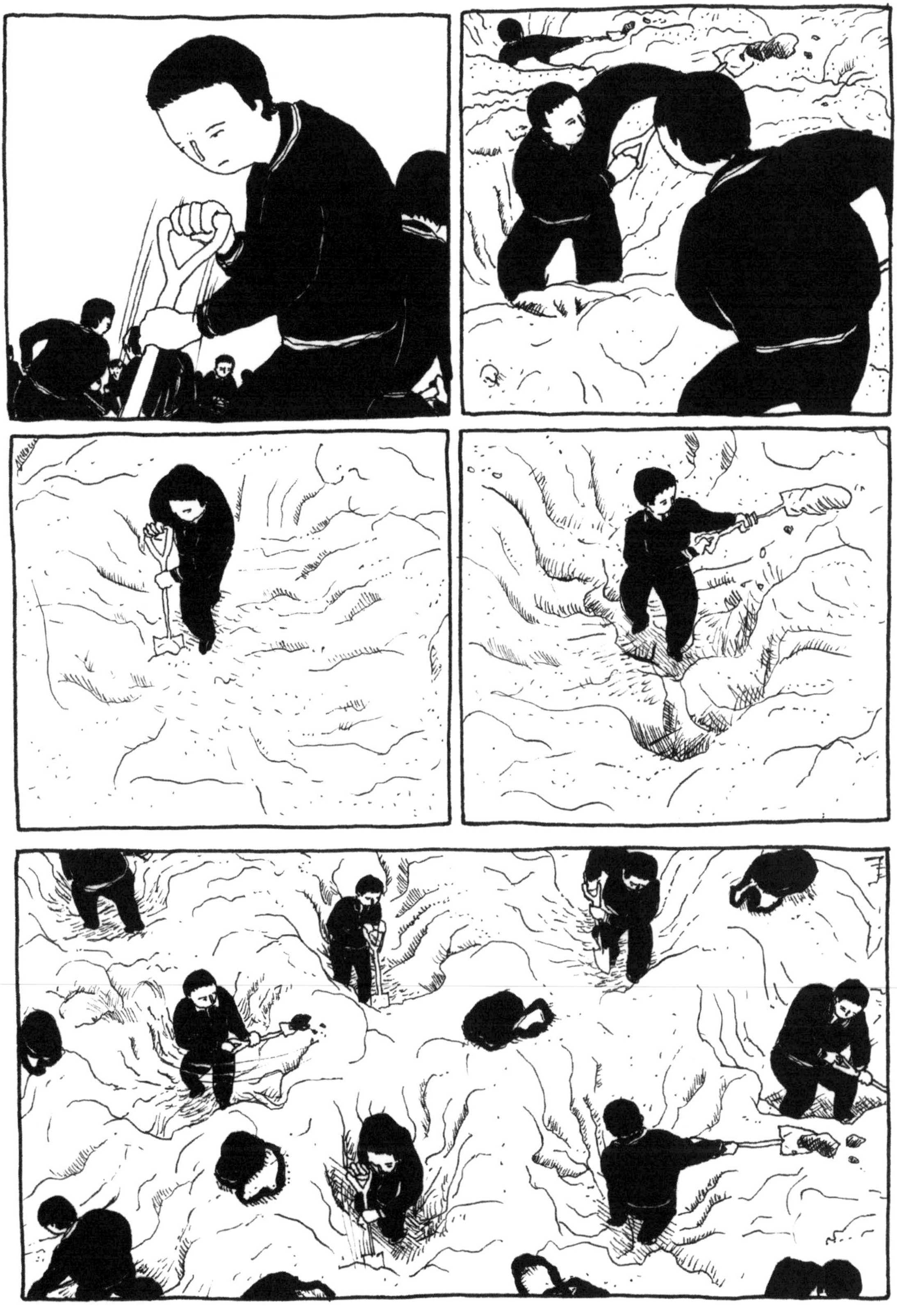

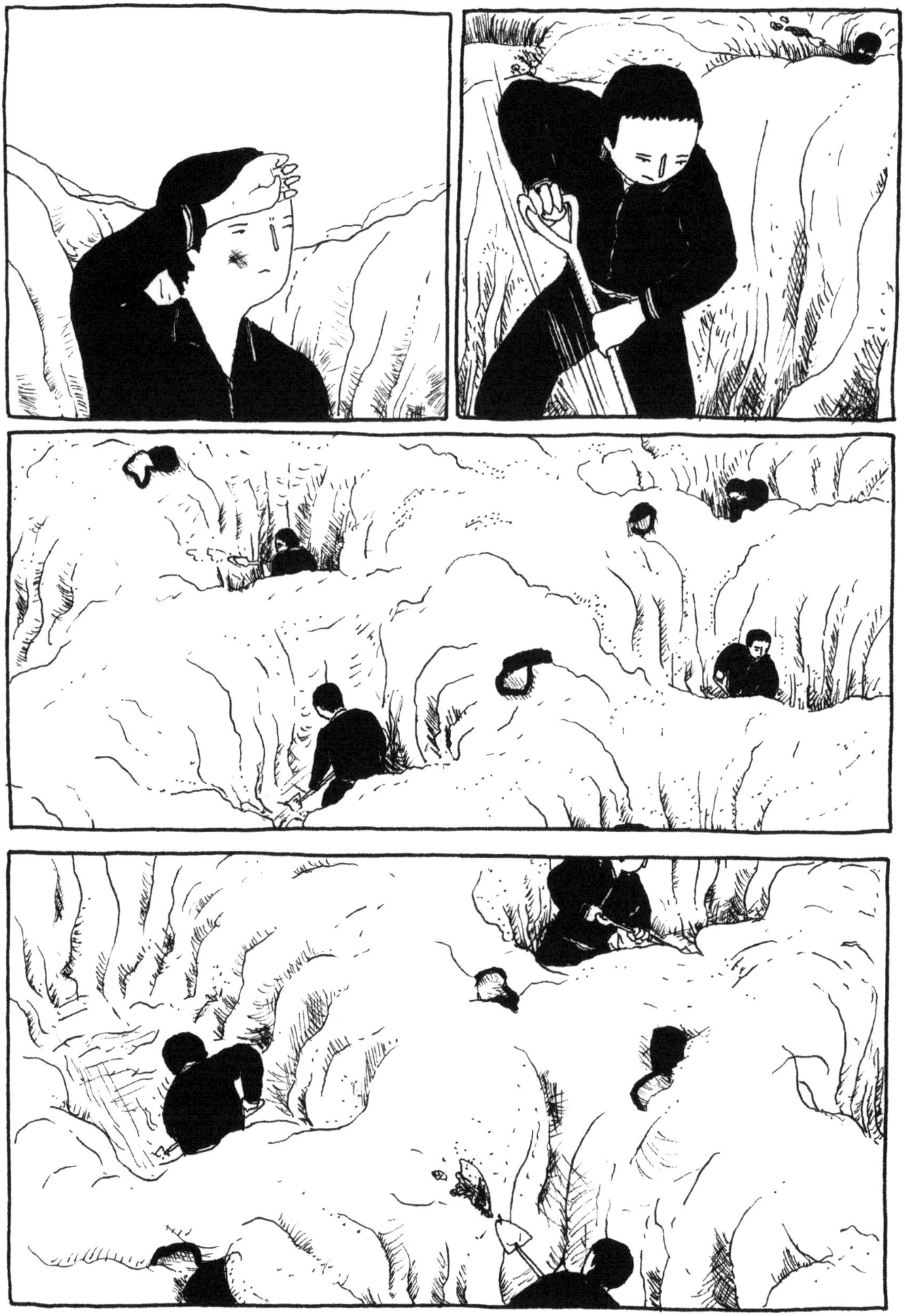

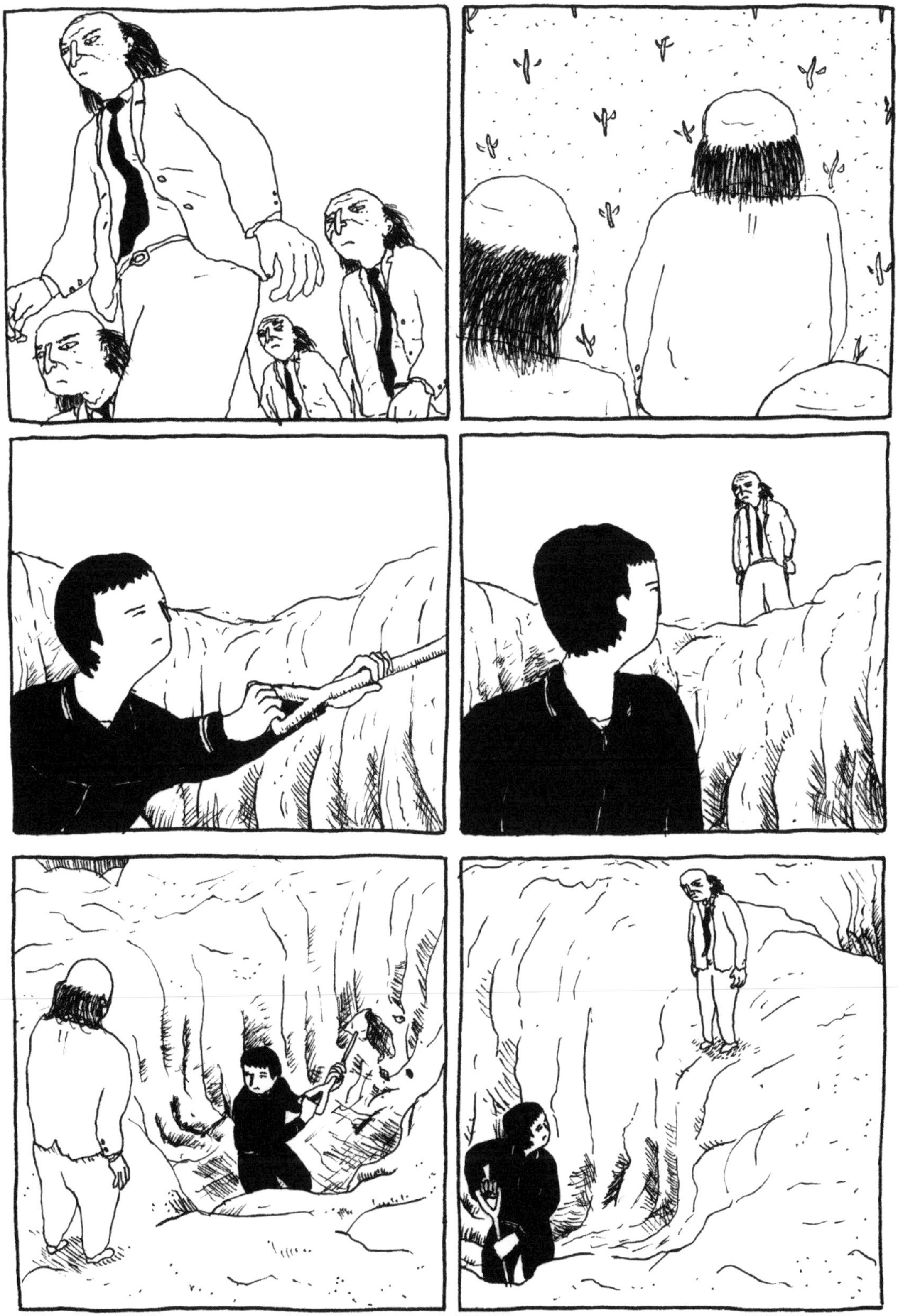

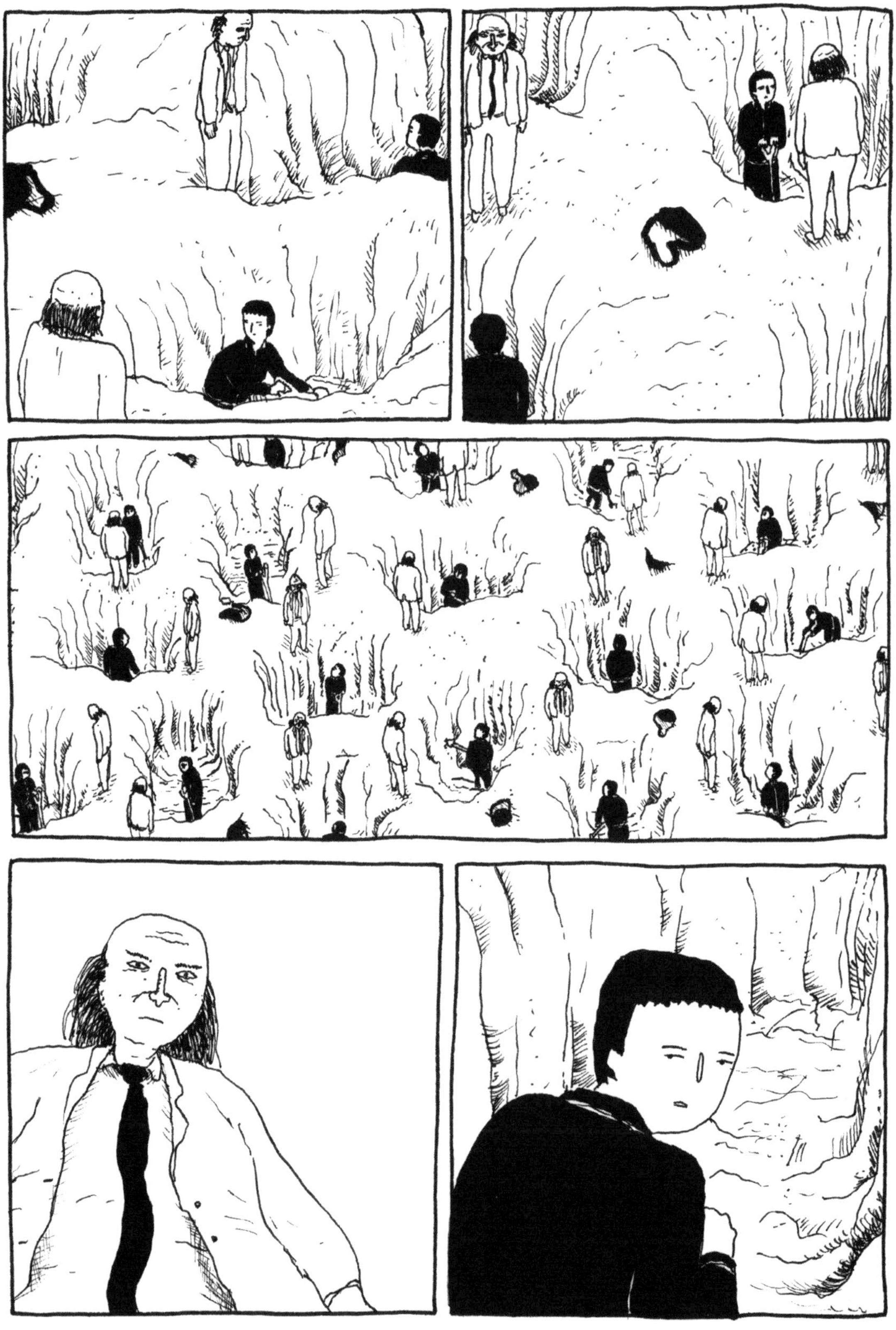

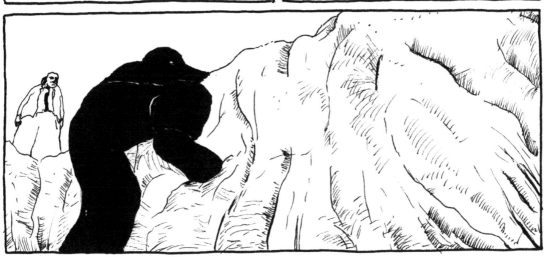

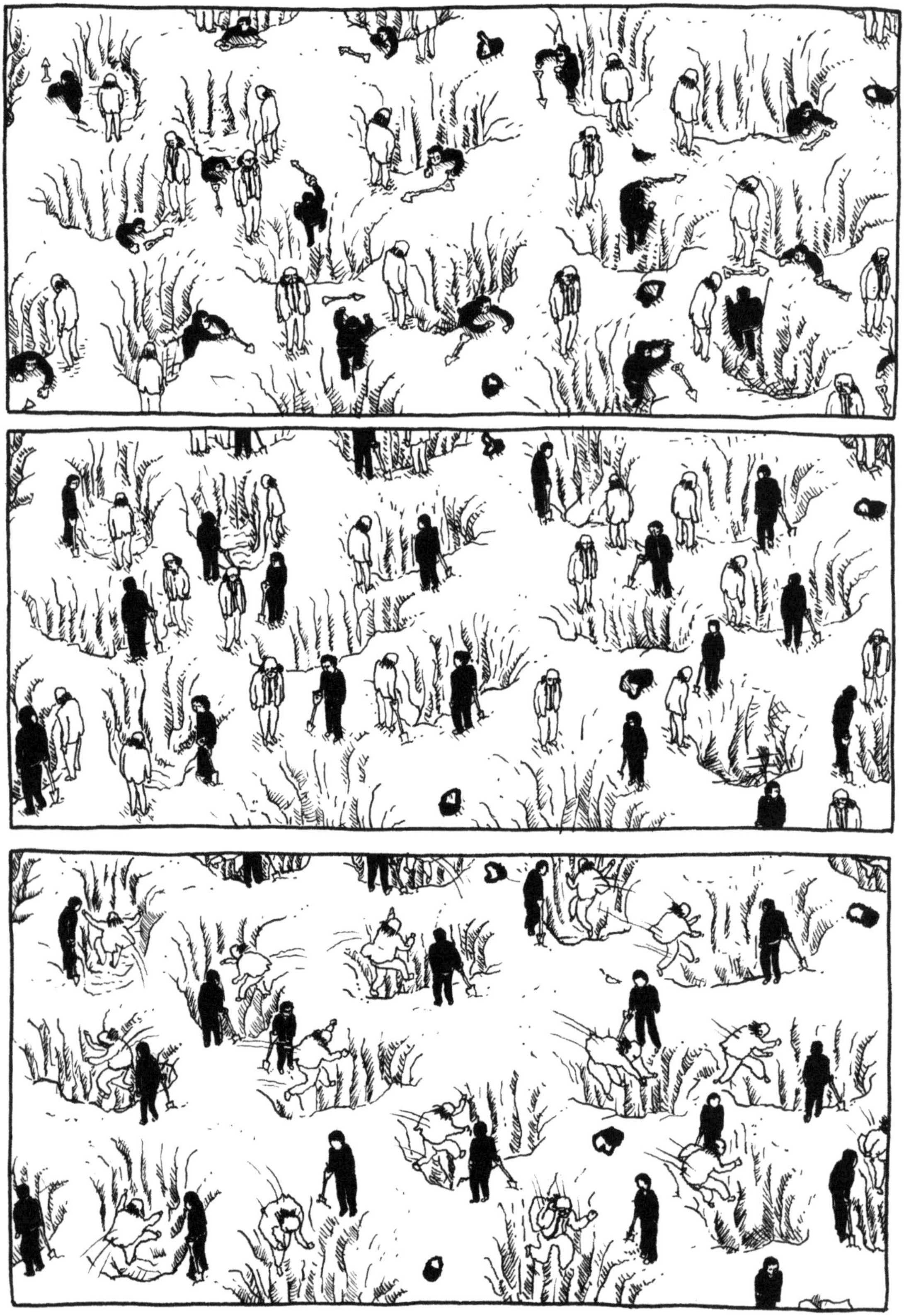

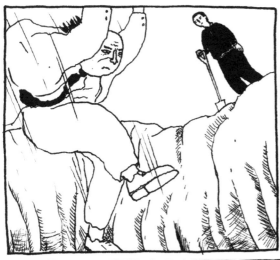

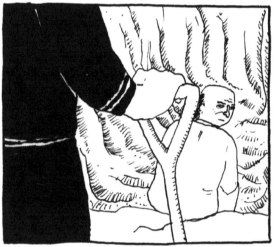
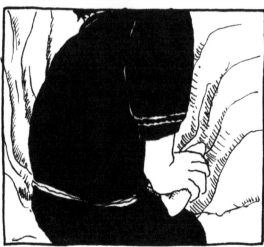

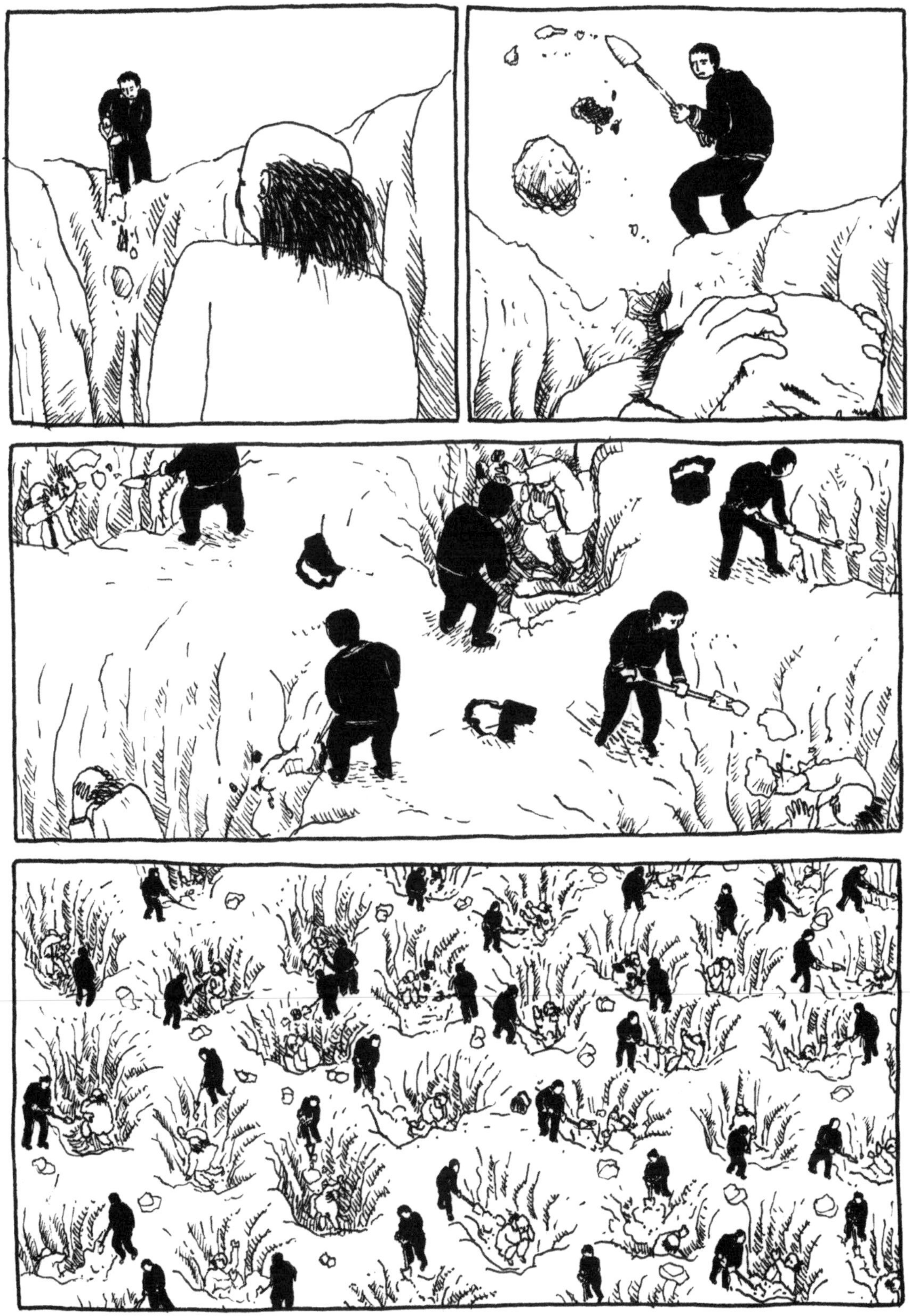

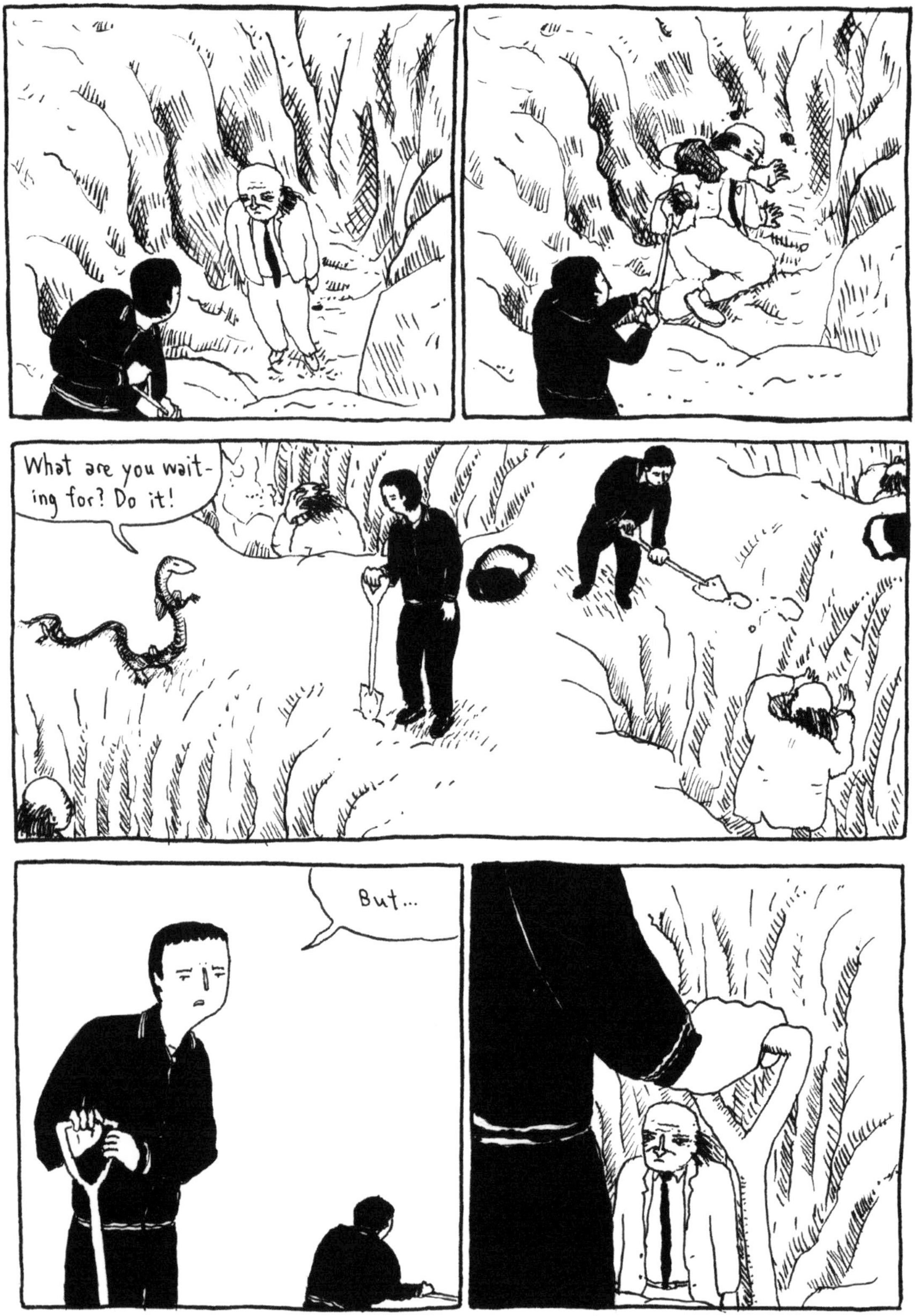
What are you wait-
ing for? Do it!
But...

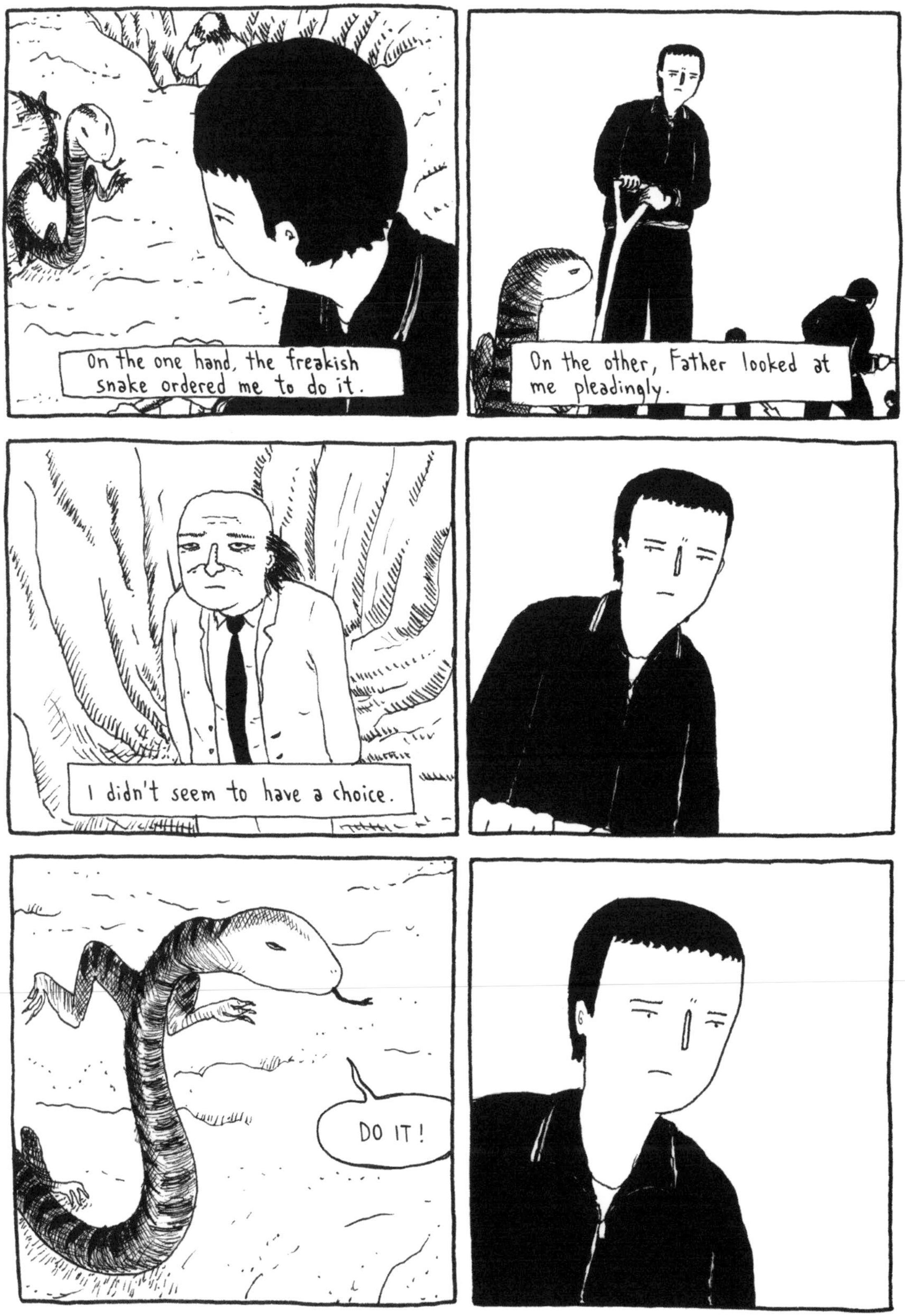
On the one hand, the freakish snake ordered me to do it.
On the other, Father looked at me pleadingly.
I didn't seem to have a choice.
DO IT!

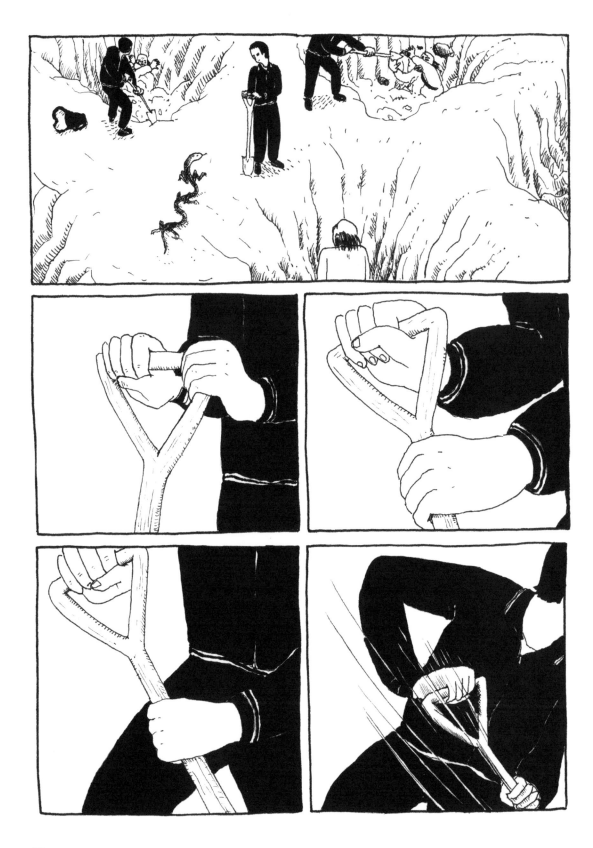

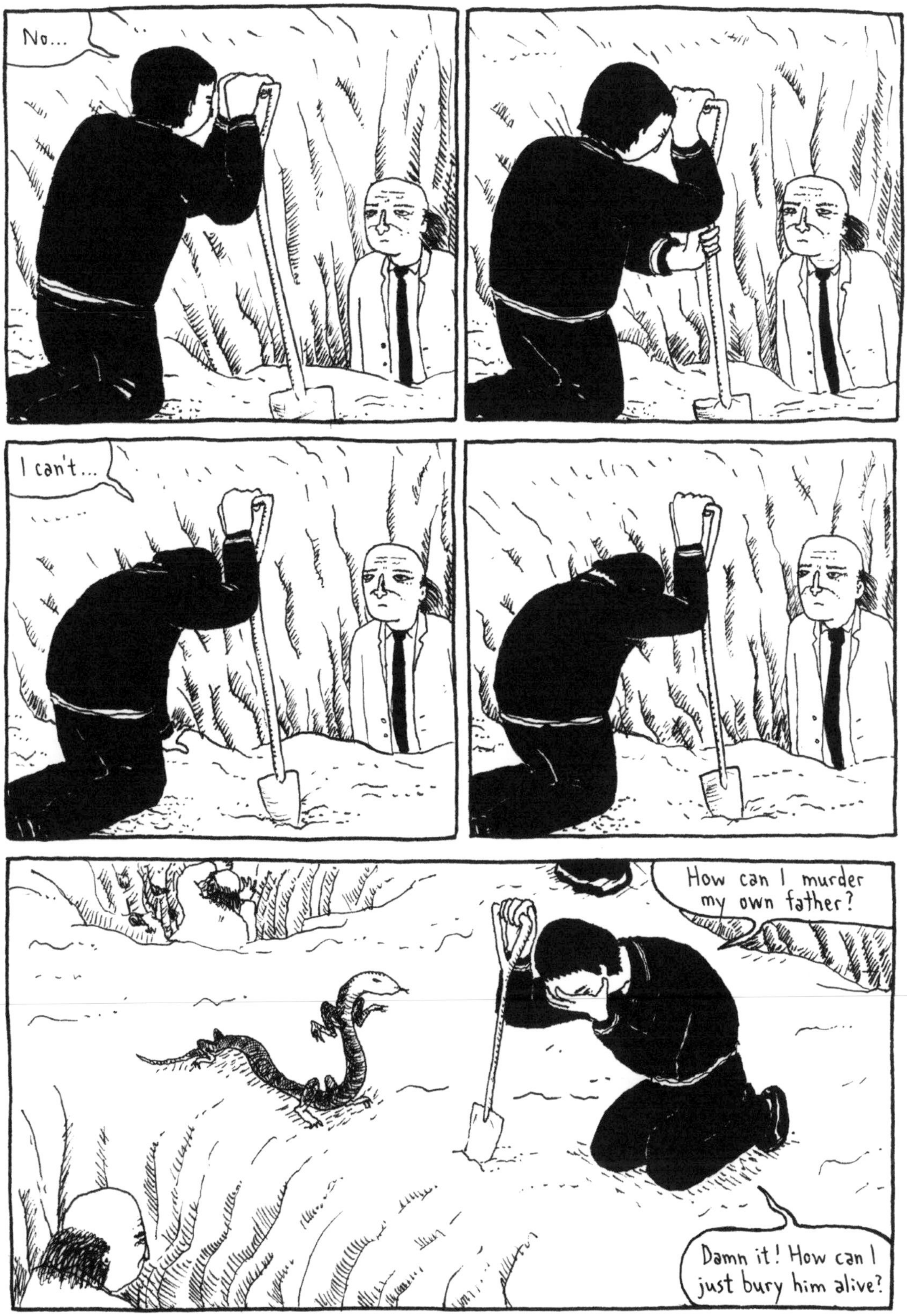
No...
I can't...
How can I murder my own father?
Damn it! How can I just bury him alive?

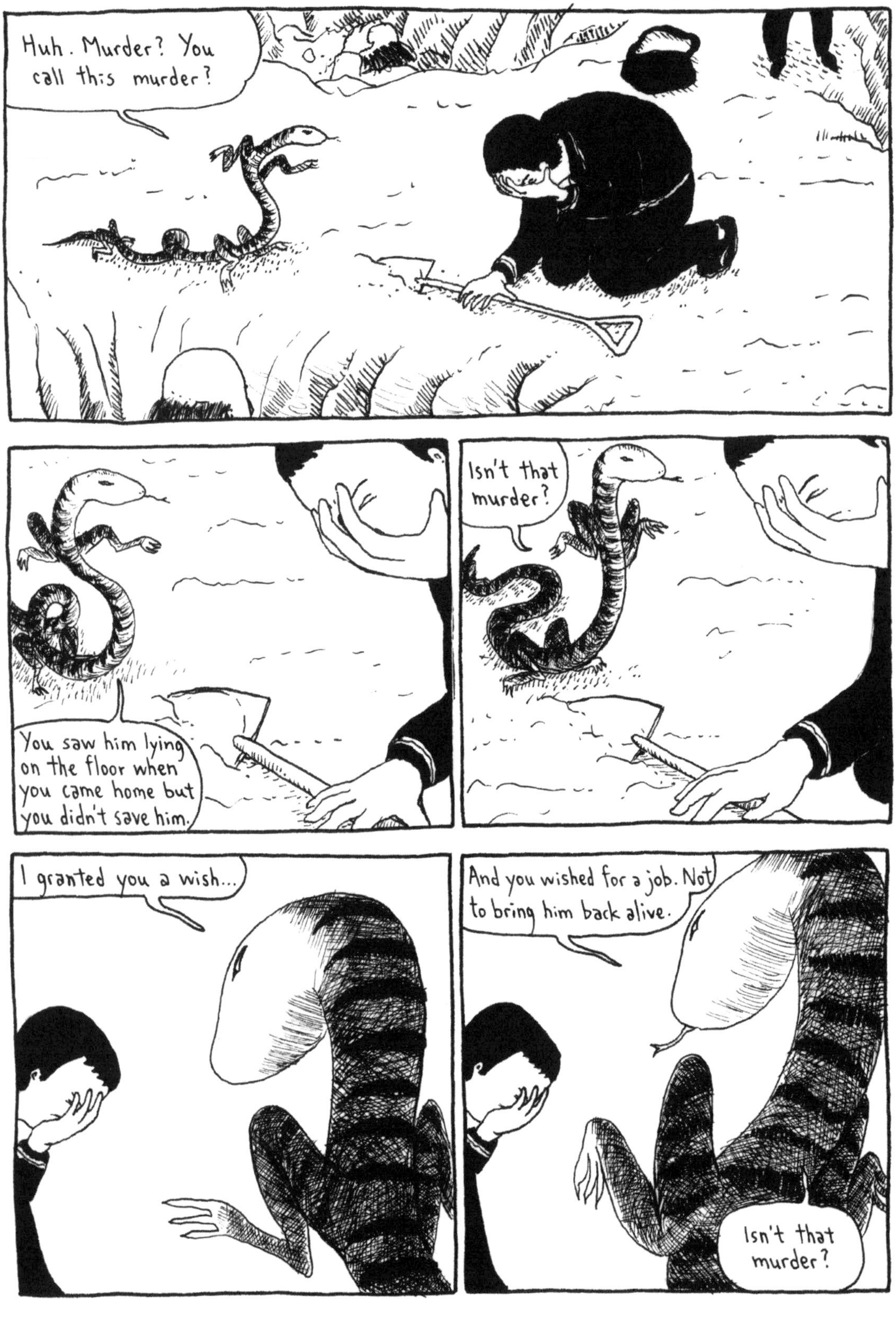
Huh. Murder? You call this murder?
You saw him lying on the floor when you came home but you didn't save him.
Isn't that murder?
I granted you a wish...
And you wished for a job. Not to bring him back alive.
Isn't that murder?

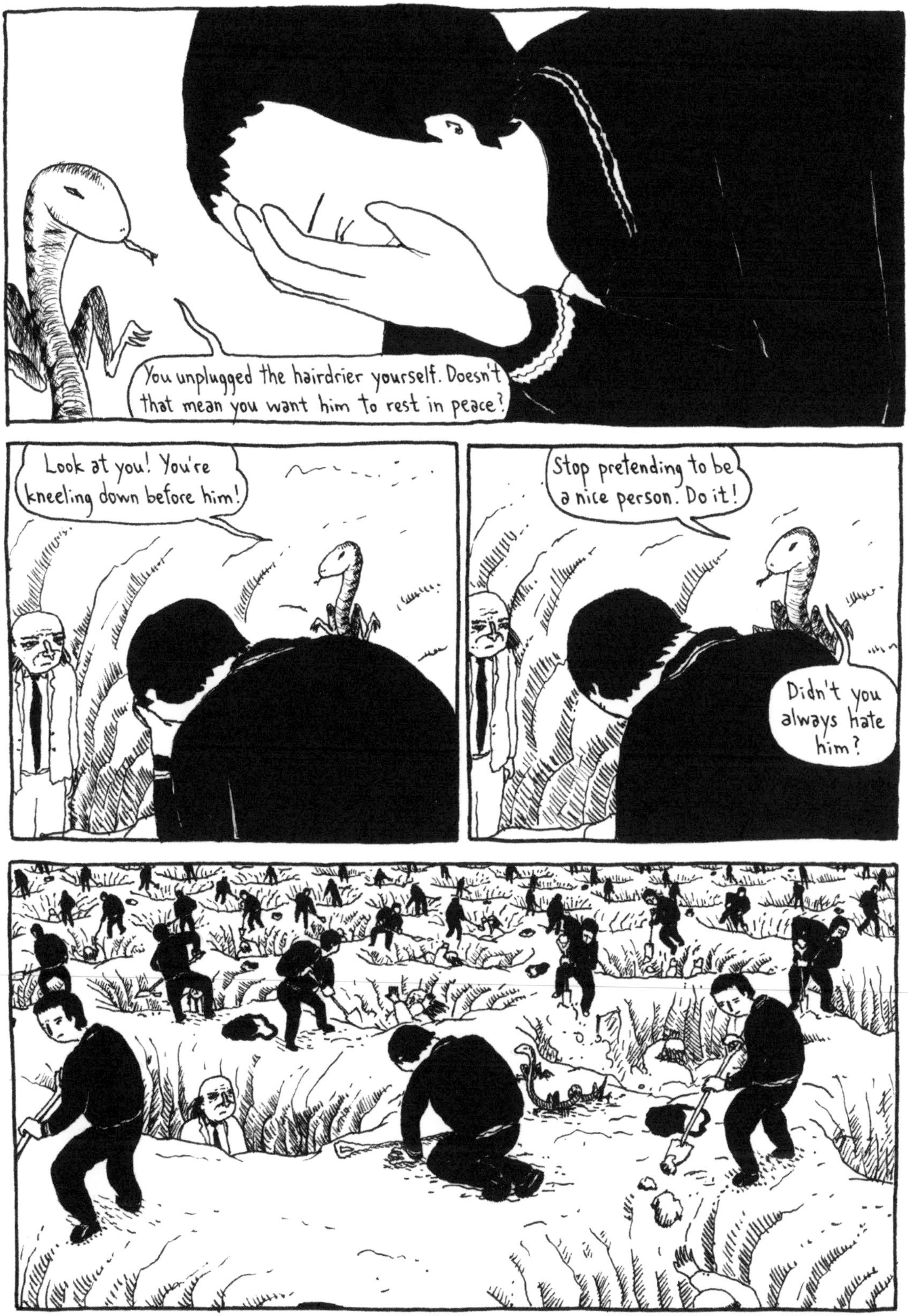
You unplugged the hairdrier yourself. Doesn't that mean you want him to rest in peace?
Look at you! You're kneeling down before him!
Stop pretending to be a nice person. Do it!
Didn't you always hate him?

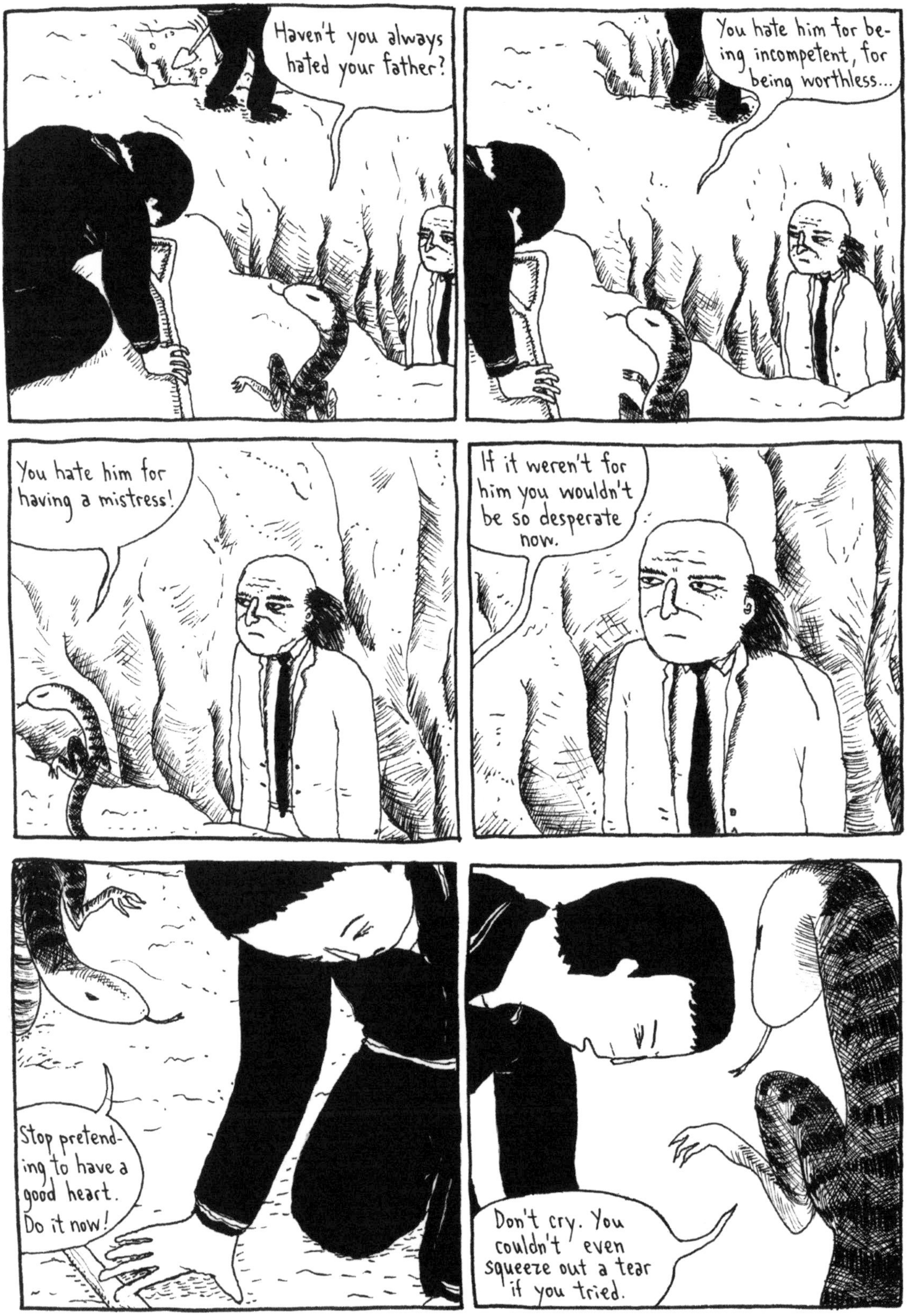
Haven't you always hated your father?
You hate him for being incompetent, for being worthless...
You hate him for having a mistress!
If it weren't for him you wouldn't be so desperate now.
Stop pretending to have a good heart. Do it now!
Don't cry. You couldn't even squeeze out a tear if you tried.

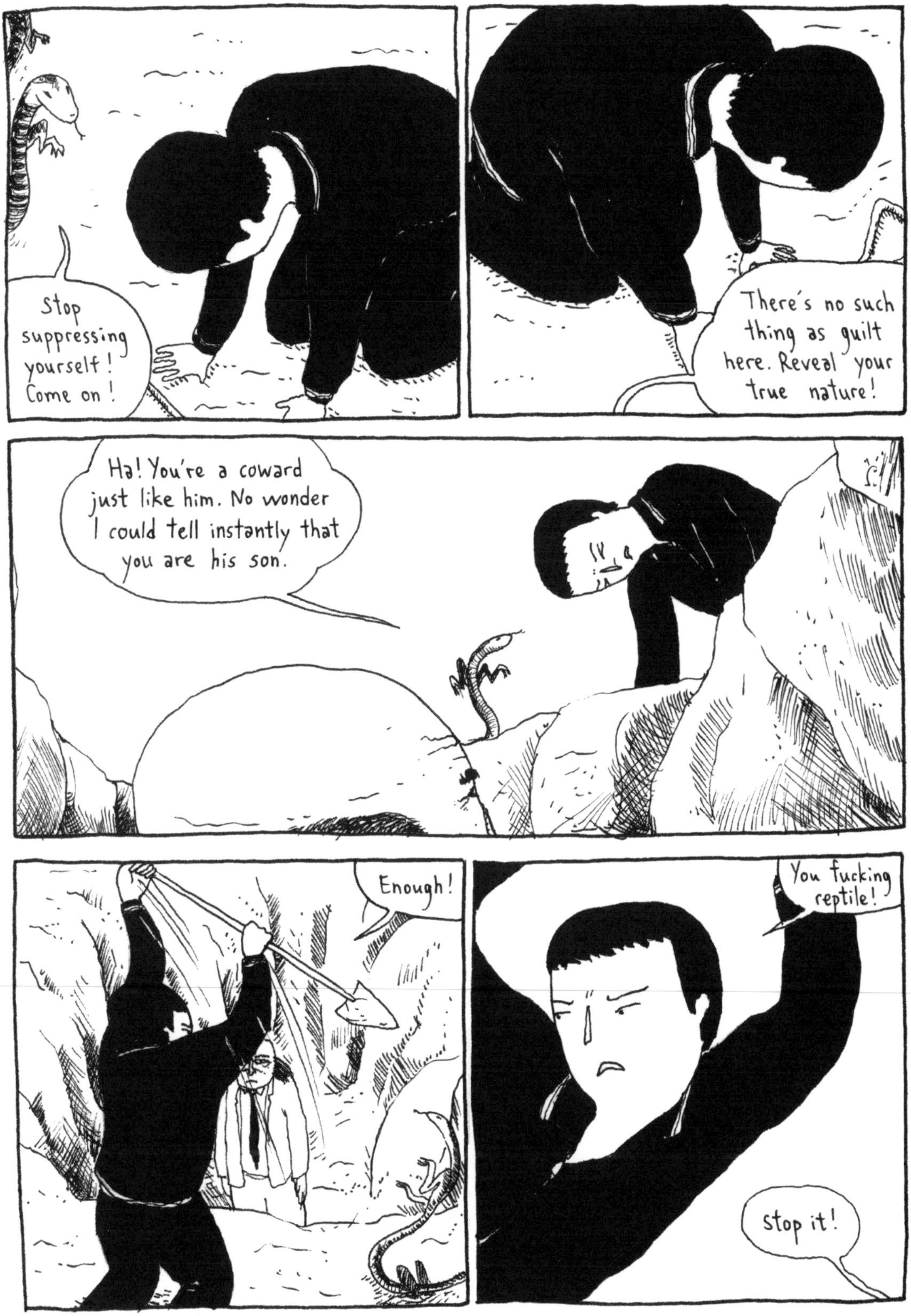
Stop suppressing yourself! Come on!
There's no such thing as guilt here. Reveal your true nature!
Ha! You're a coward just like him. No wonder I could tell instantly that you are his son.
Enough!
You fucking reptile!
Stop it!

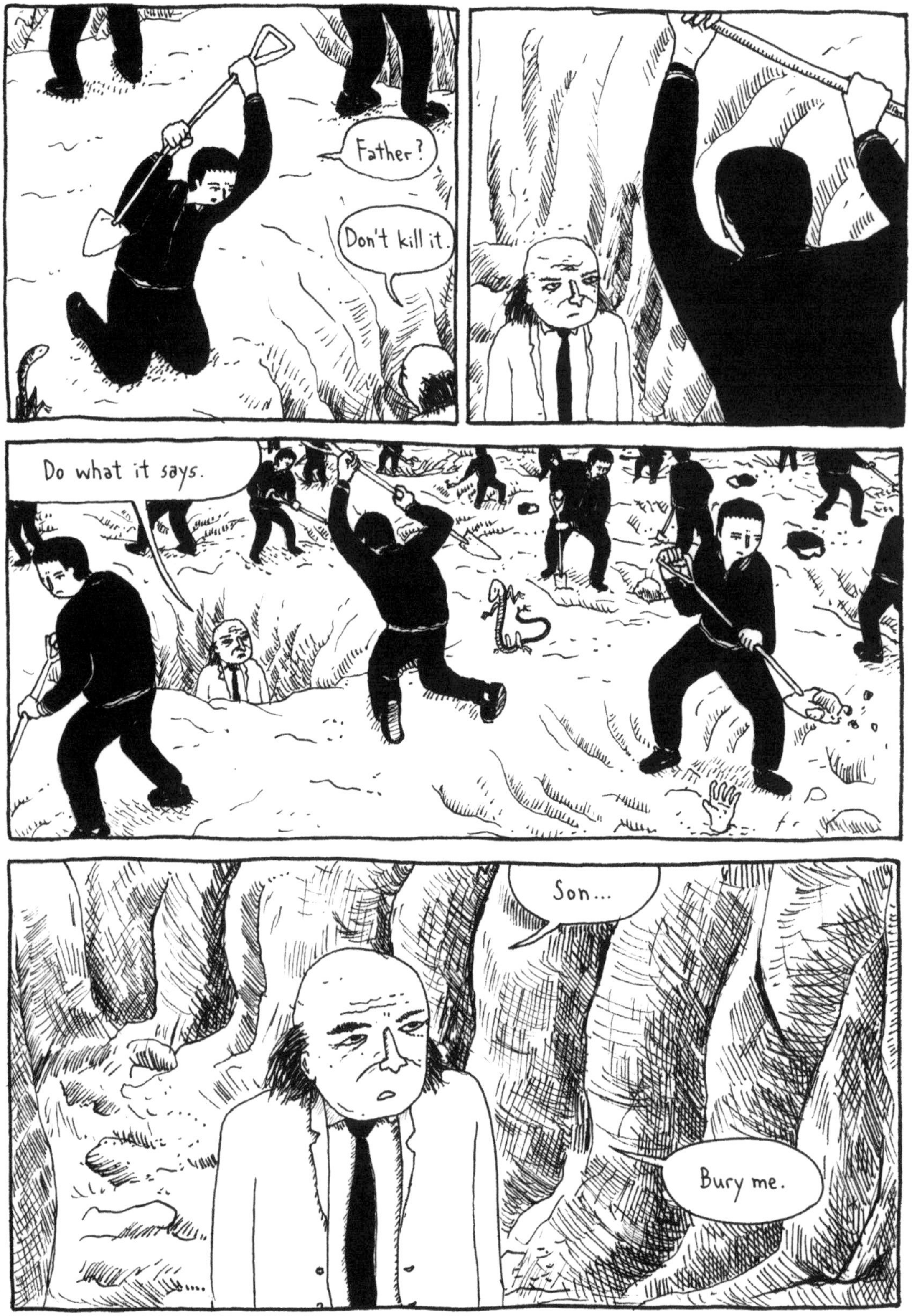
Father?
Don't kill it.
Do what it says.
Son...
Bury me.

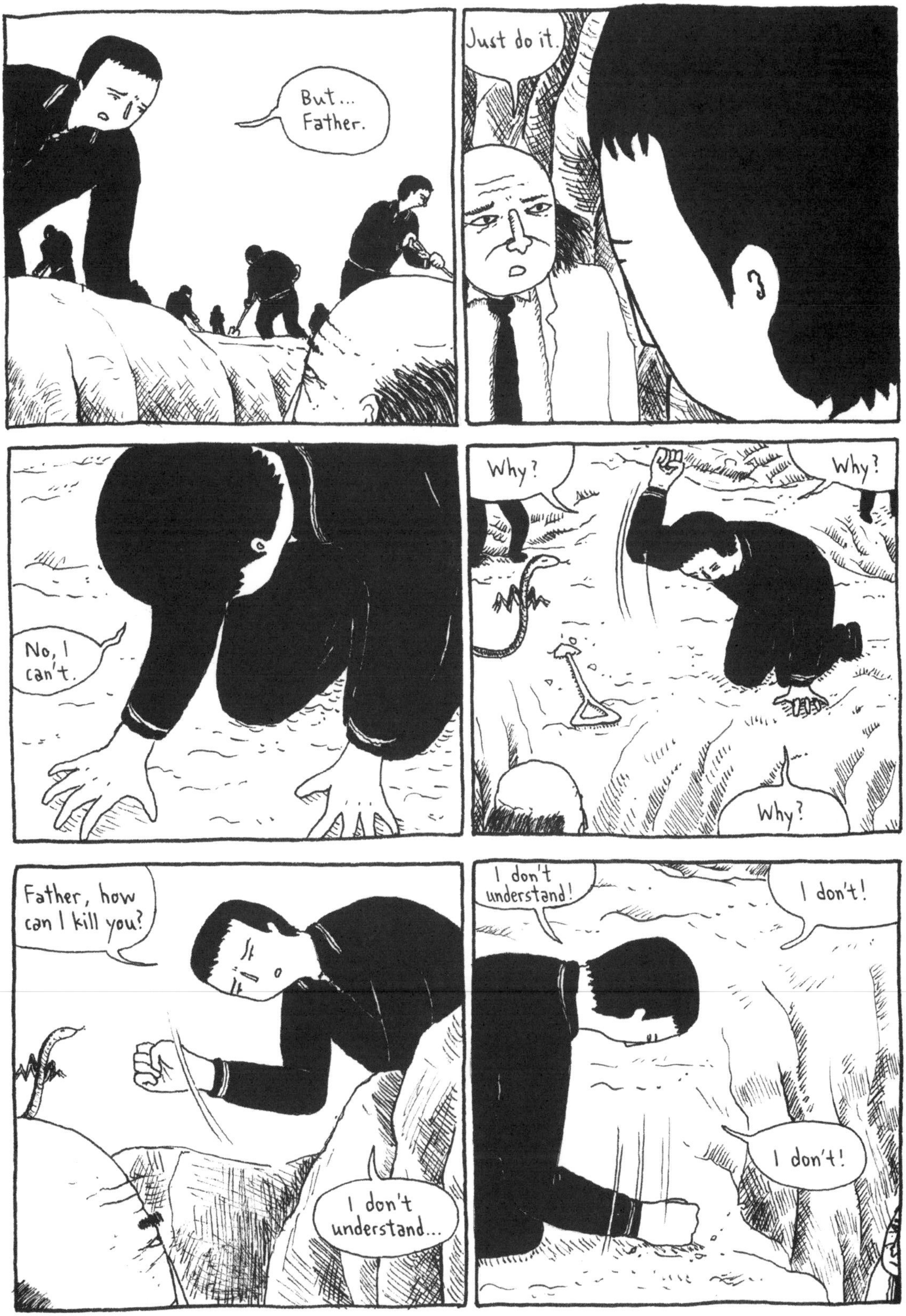
But... Father.
Just do it.
No, I can't.
Why?
Why?
Why?
Father, how can I kill you?
I don't understand...
I don't understand!
I don't!
I don't!

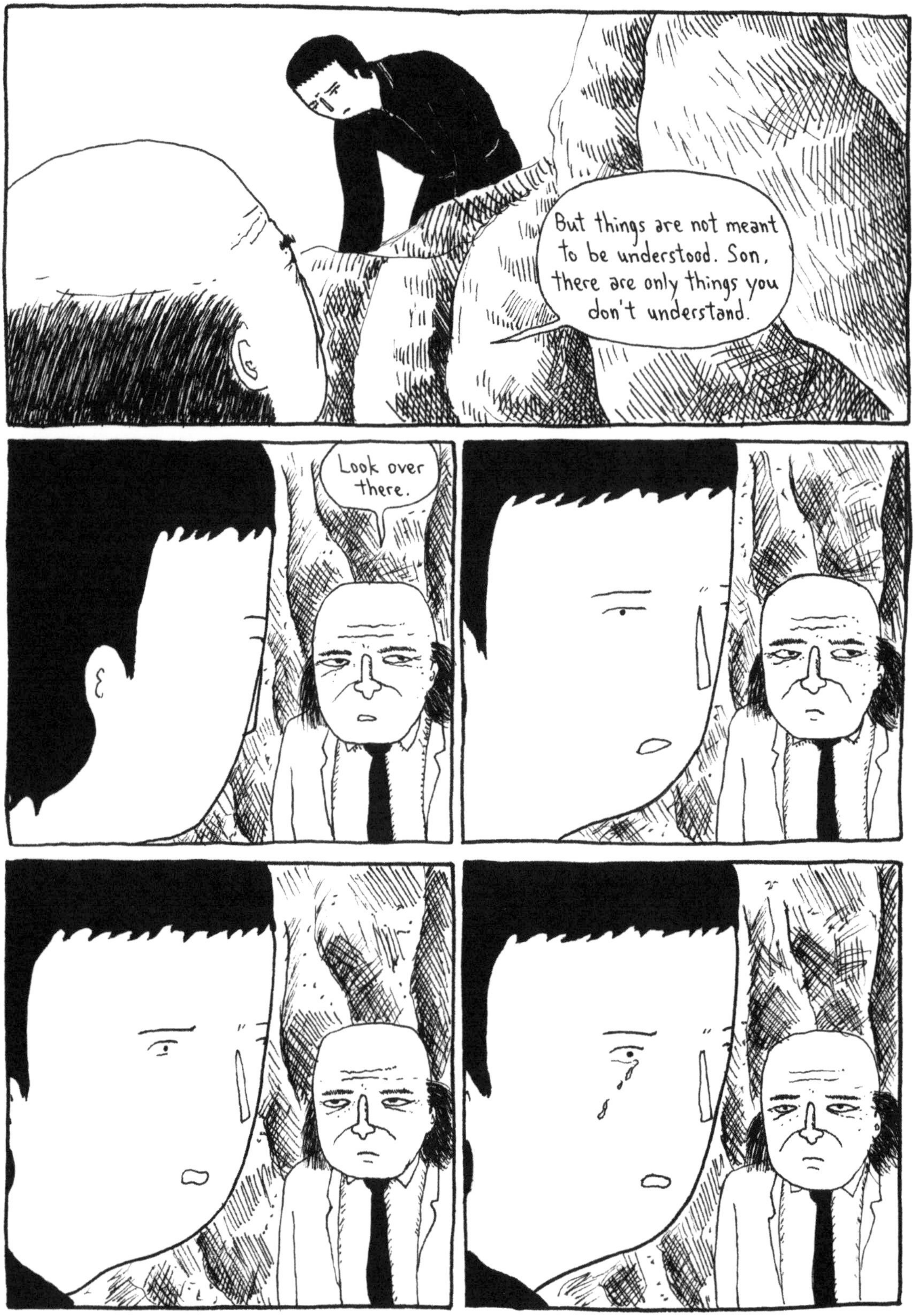
But things are not meant to be understood. Son, there are only things you don't understand.
Look over there.

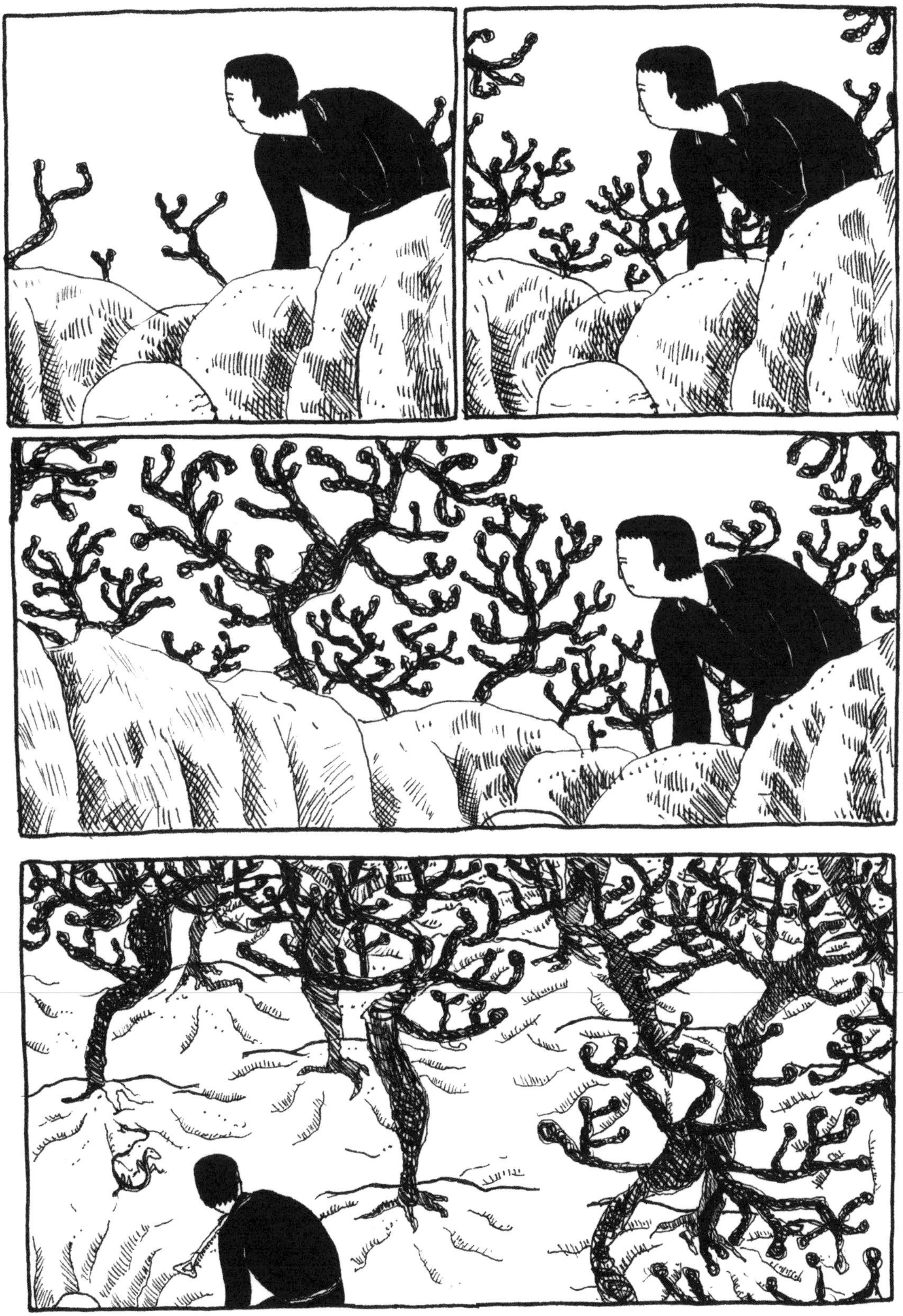

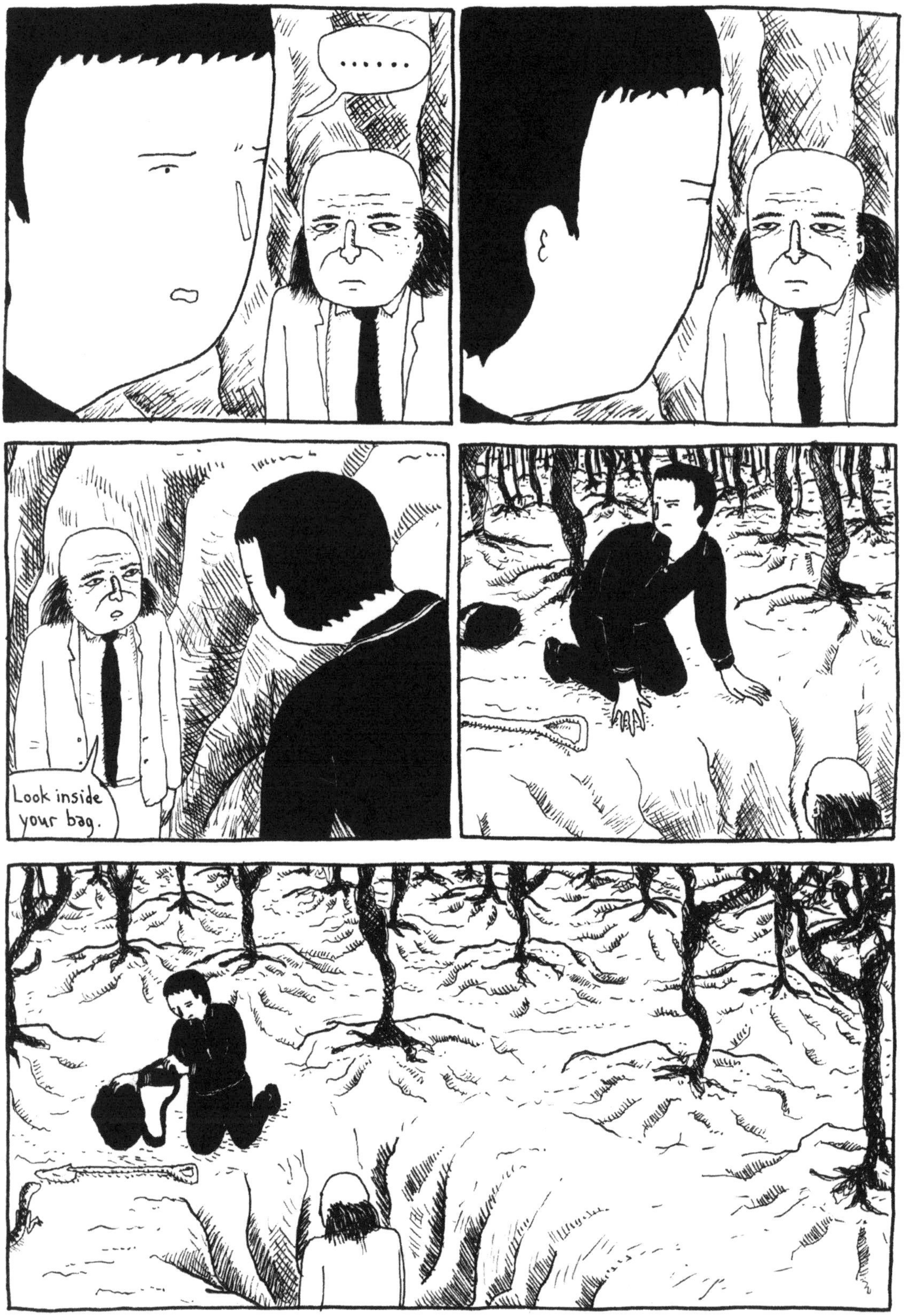
......
Look inside your bag.

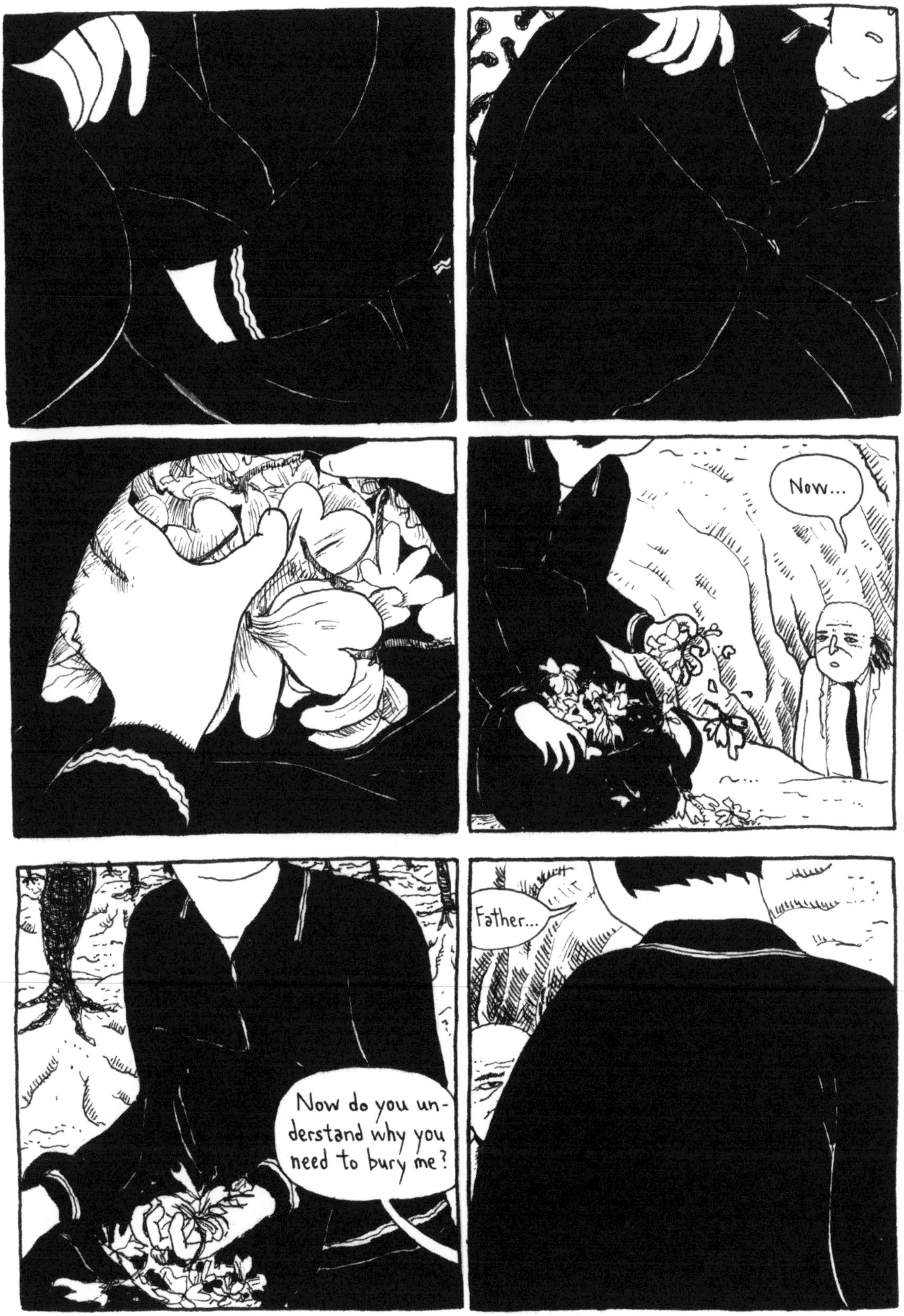
Now...
Now do you understand why you need to bury me?
Father...

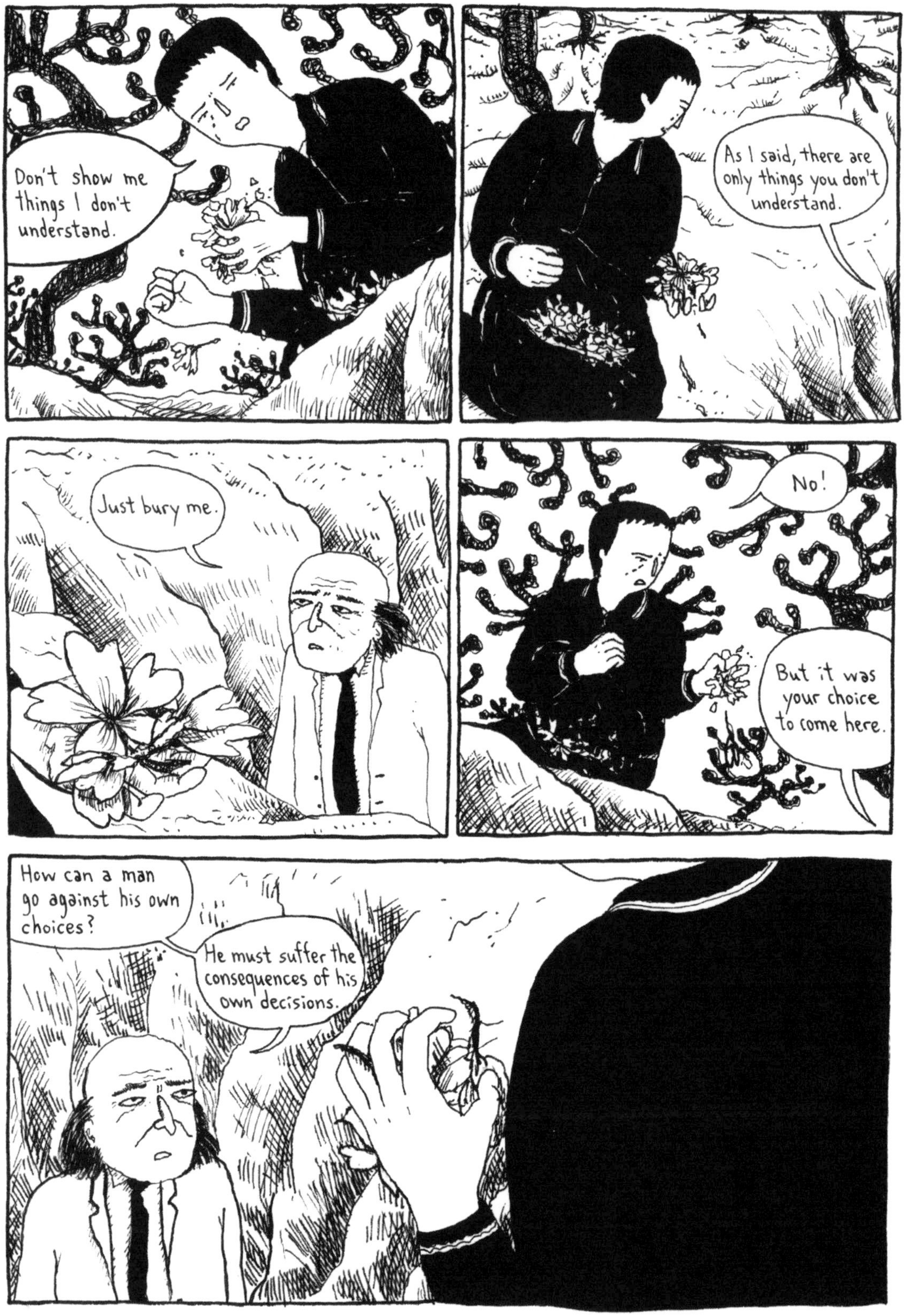
Don't show me things I don't understand.
As I said, there are only things you don't understand.
Just bury me.
No!
But it was your choice to come here.
How can a man go against his own choices?
He must suffer the consequences of his own decisions.

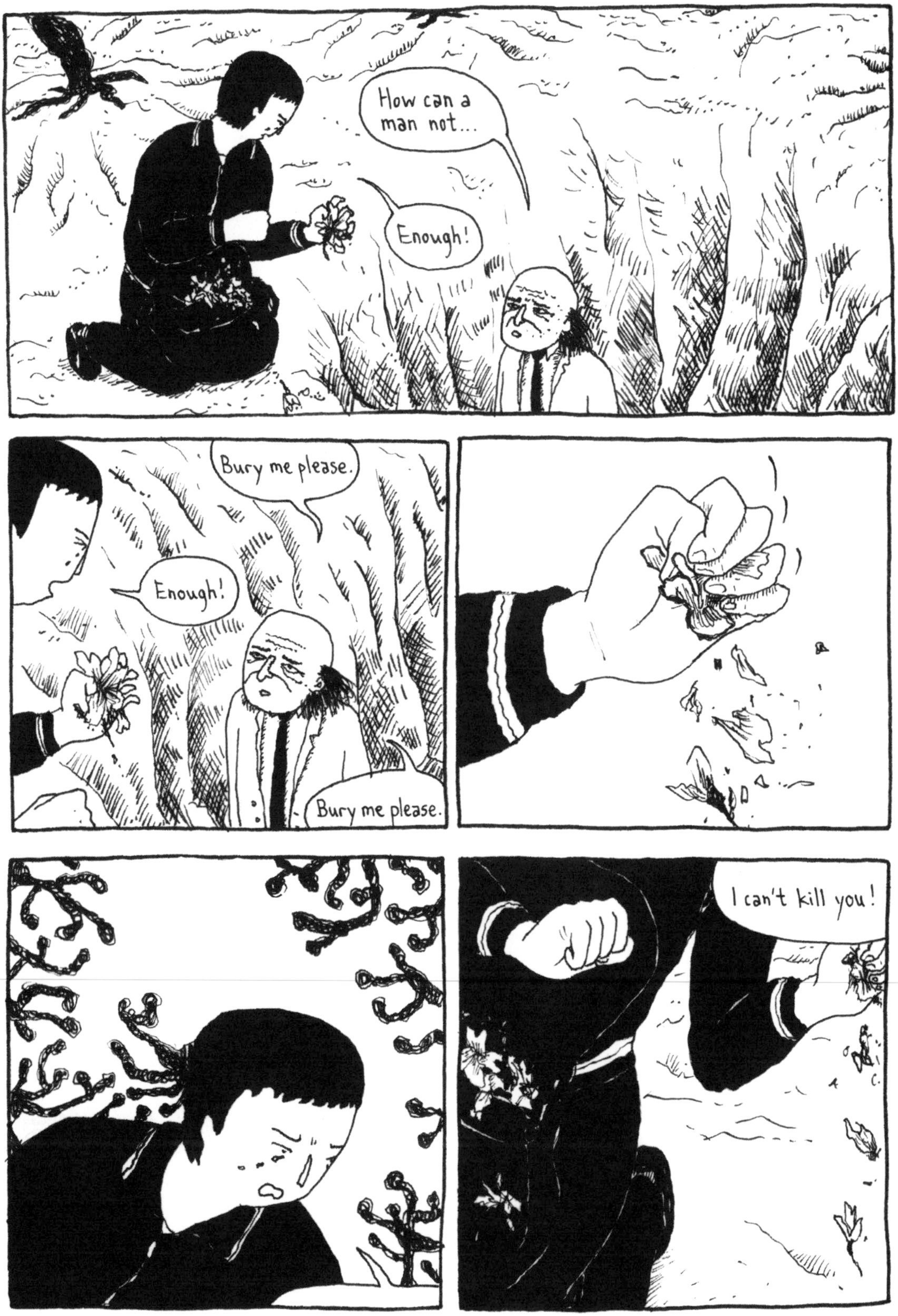
How can a man not...
Enough!
Bury me please.
Enough!
Bury me please.
I can't kill you!

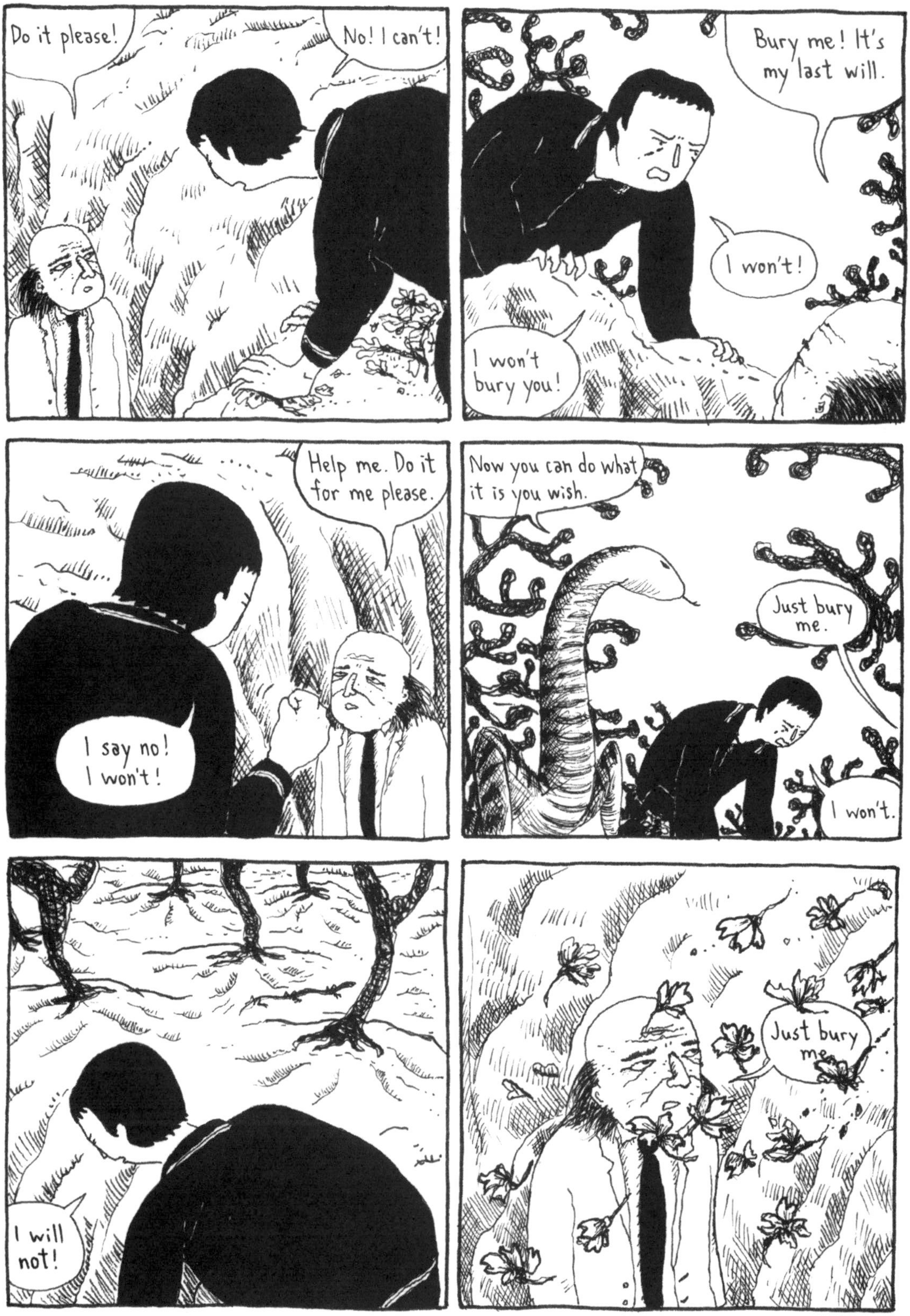

Do it please!
No! I can't!
Bury me! It's my last will.
I won't!
I won't bury you!
Help me. Do it for me please.
I say no! I won't!
Now you can do what it is you wish.
Just bury me.
I won't.
I will not!
Just bury me.

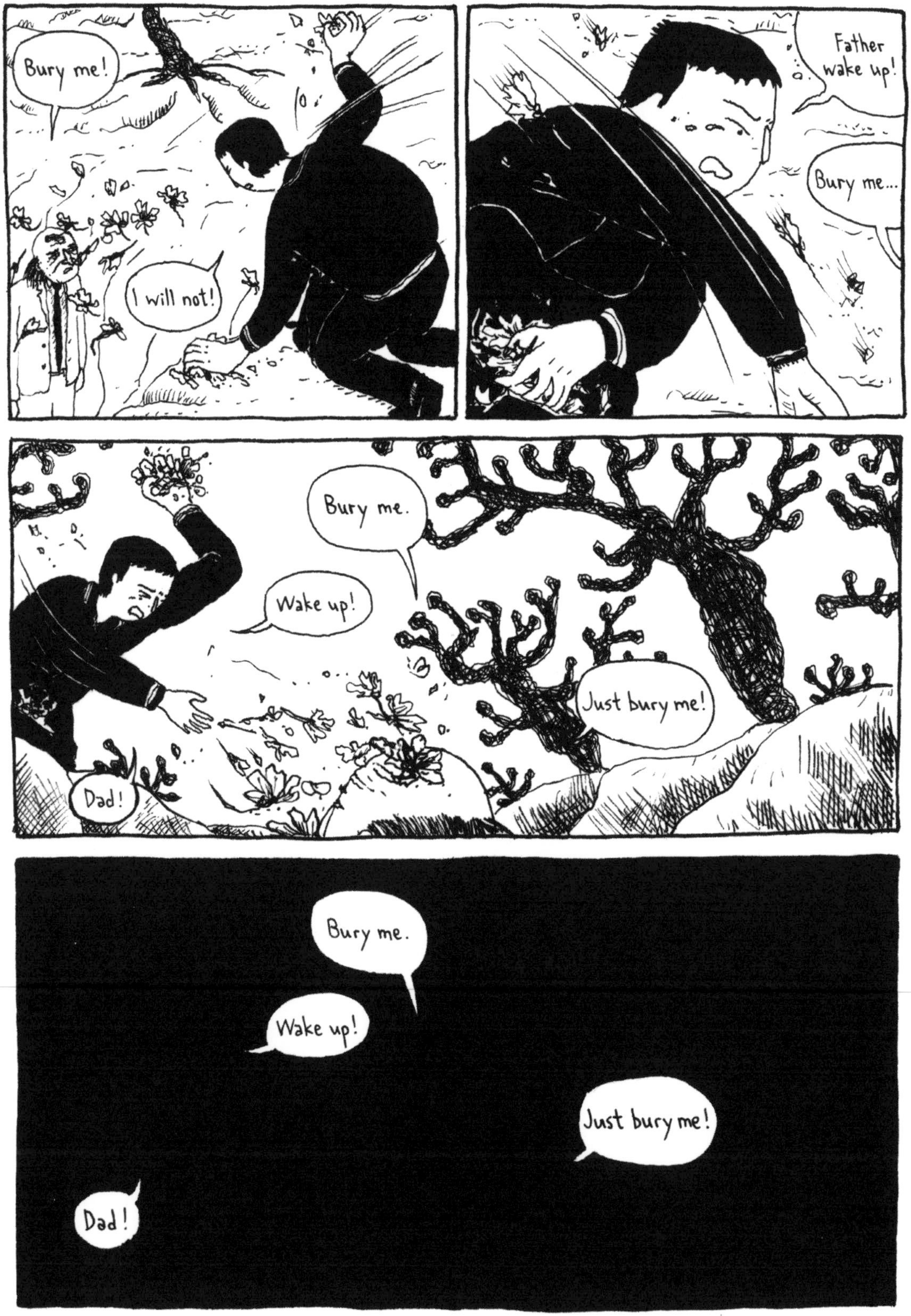
Bury me!
I will not!
Father wake up!
Bury me...
Bury me.
Wake up!
Just bury me!
Dad!
Bury me.
Wake up!
Just bury me!
Dad!

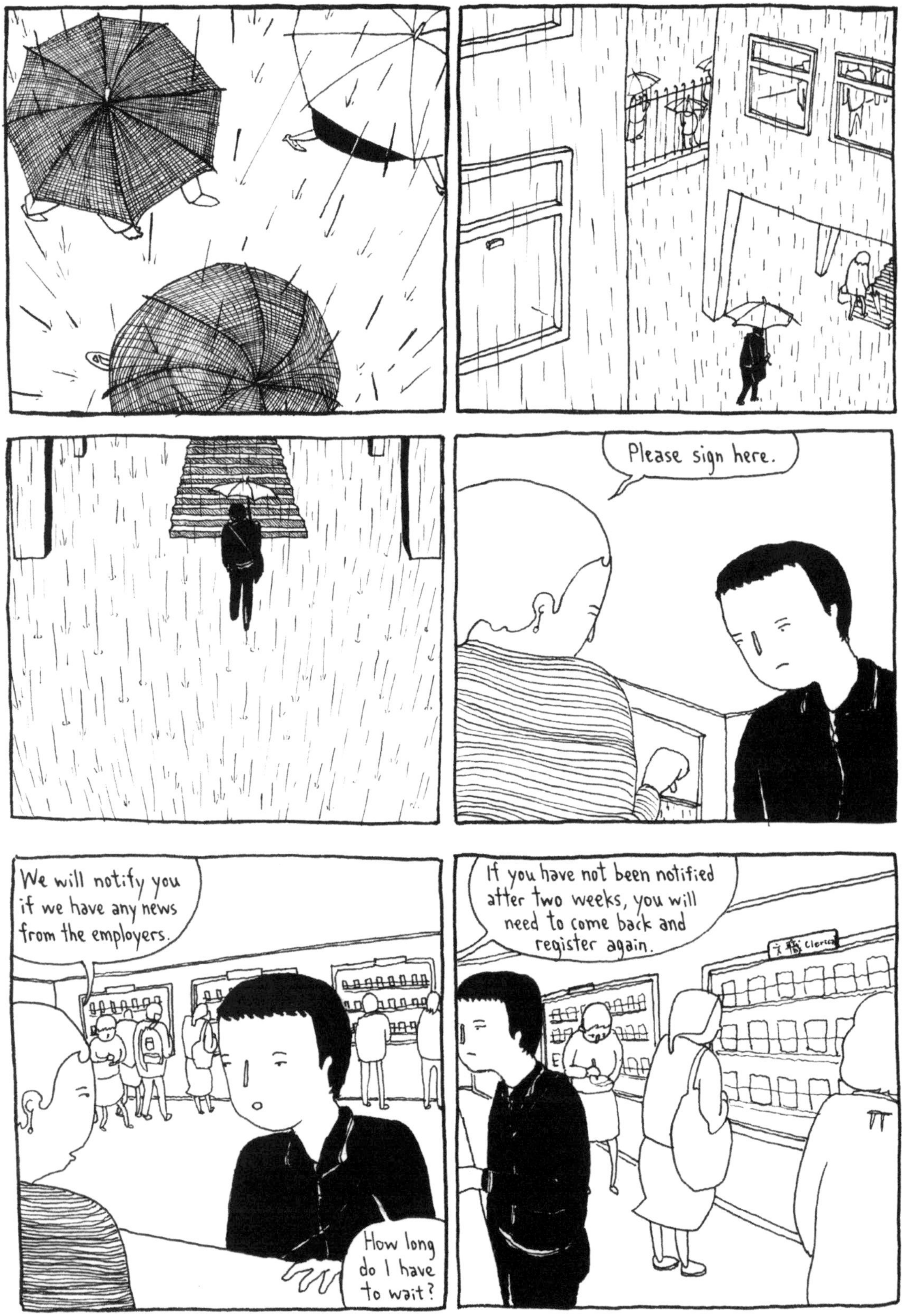
Please sign here.
We will notify you if we have any news from the employers.
How long do I have to wait?
If you have not been notified after two weeks, you will need to come back and register again.

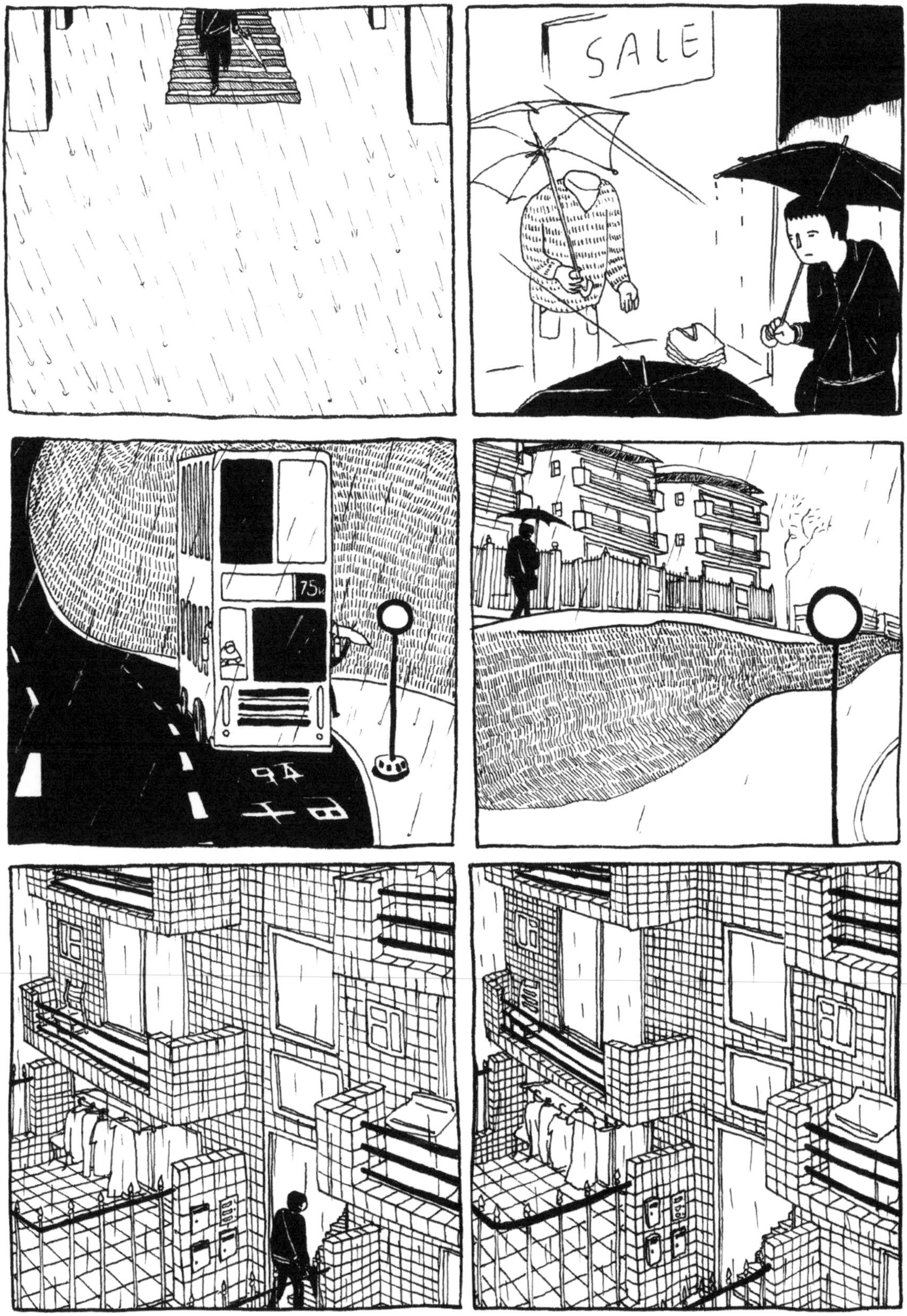
SALE
75K

Sorry

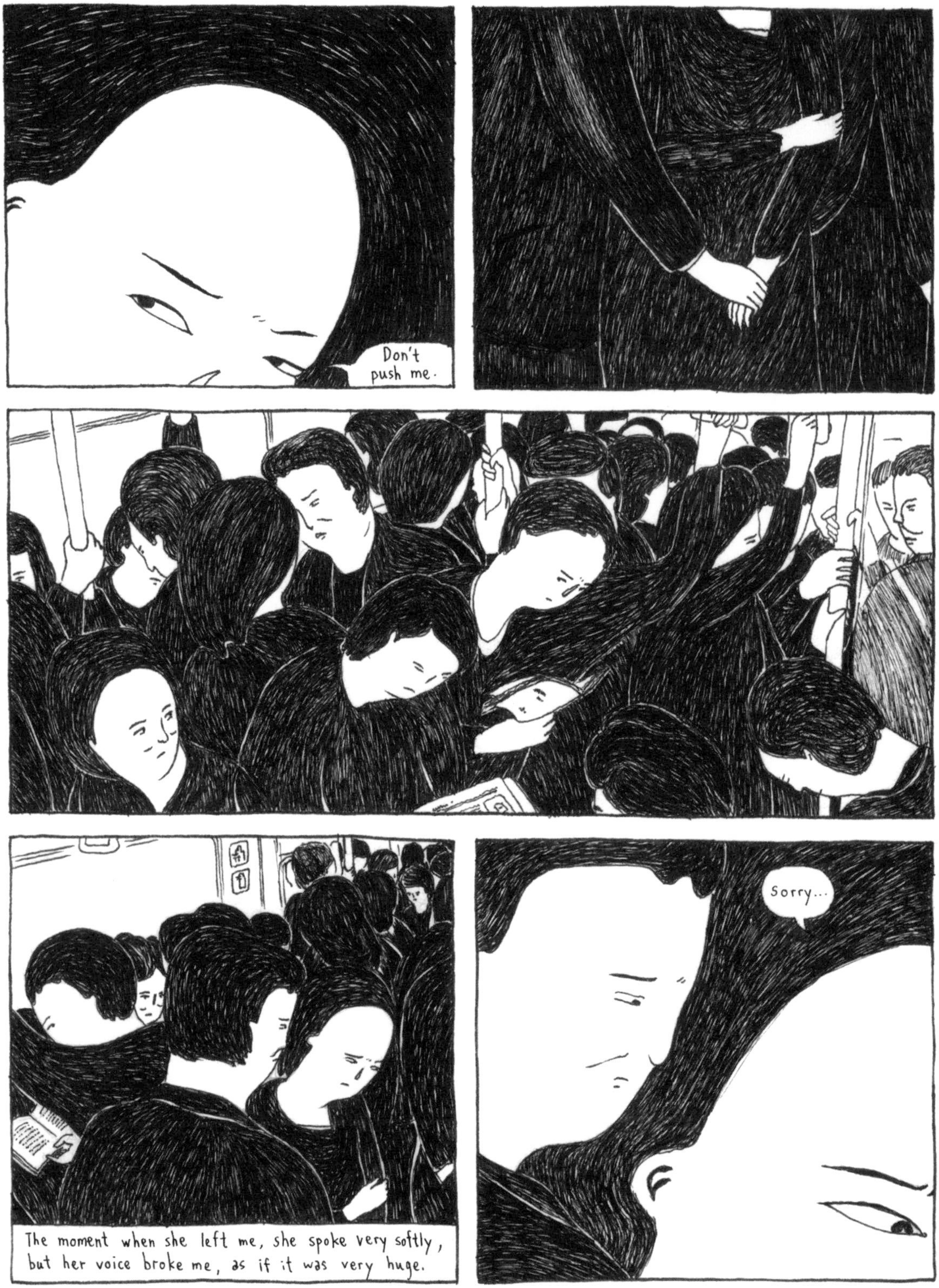
Don't push me.
The moment when she left me, she spoke very softly, but her voice broke me, as if it was very huge.
Sorry...

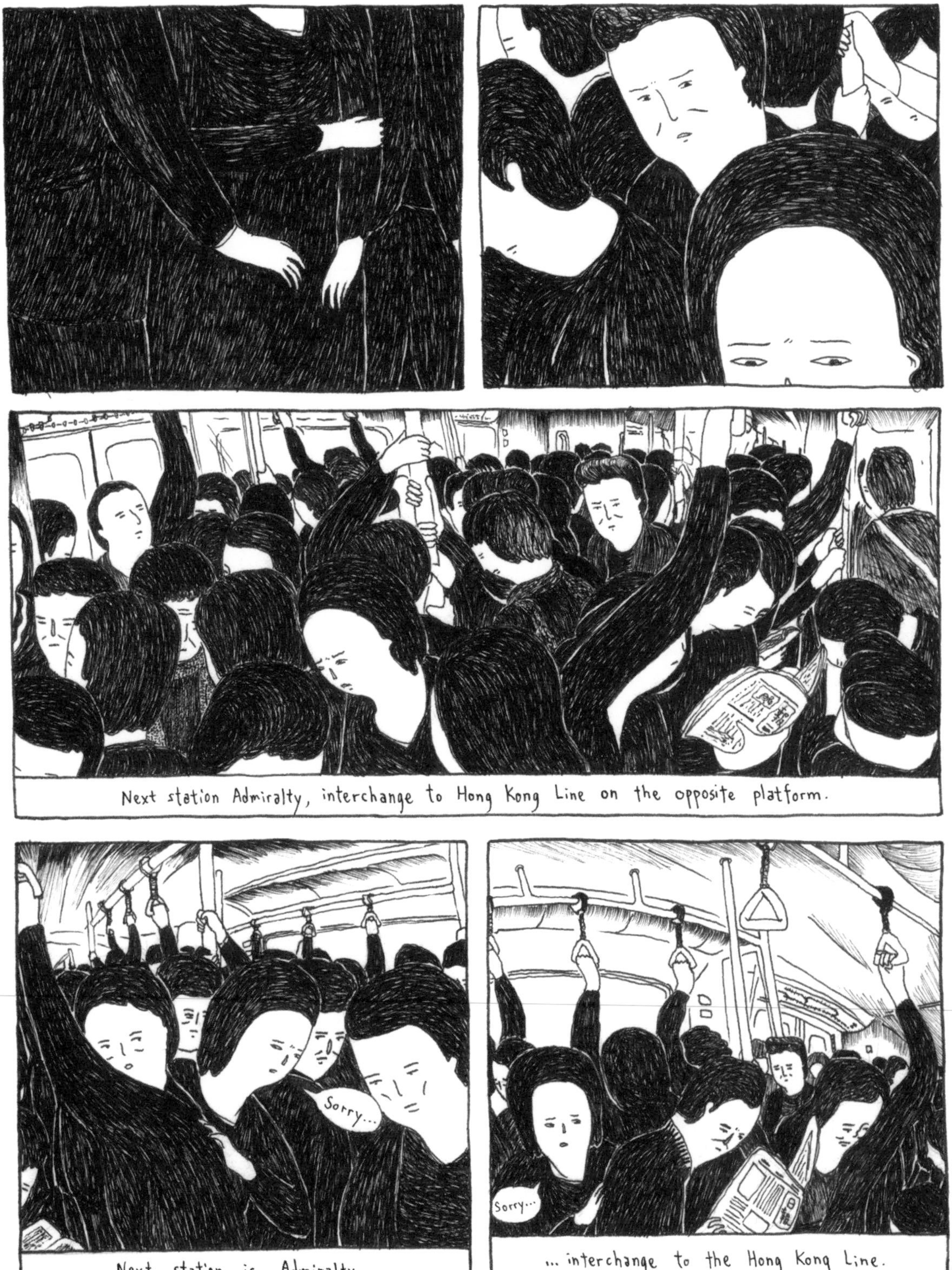
Next station Admiralty, interchange to Hong Kong Line on the opposite platform.
Sorry...
Next station is Admiralty...
Sorry...
... interchange to the Hong Kong Line.

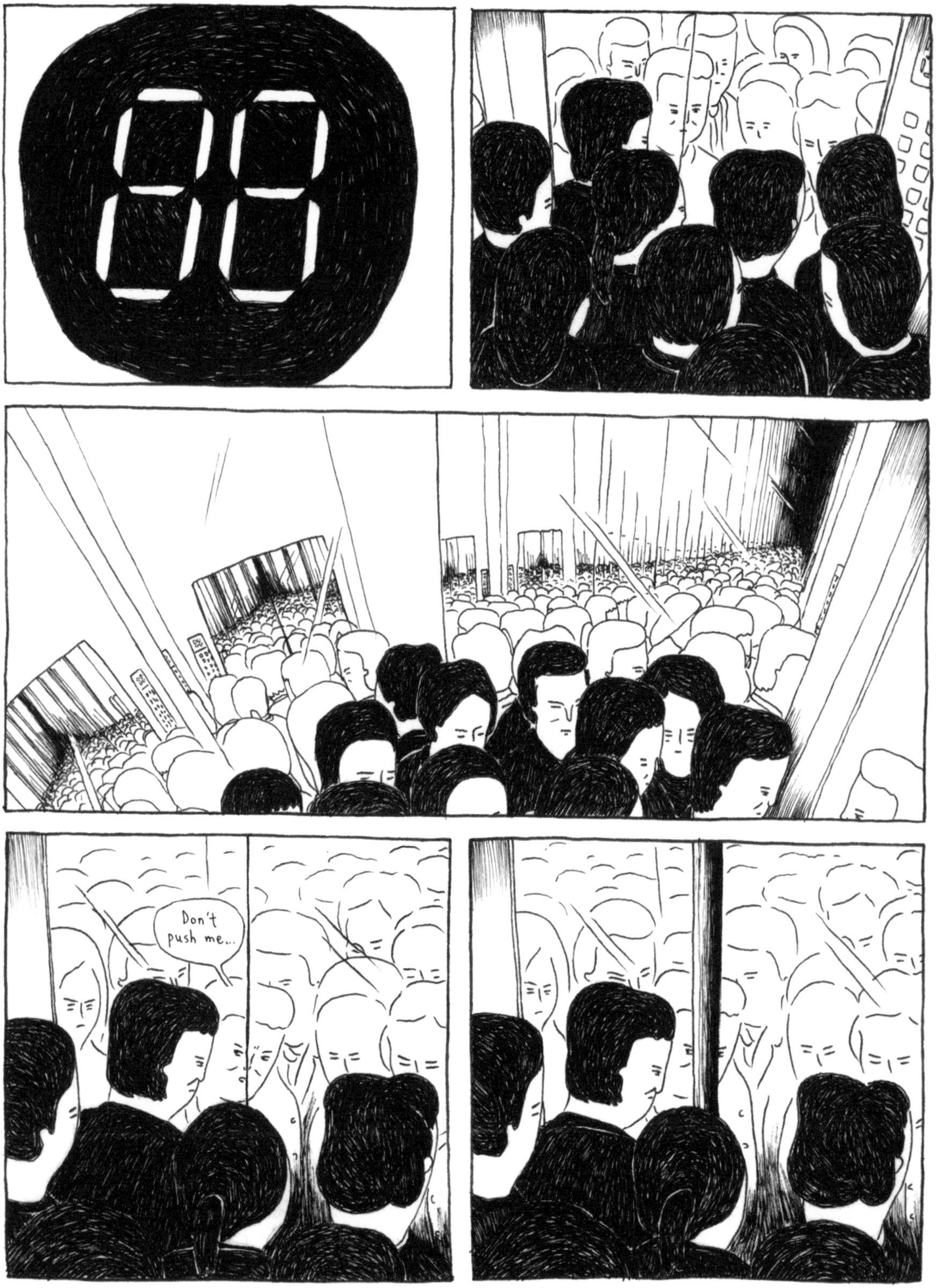
Don't push me...

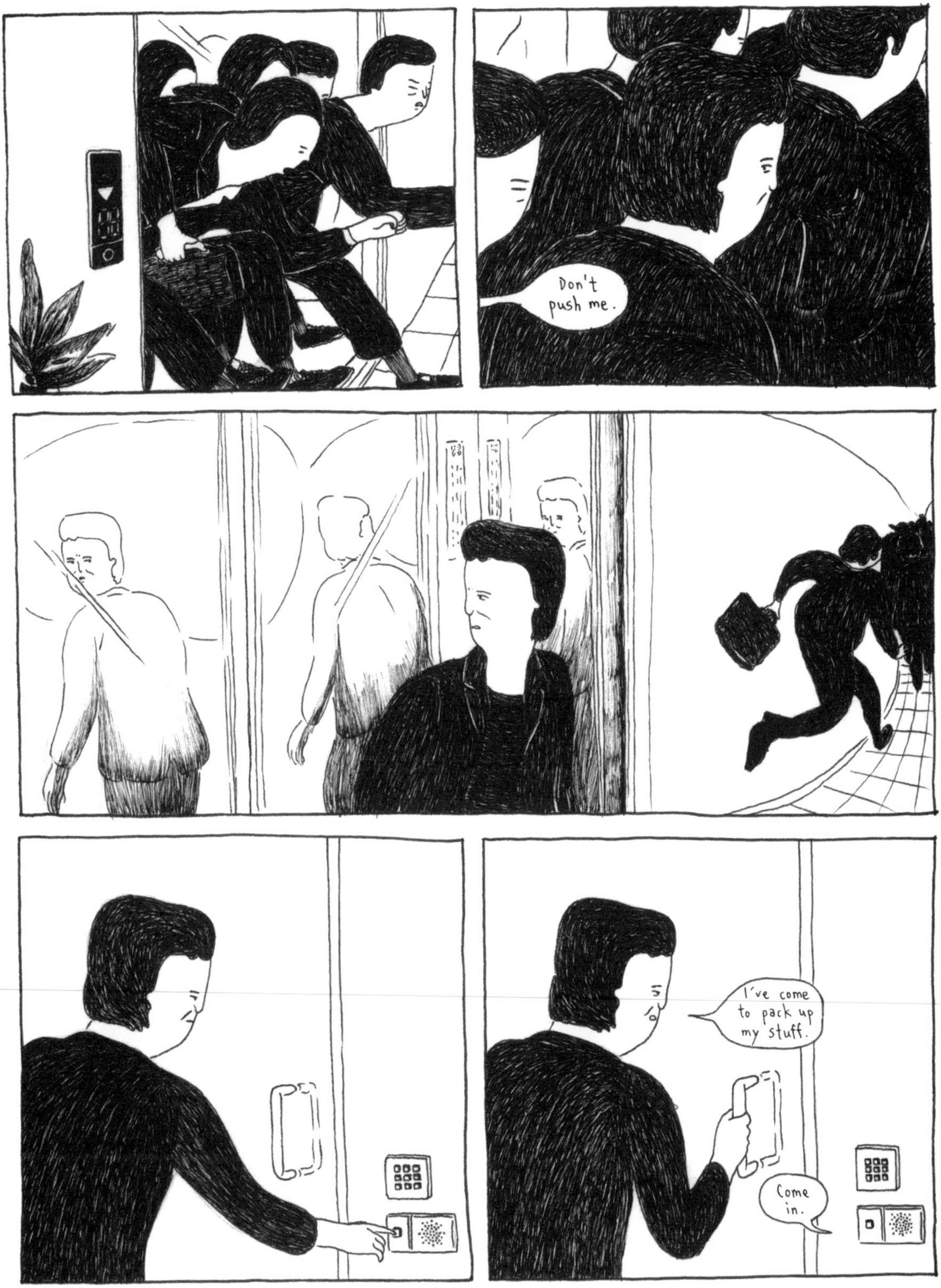
Don't push me.
I've come to pack up my stuff.
Come in.

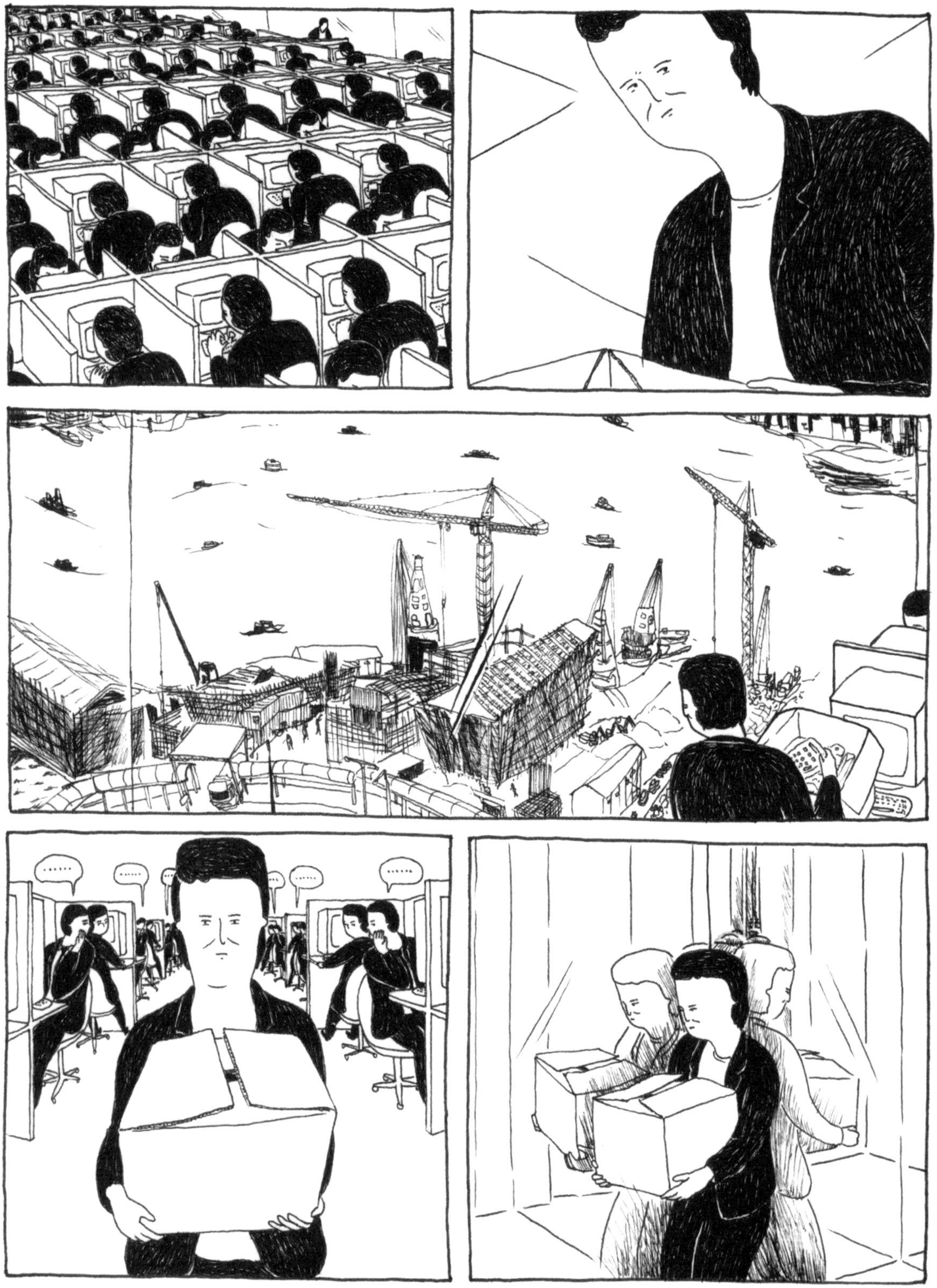

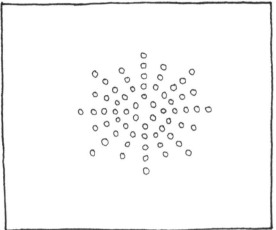

Admiralty, disembark on the right.

Admiralty, doors will open on the right.

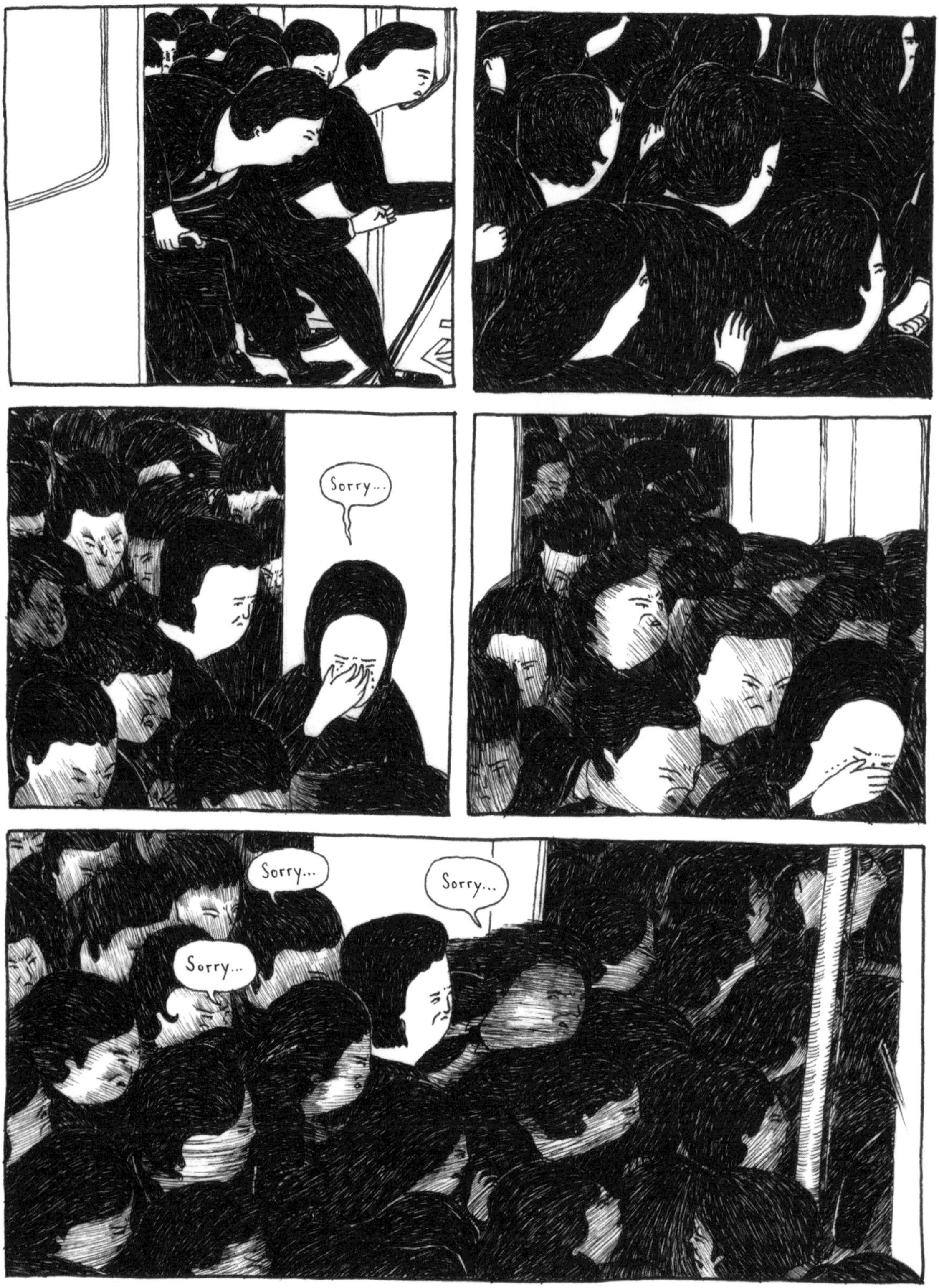
Sorry...
Sorry...
Sorry...
Sorry...

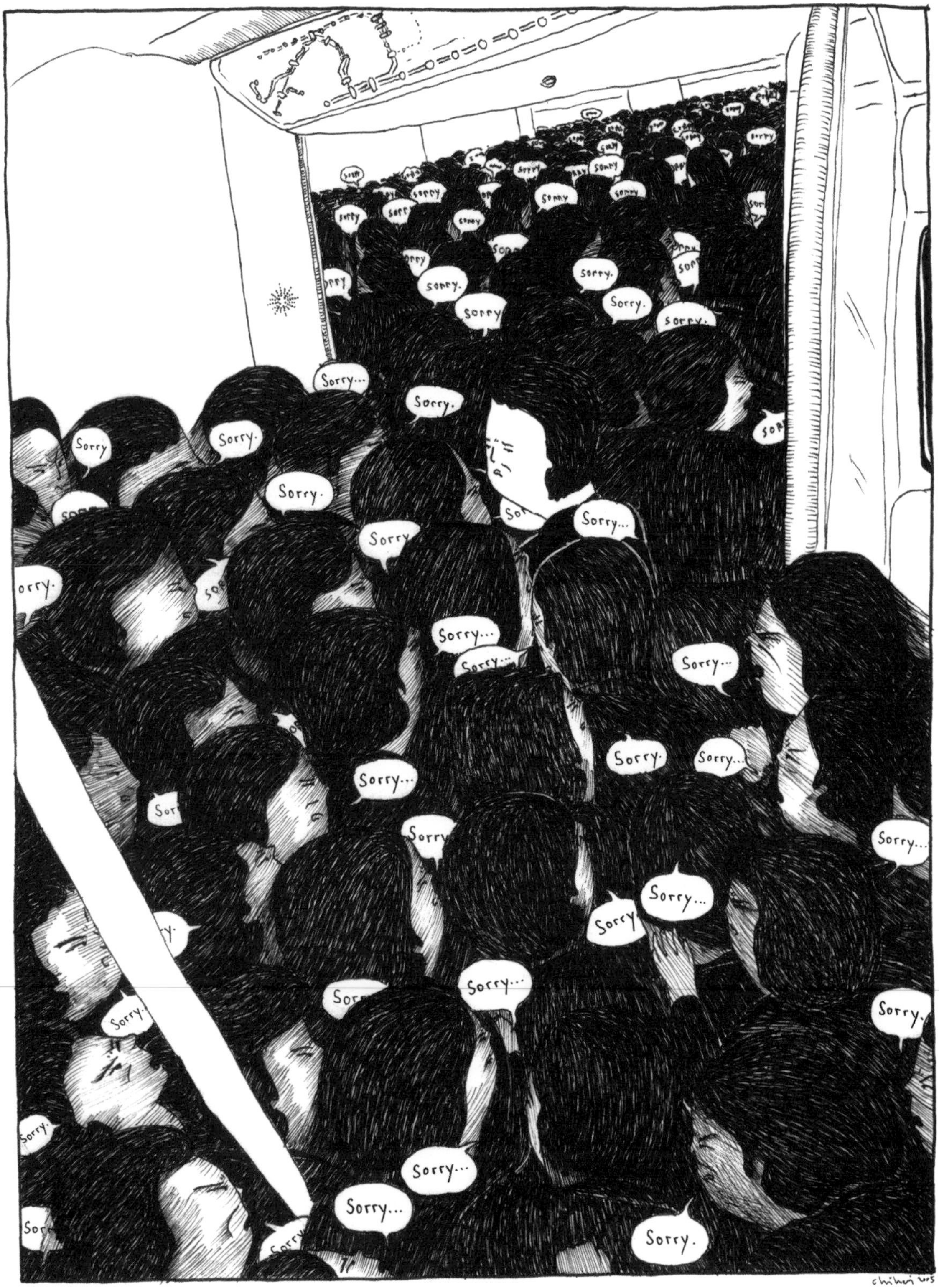
sorry
sorry.
sorry.
sorry.
Sorry.
sorry.
Sorry...
Sorry.
Sorry
Sorry.
Sorry.
Sorry...
Sorry...
Sorry...
Sorry.
Sorry...
Sorry...
Sorry...
Sorry.
Sorry...
Sorry...
Sorry.
Sorry.
Sorry...
Sorry...
Sorry.

# Canine

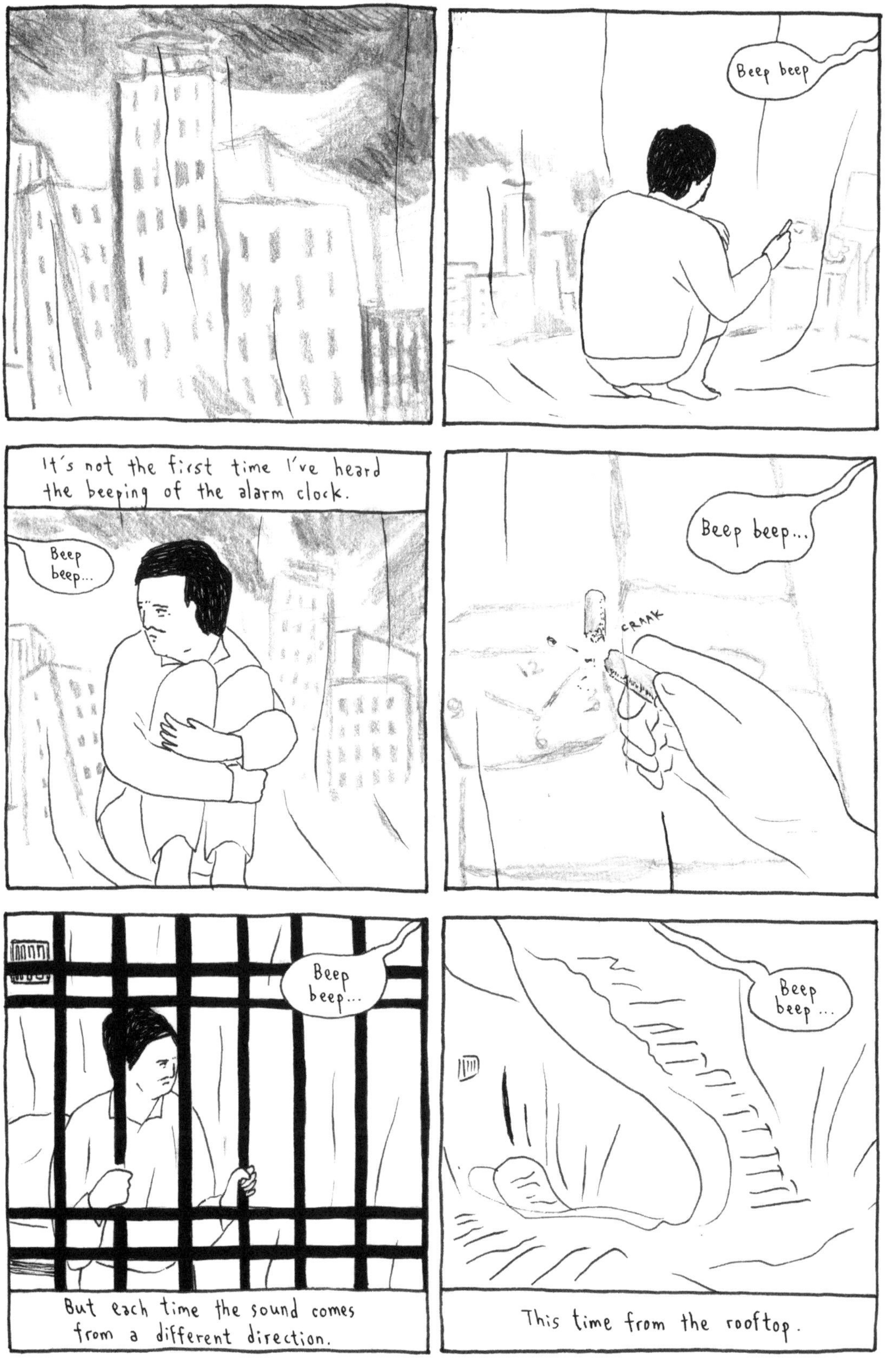
Beep beep
It's not the first time I've heard the beeping of the alarm clock.
Beep beep...
Beep beep...
CRAAK
Beep beep...
But each time the sound comes from a different direction.
Beep beep...
This time from the rooftop.

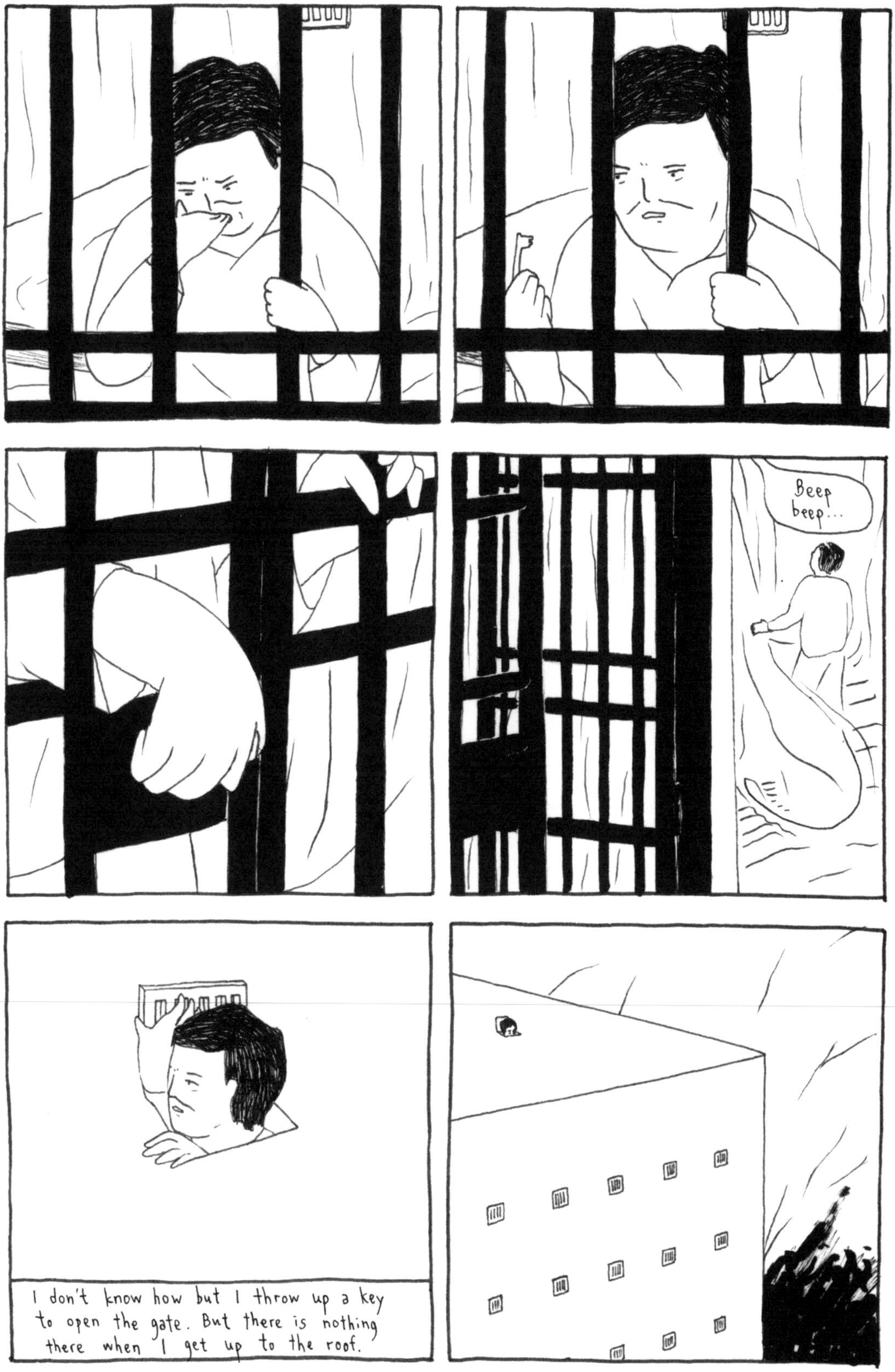
Beep beep...
I don't know how but I throw up a key to open the gate. But there is nothing there when I get up to the roof.

Back in my room, I discover a creature occupying my bed.

Like an invertebrate, churning and moaning.

Then I take the opportunity to escape.

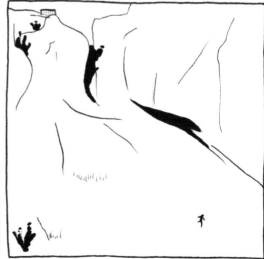

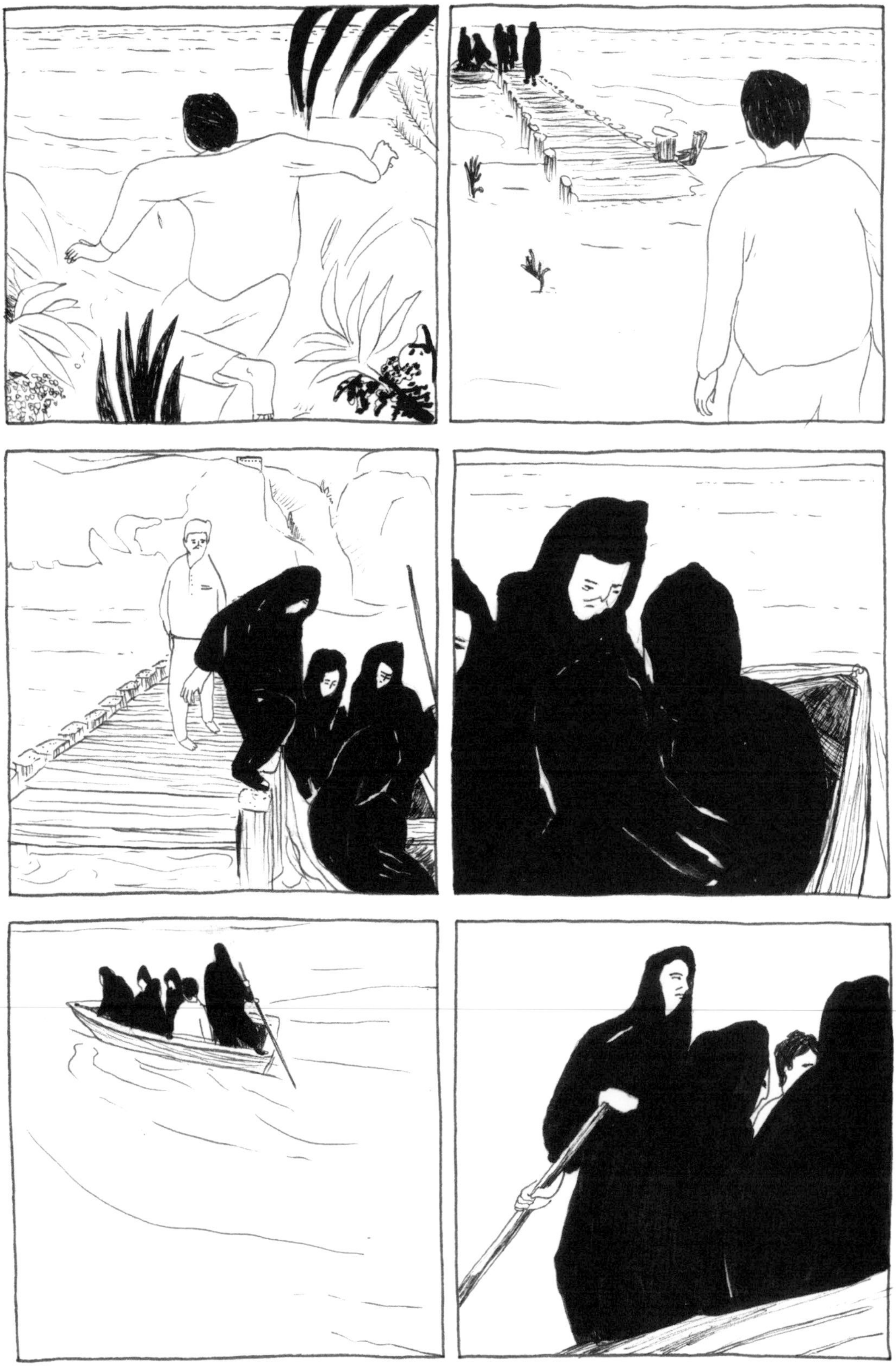

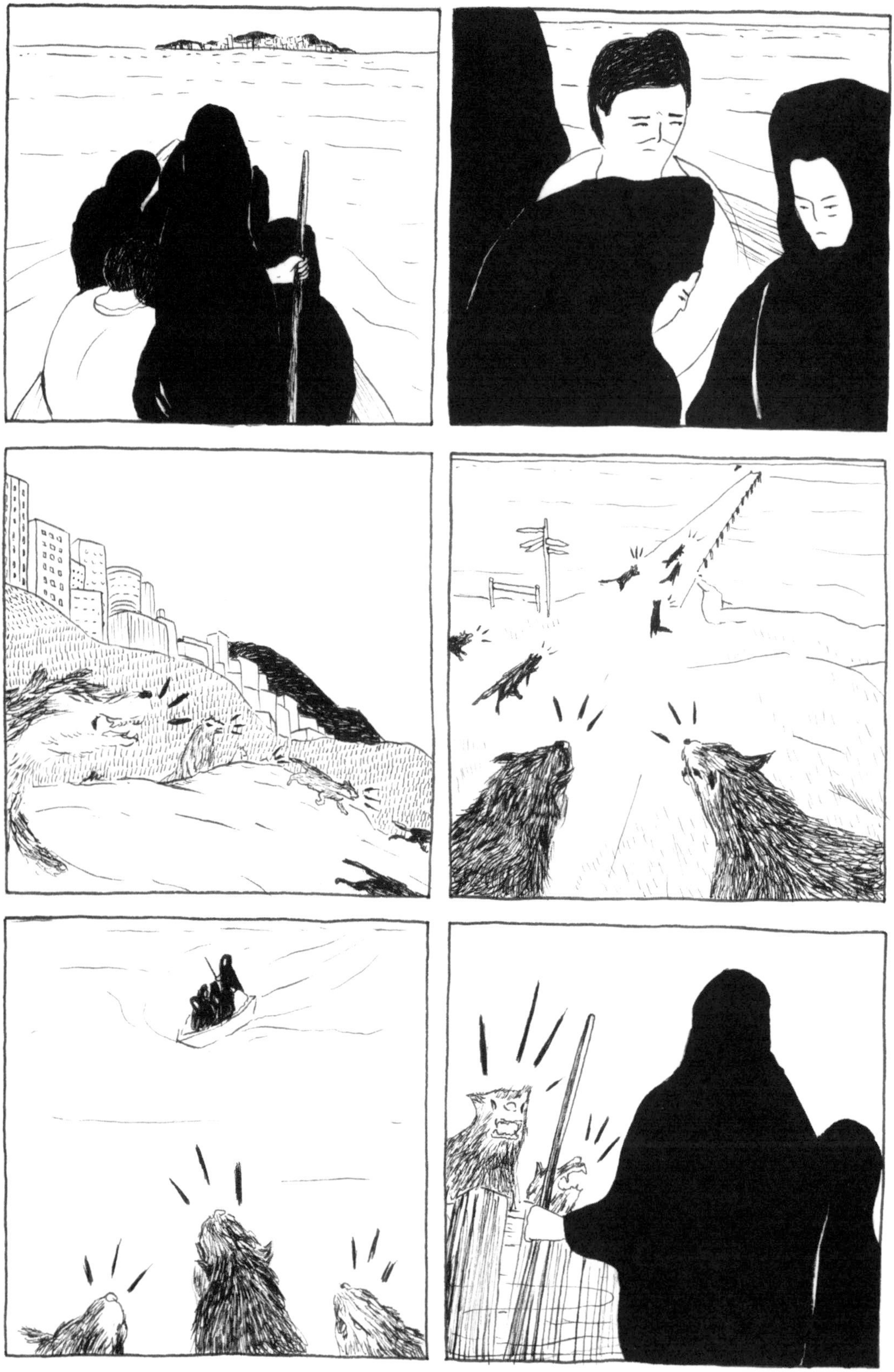

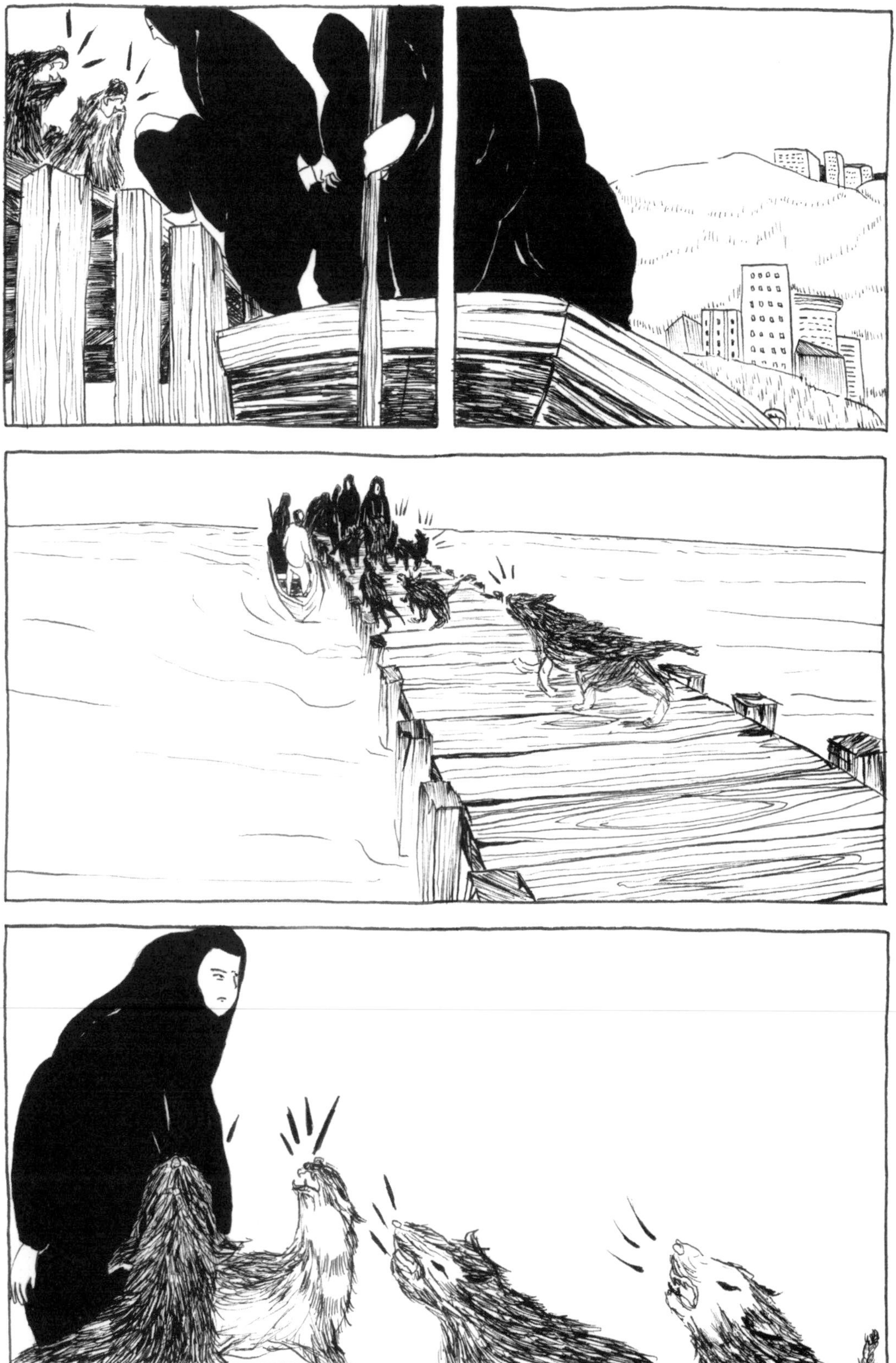

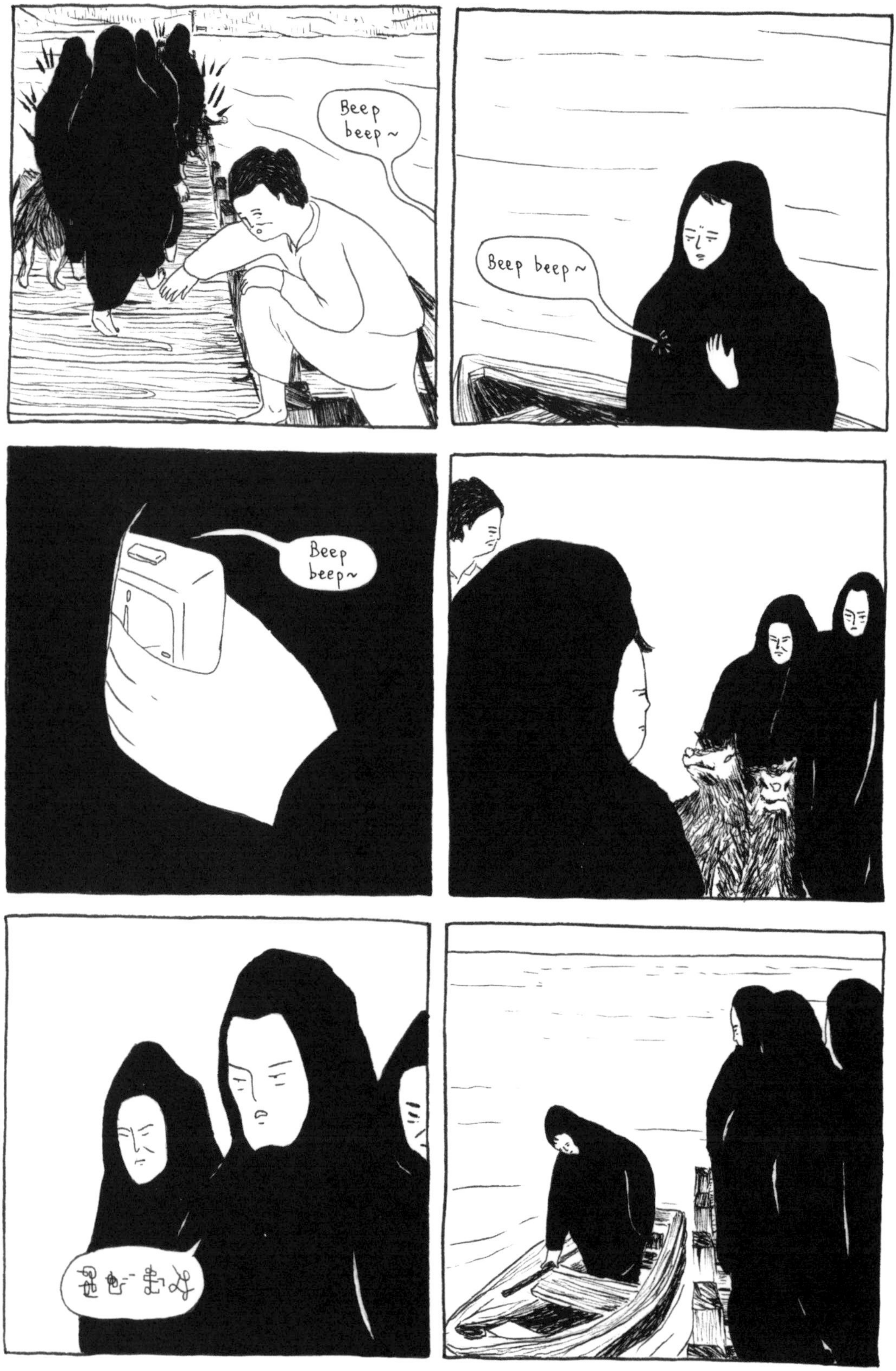
Beep beep~
Beep beep~
Beep beep~

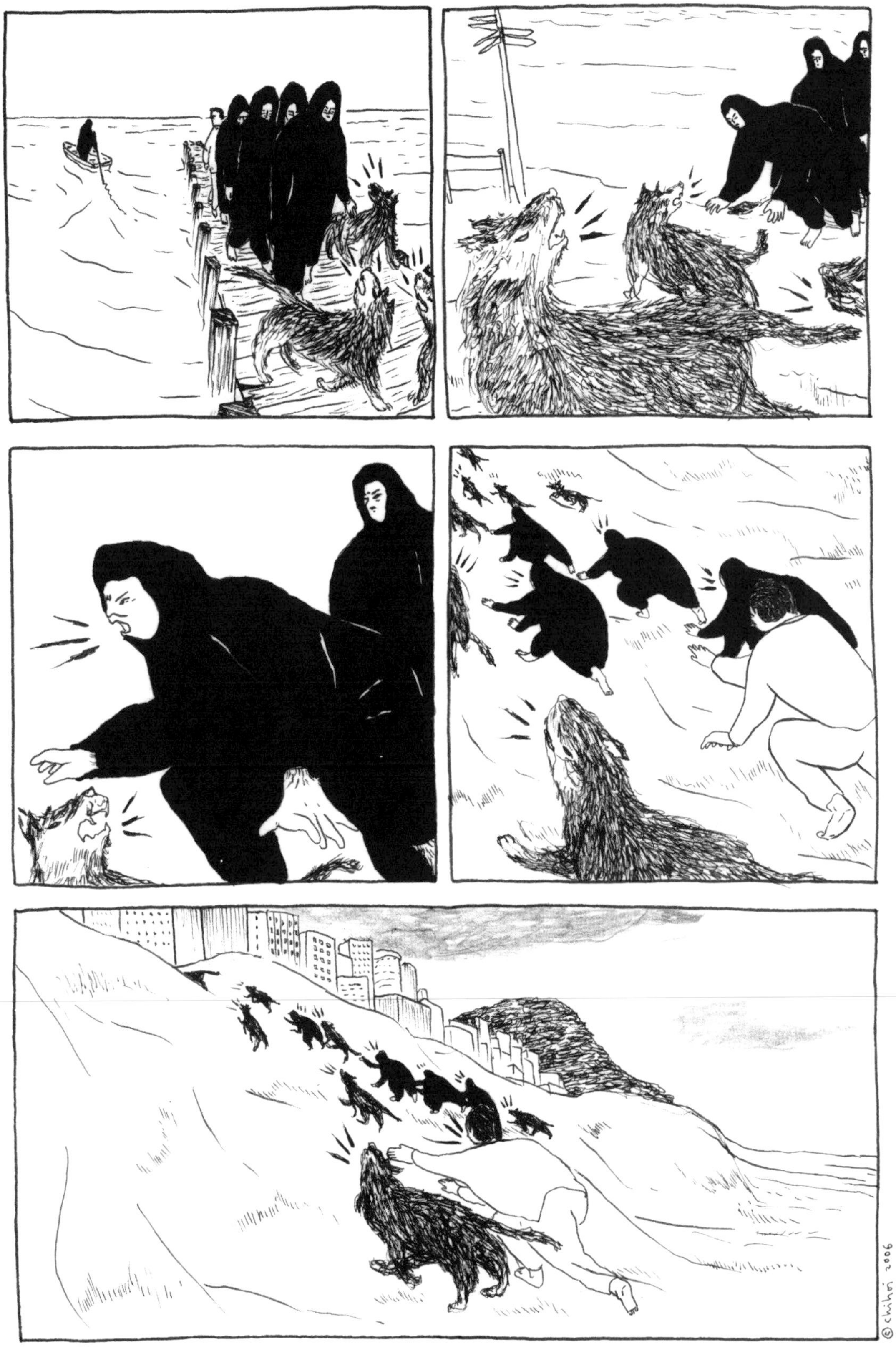
©chihoi 2006

# The Sea

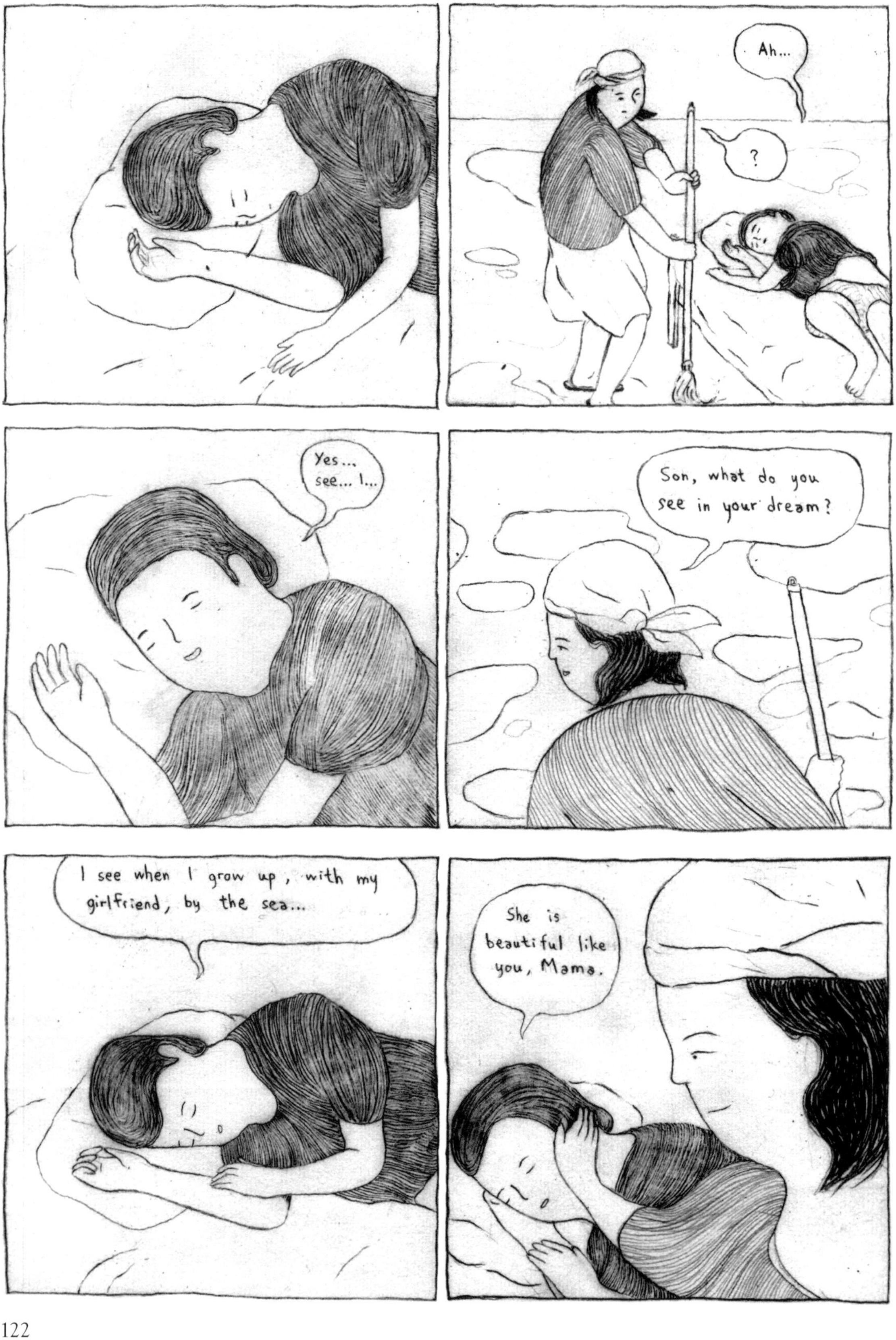
Ah...
?
Yes... see... I...
Son, what do you see in your dream?
I see when I grow up, with my girlfriend, by the sea...
She is beautiful like you, Mama.

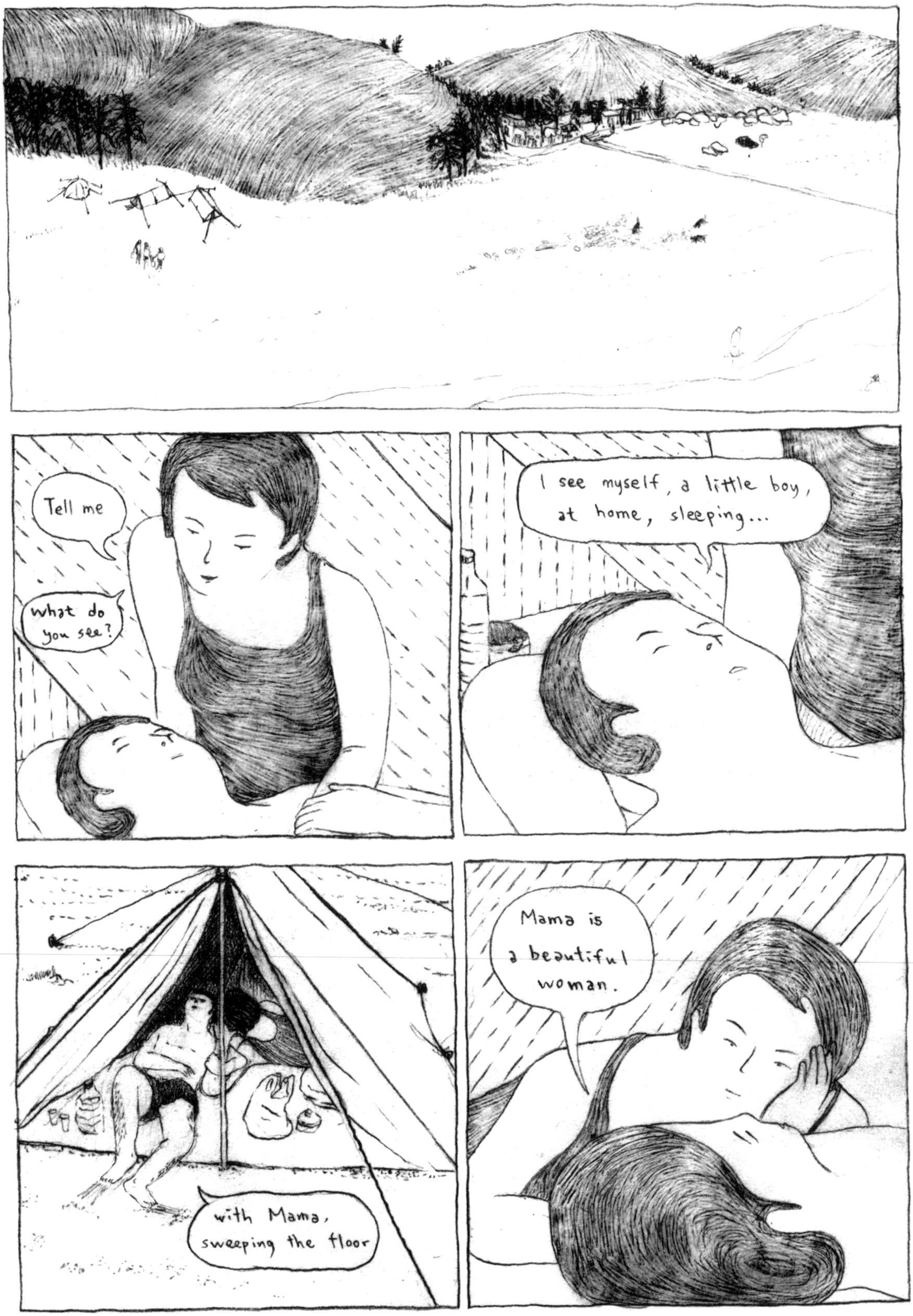
Tell me
what do you see?
I see myself, a little boy, at home, sleeping...
with Mama, sweeping the floor
Mama is a beautiful woman.

There is so much water to sweep away.
Sometimes she bends her back too much.

I don't know when I woke up.
But Mama has already gone.

And all the puddles on the floor
have merged into one.

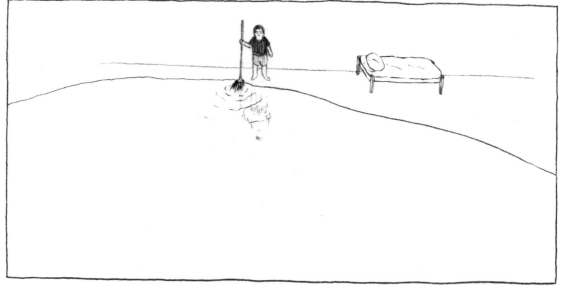

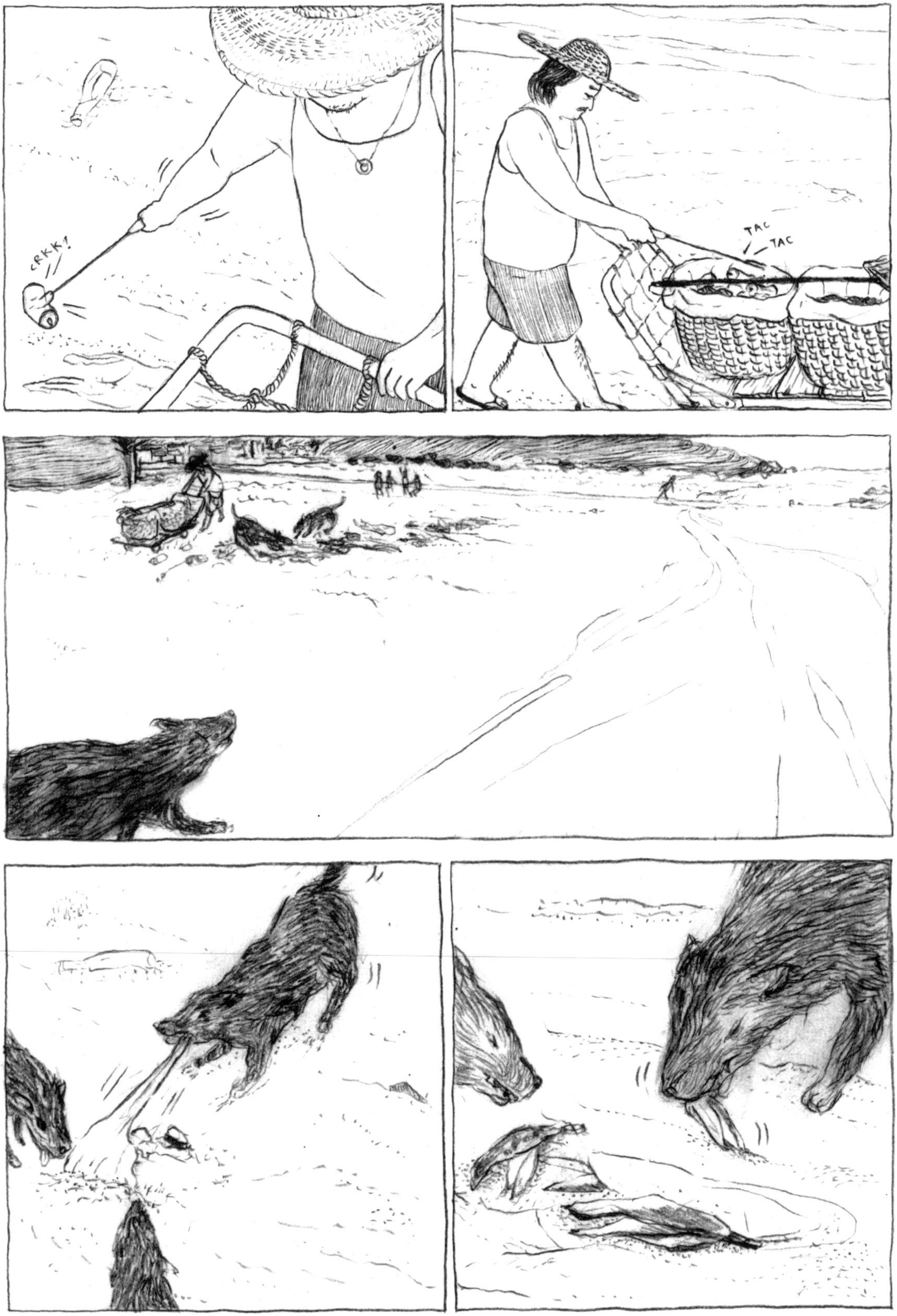
CRKK!
TAC
TAC

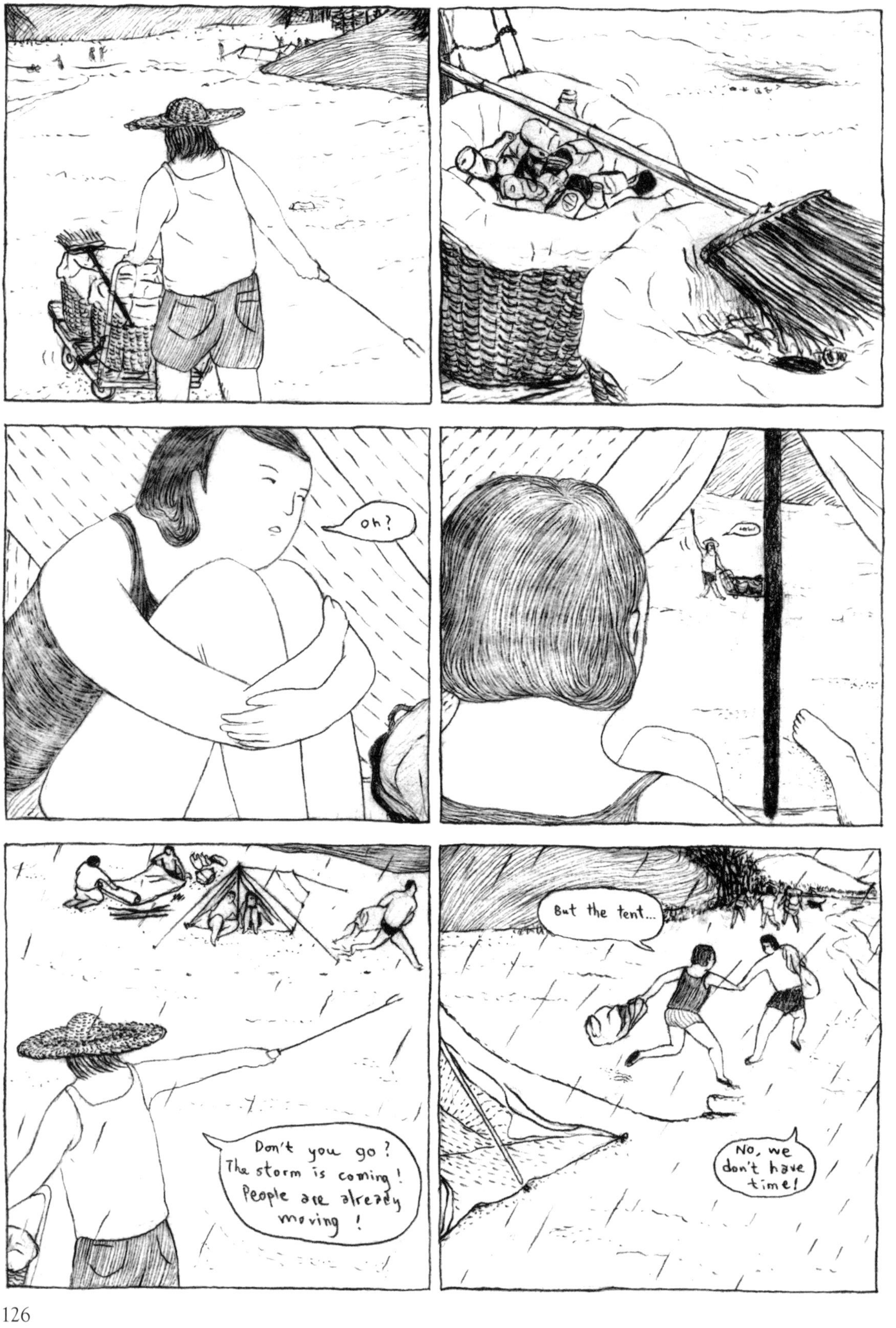
oh?
Don't you go? The storm is coming! People are already moving!
But the tent...
No, we don't have time!

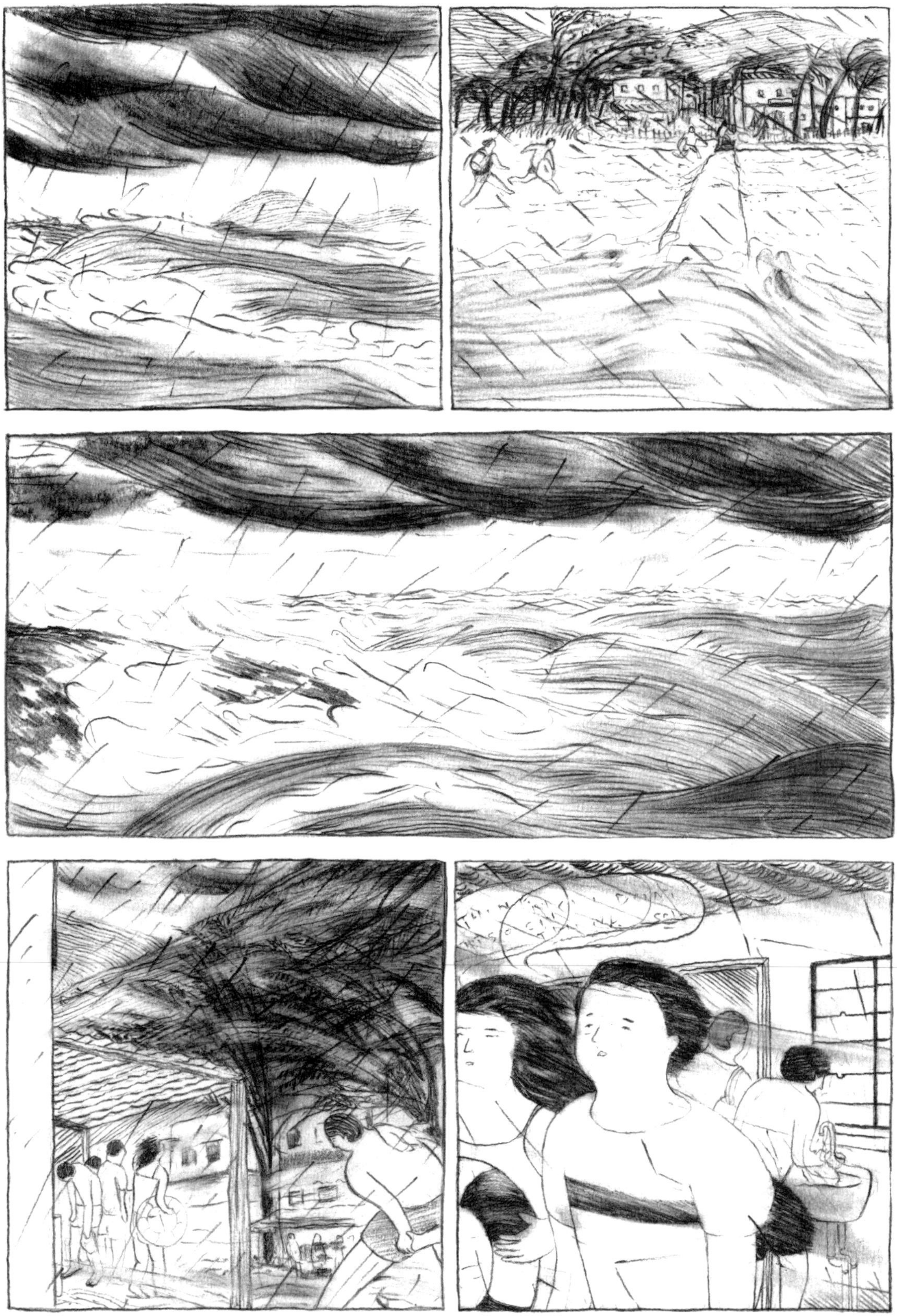

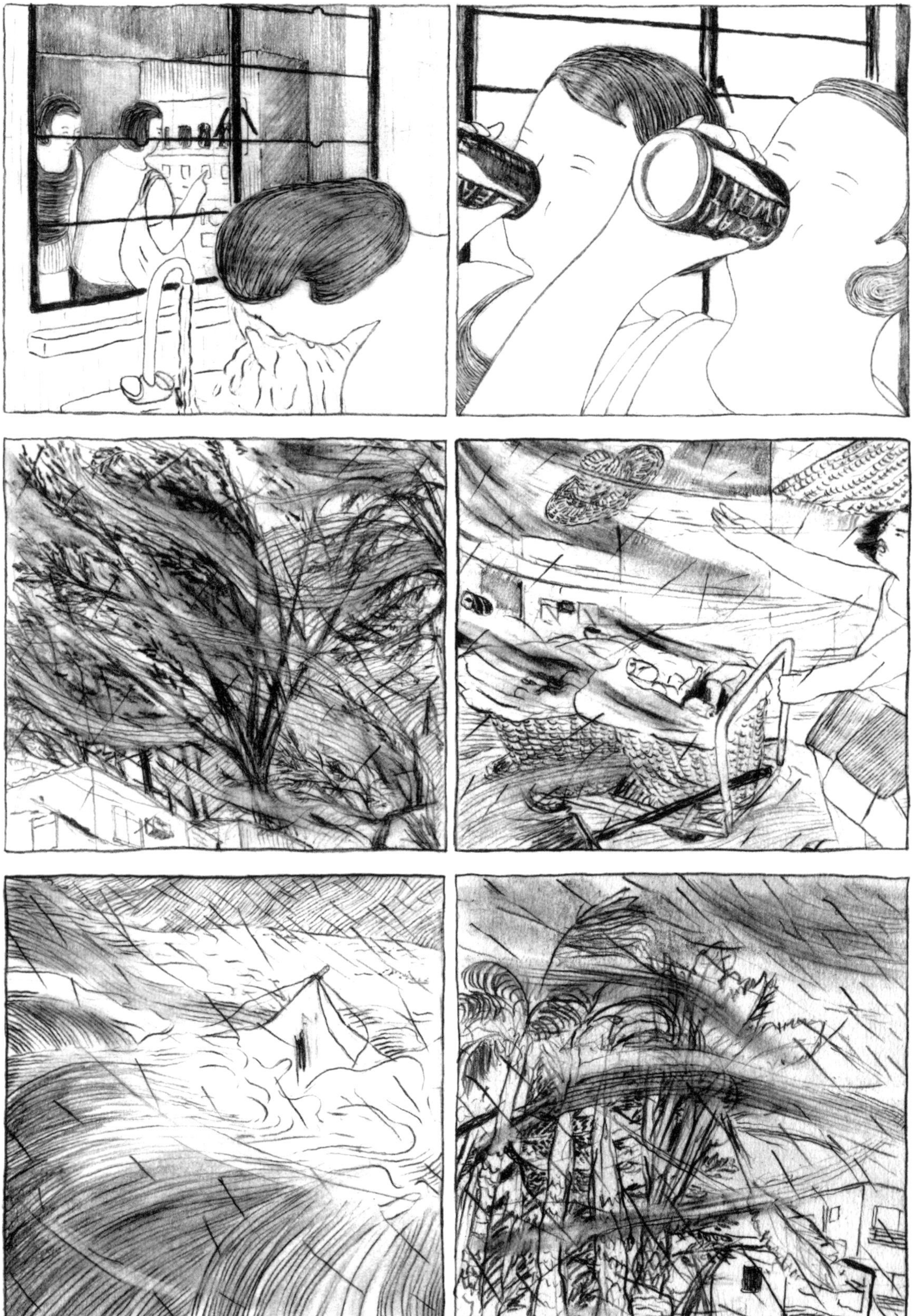
SWEAT

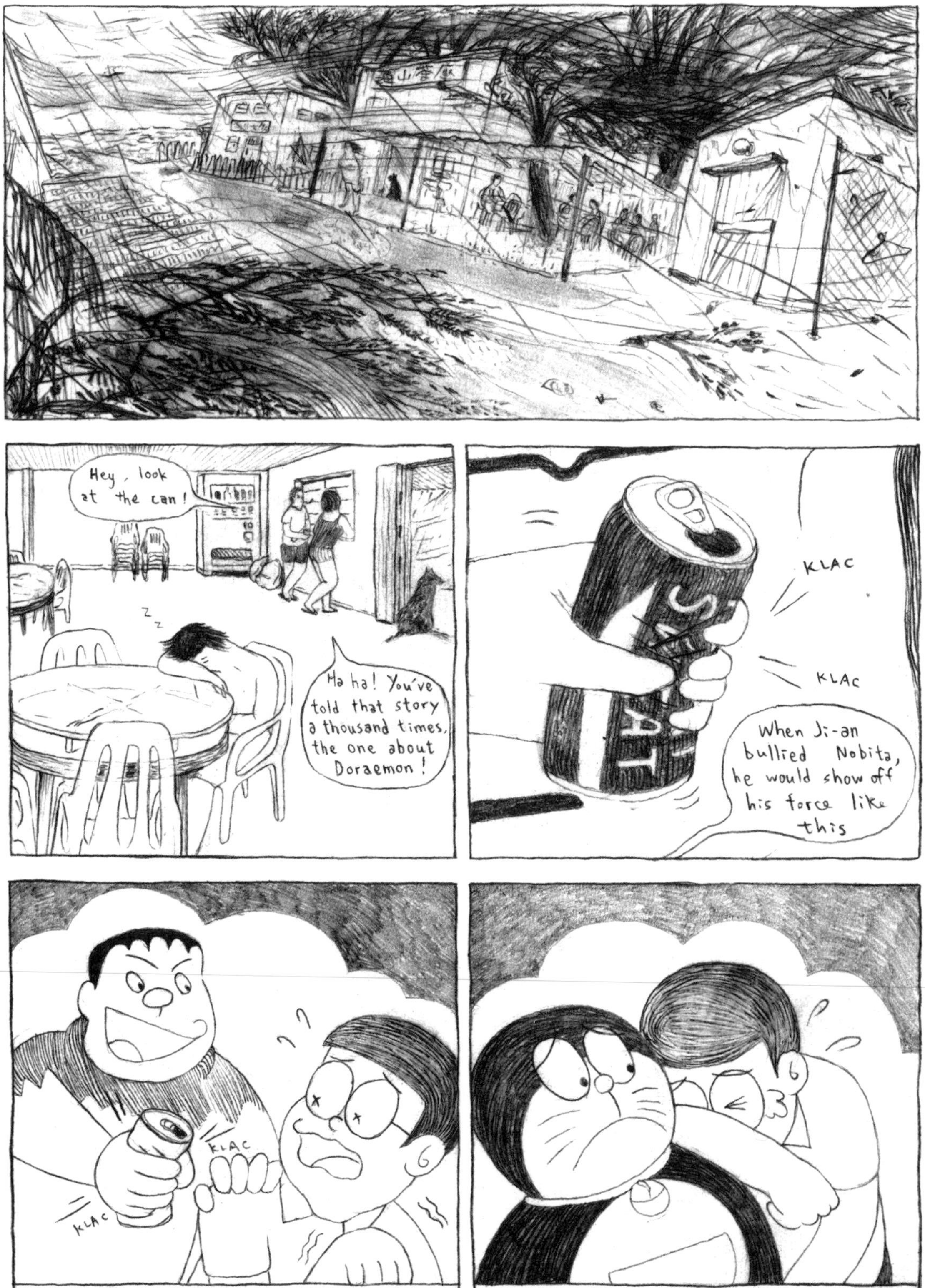

Hey, look at the can!
Ha ha! You've told that story a thousand times, the one about Doraemon!
KLAC
KLAC
When Ji-an bullied Nobita, he would show off his force like this
KLAC
KLAC
Nobita got really scared and he turned to Doraemon for help.
You see either Ji-an is really strong, or Nobita is really fragile.

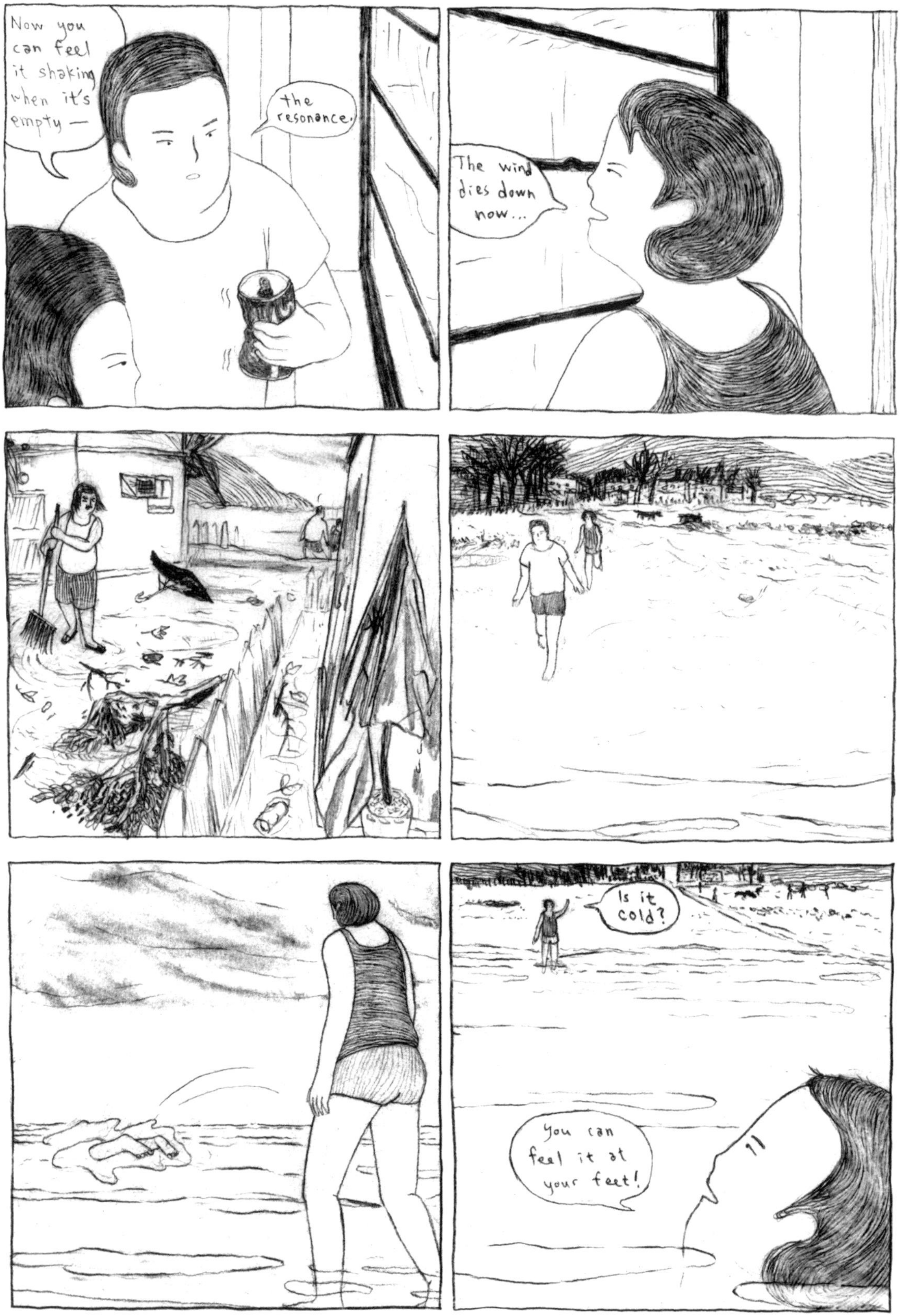
Now you can feel it shaking when it's empty —
the resonance.
The wind dies down now...
Is it cold?
You can feel it at your feet!

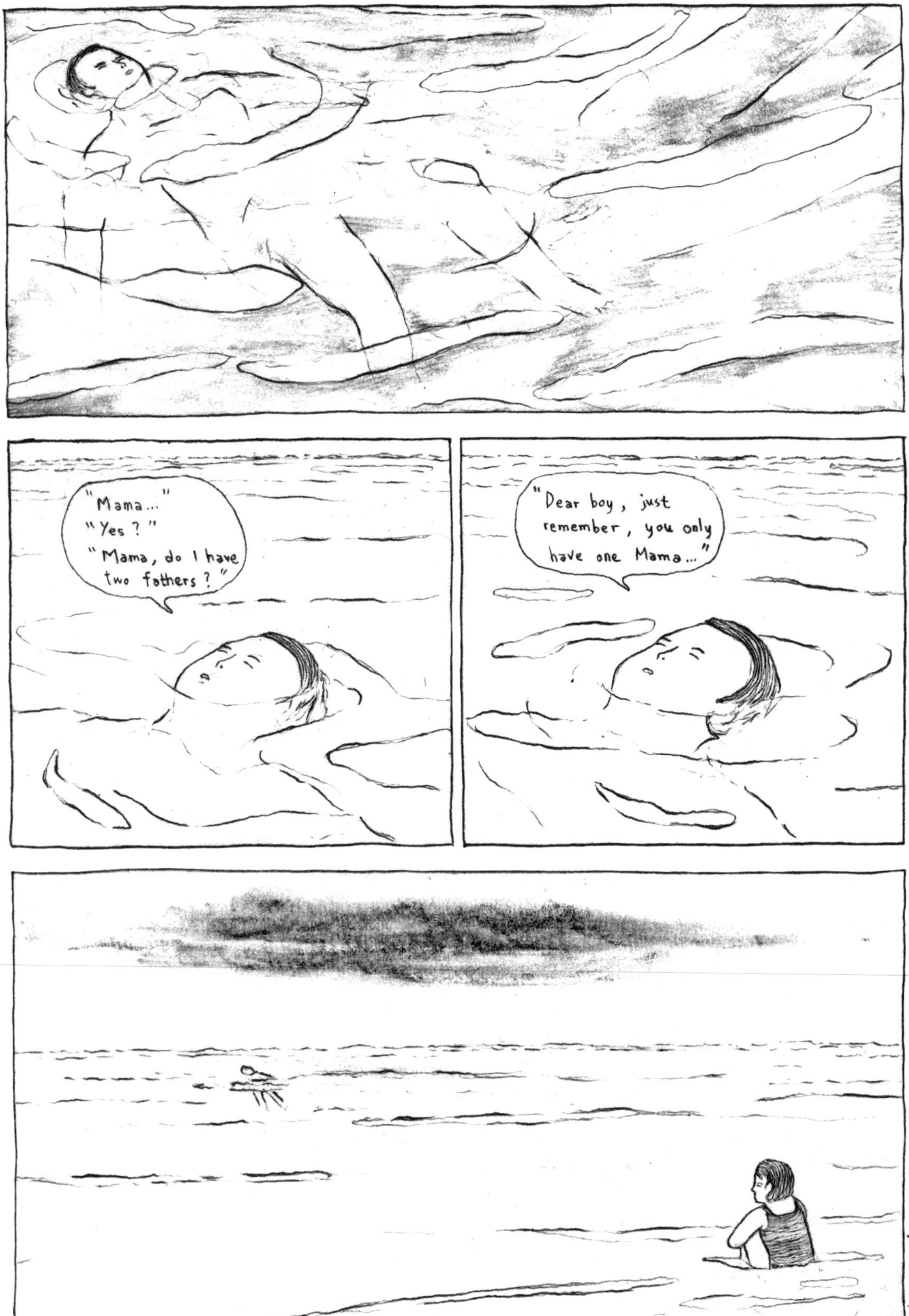
"Mama..."
"Yes?"
"Mama, do I have two fathers?"
"Dear boy, just remember, you only have one Mama..."

# I'm with my Saint

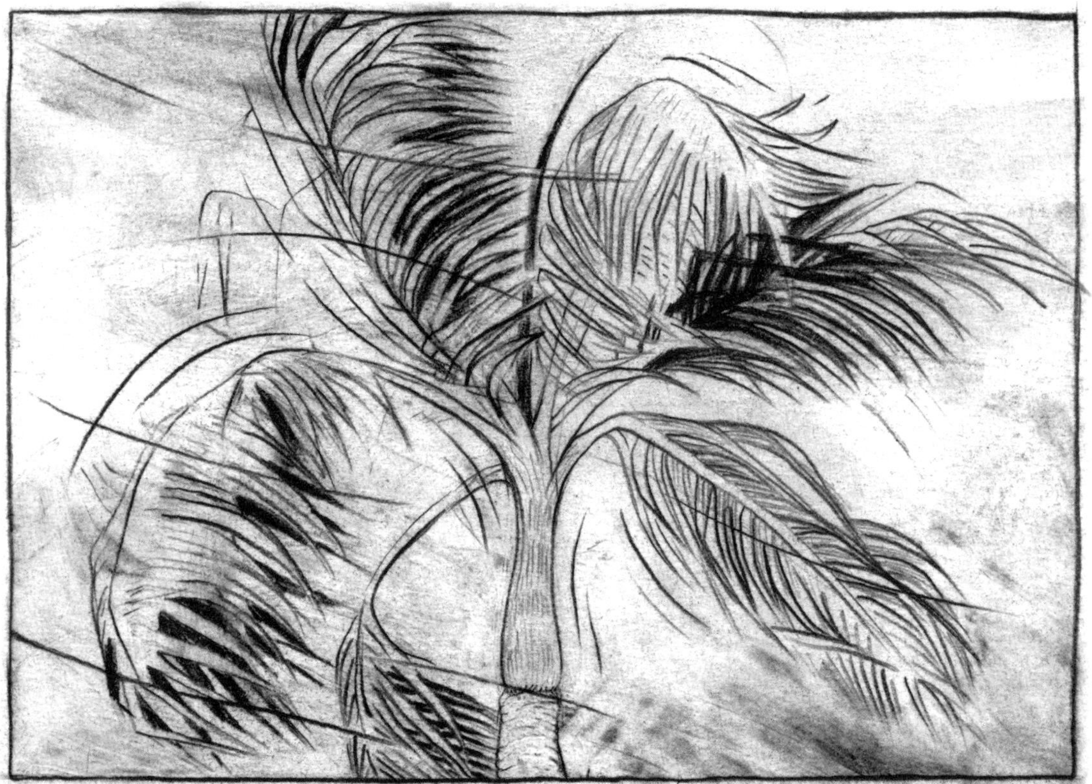

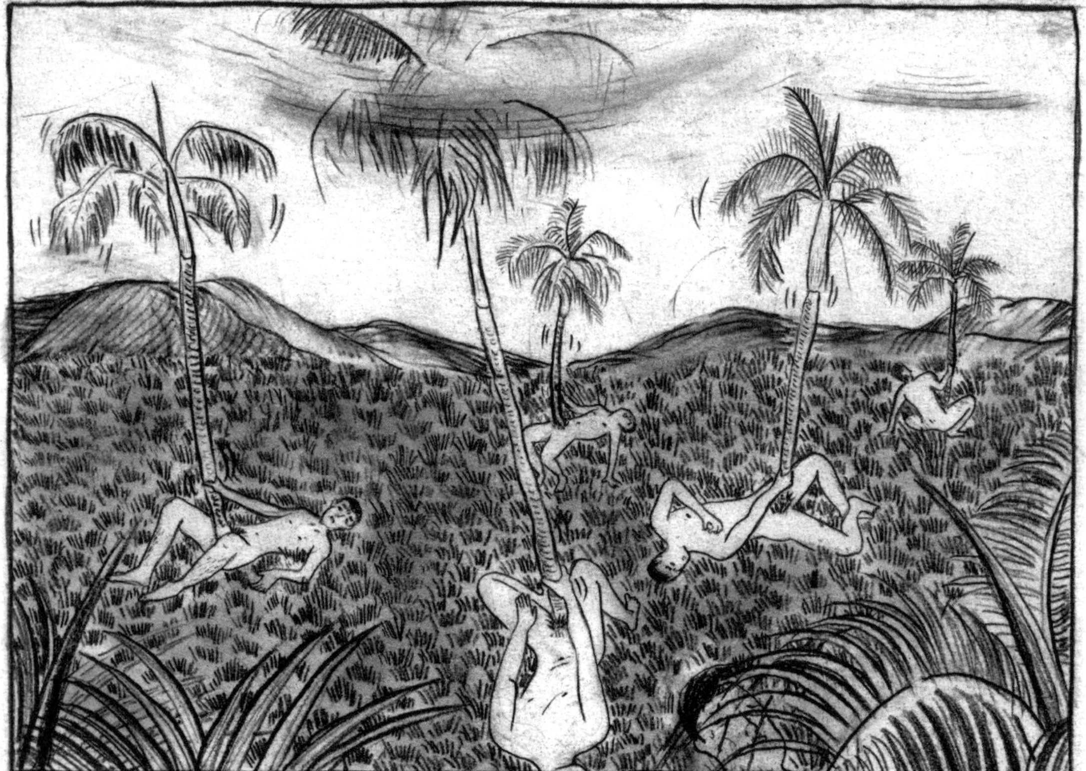

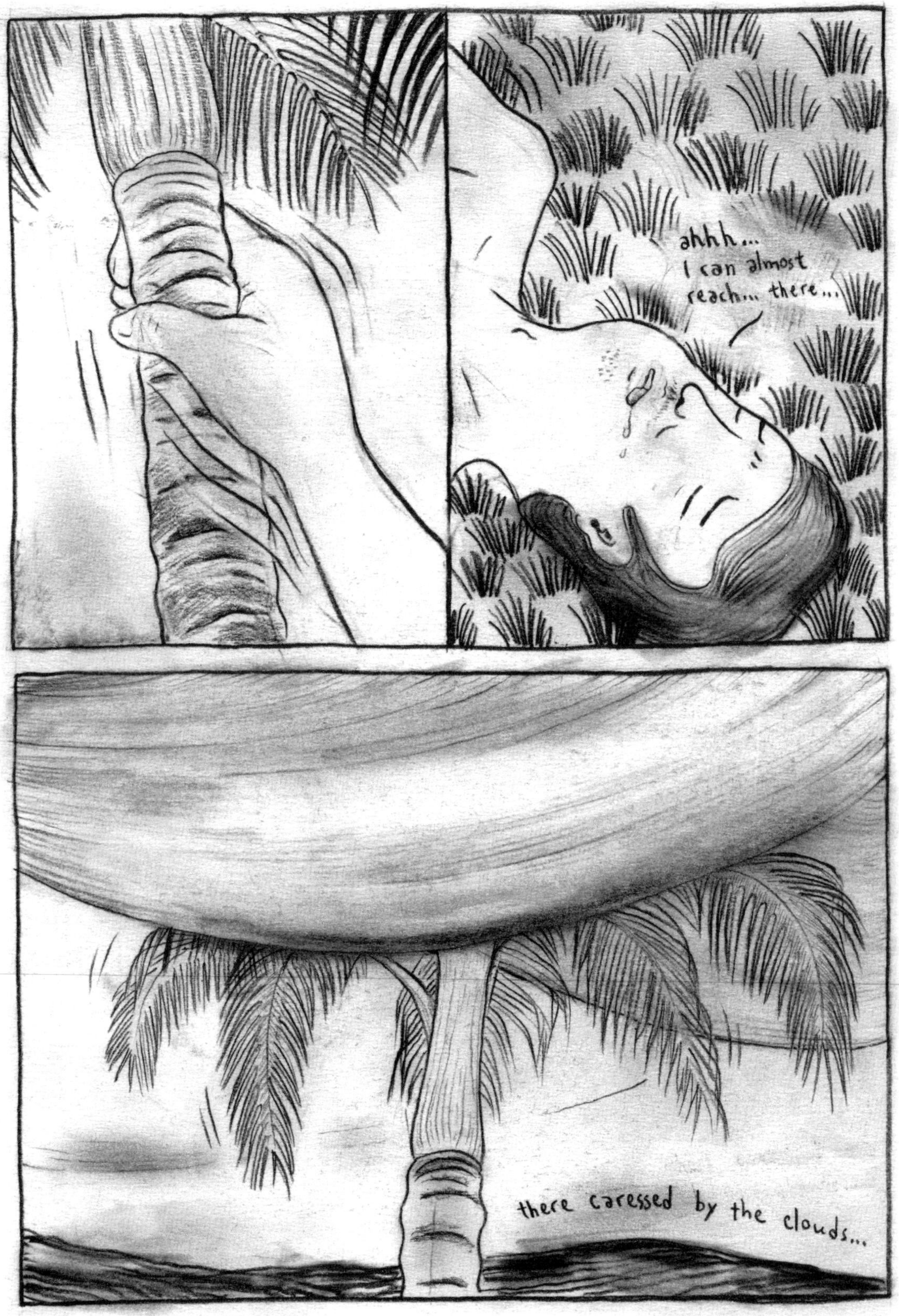
ahhh...
I can almost
reach... there...
there caressed by the clouds...

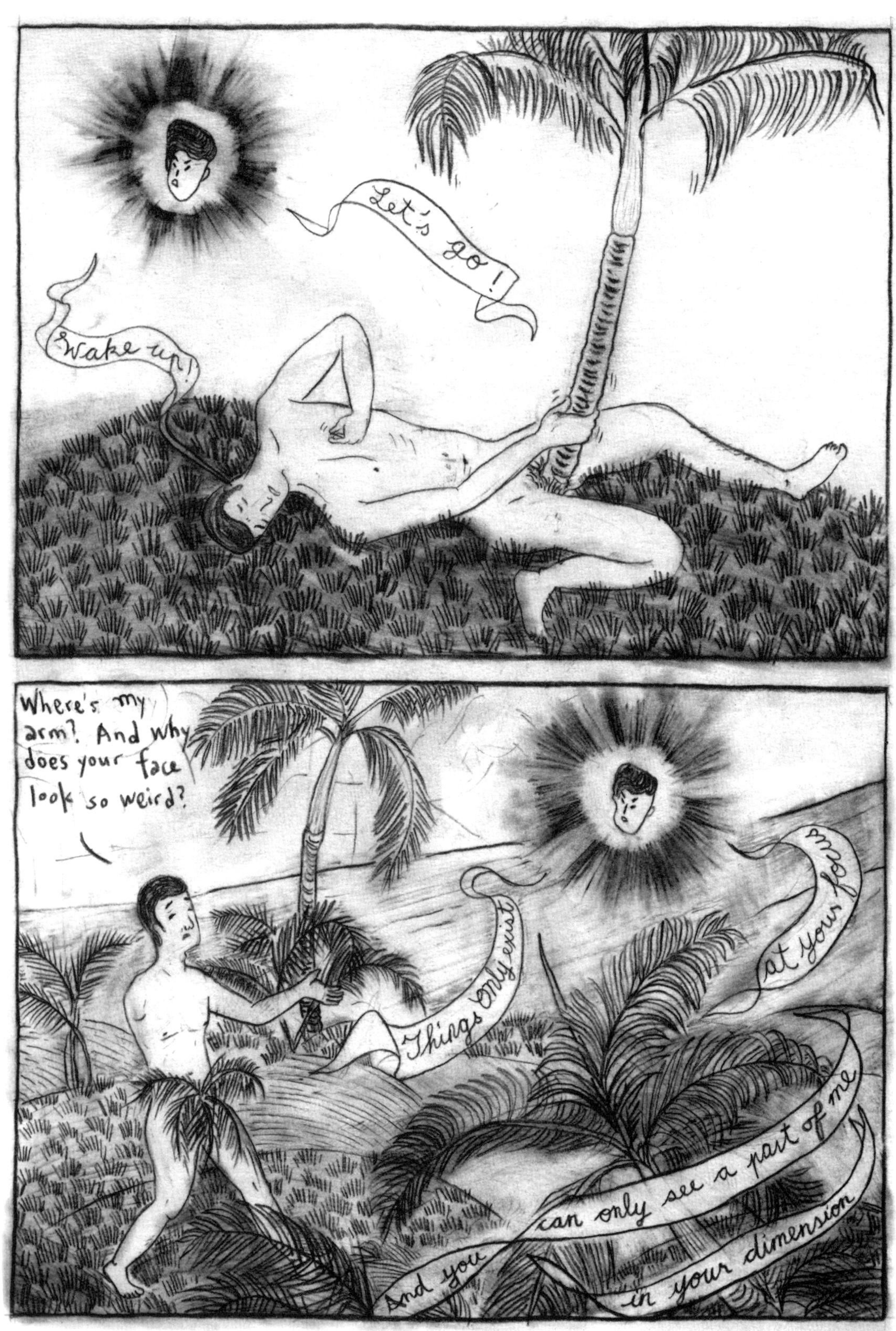
Wake up!
Let's go!
Where's my arm? And why does your face look so weird?
Things only exist
at your focus
And you can only see a part of me
in your dimension

Focus ?
But what are these palm trees for ? Why this monoculture ?
How can you tell they are palms not coconuts ?

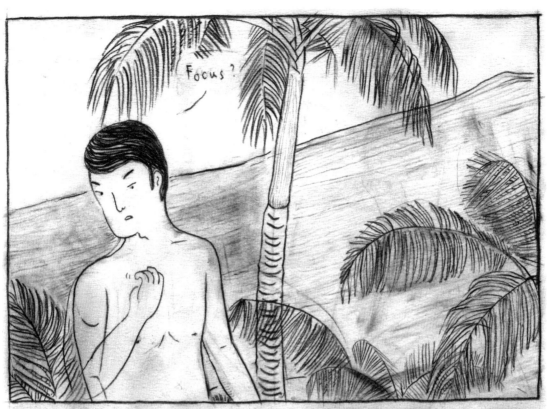

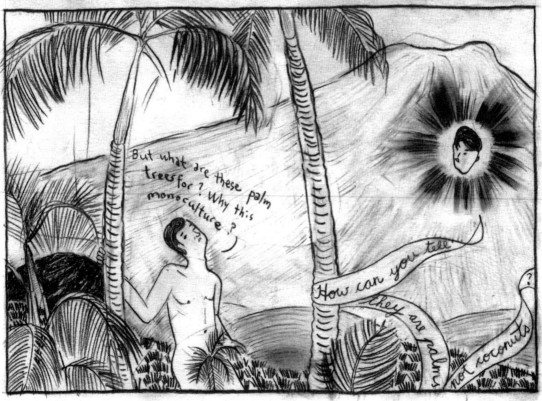

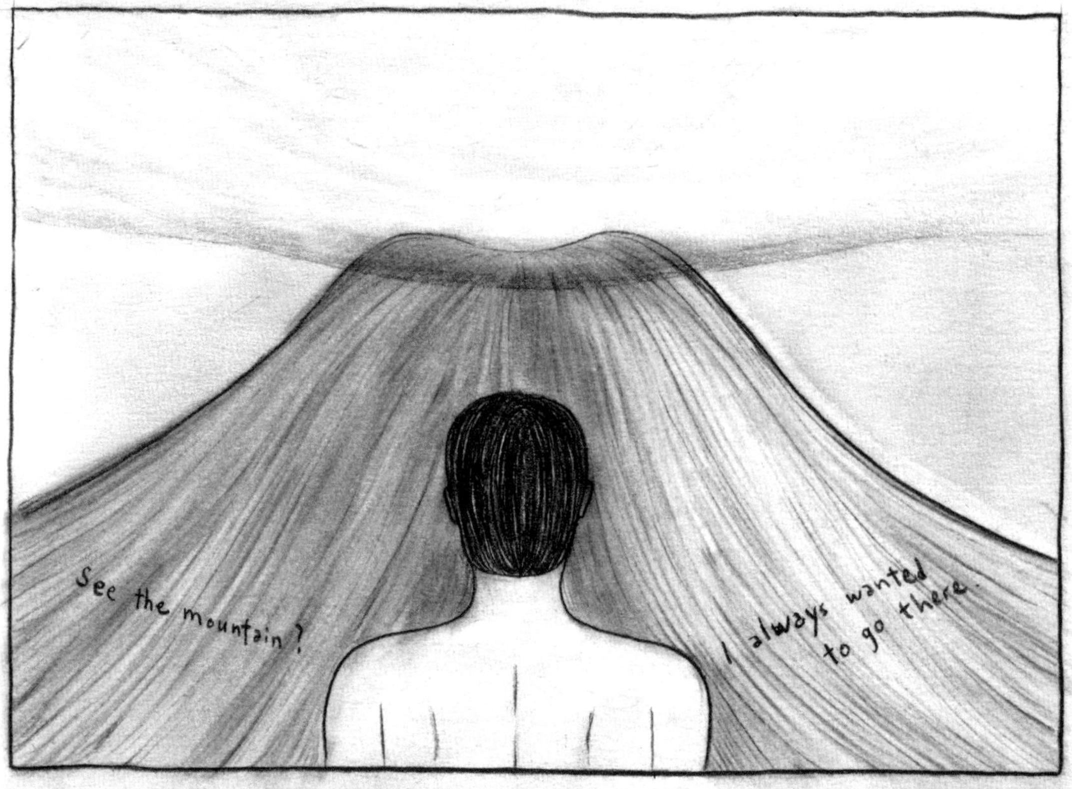
See the mountain?
I always wanted to go there.

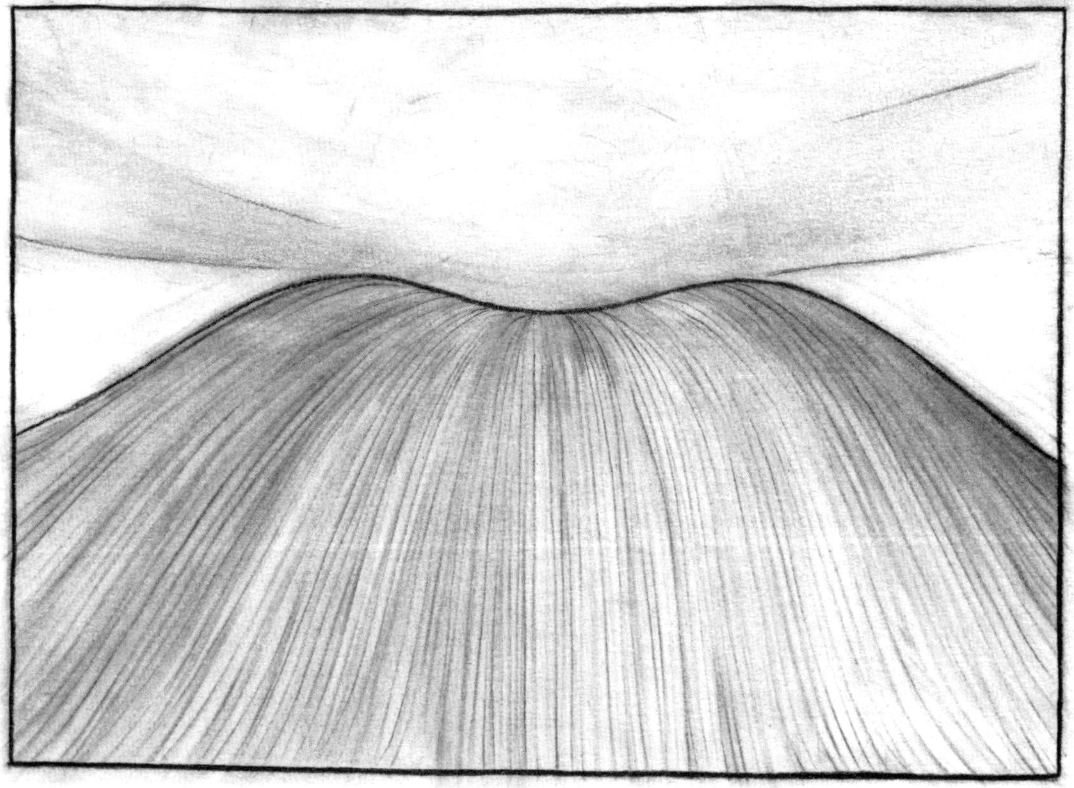

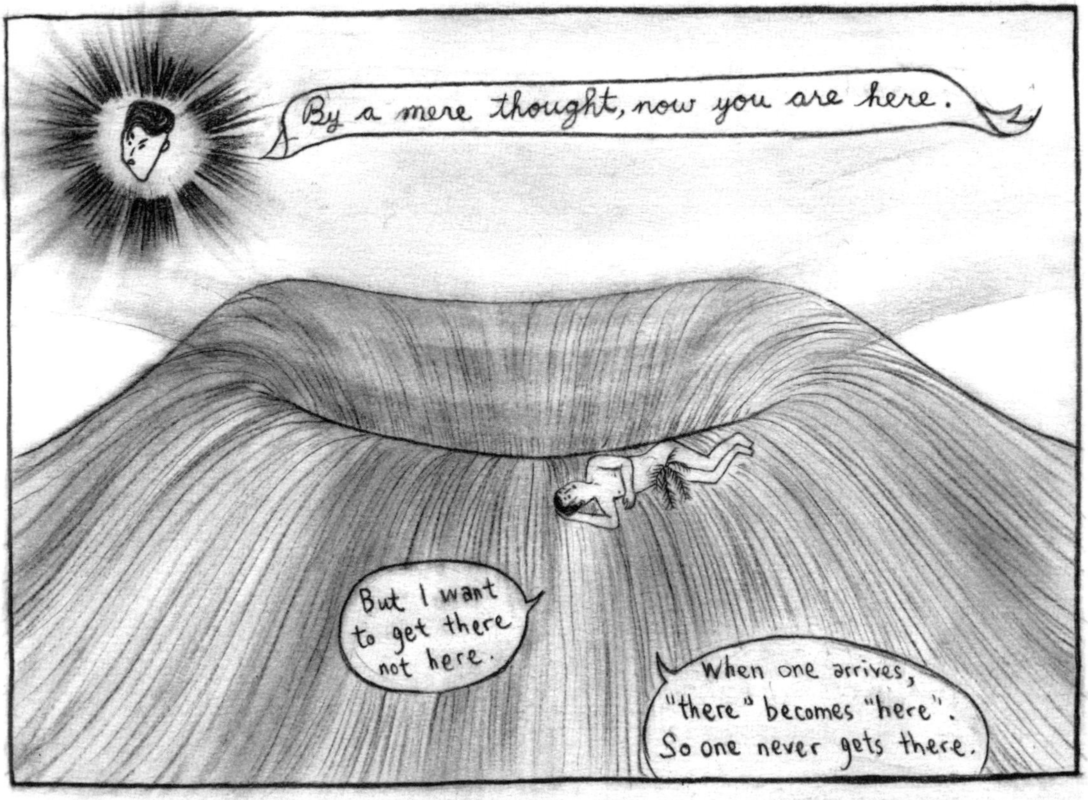
By a mere thought, now you are here.
But I want to get there not here.
When one arrives, "there" becomes "here". So one never gets there.

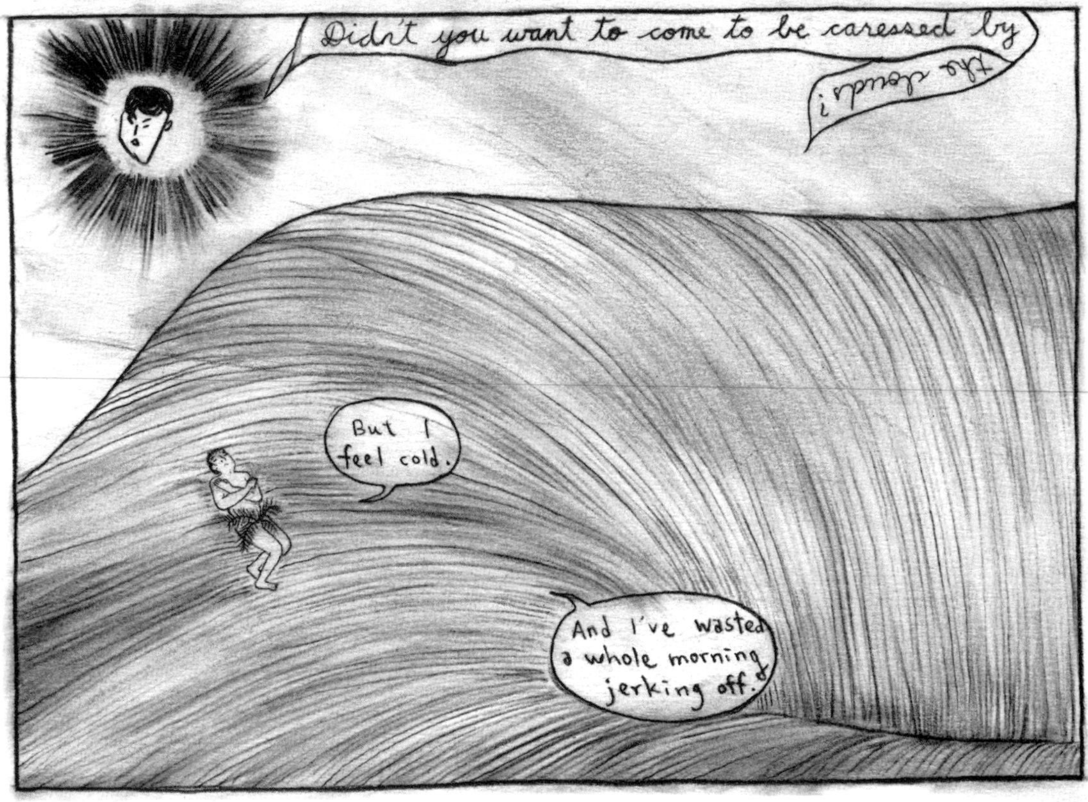
Didn't you want to come to be caressed by the clouds?
But I feel cold.
And I've wasted a whole morning jerking off.

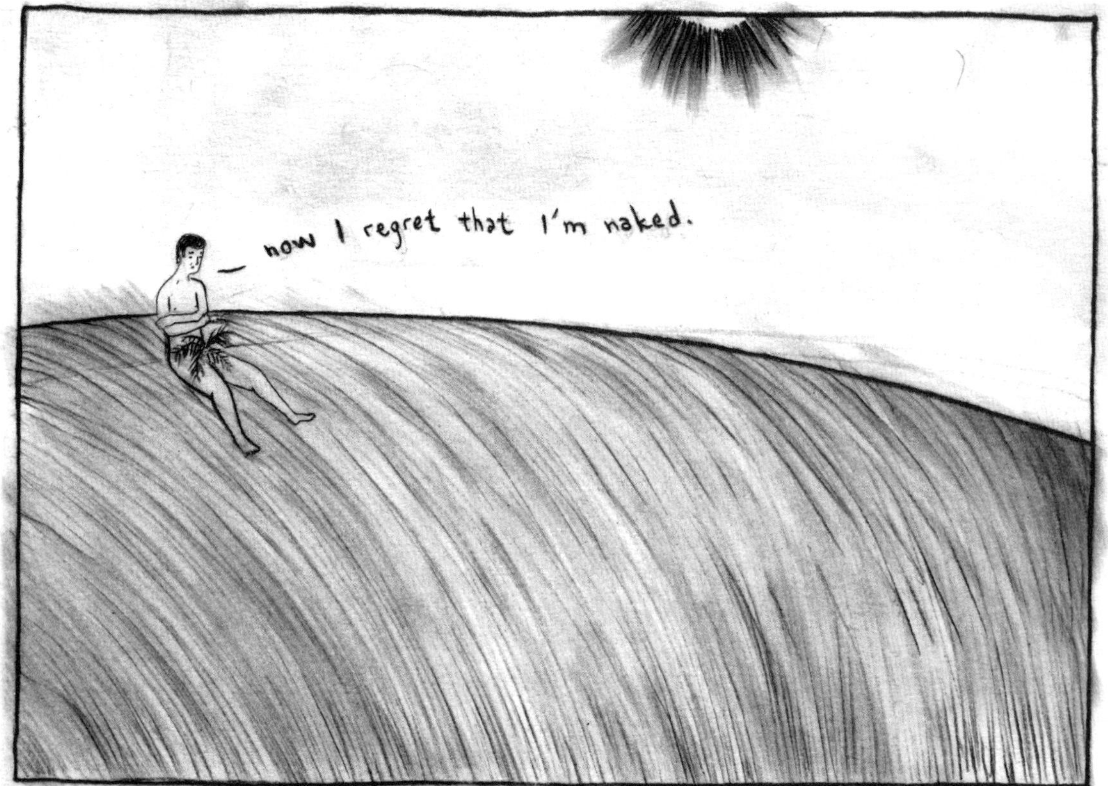
— now I regret that I'm naked.

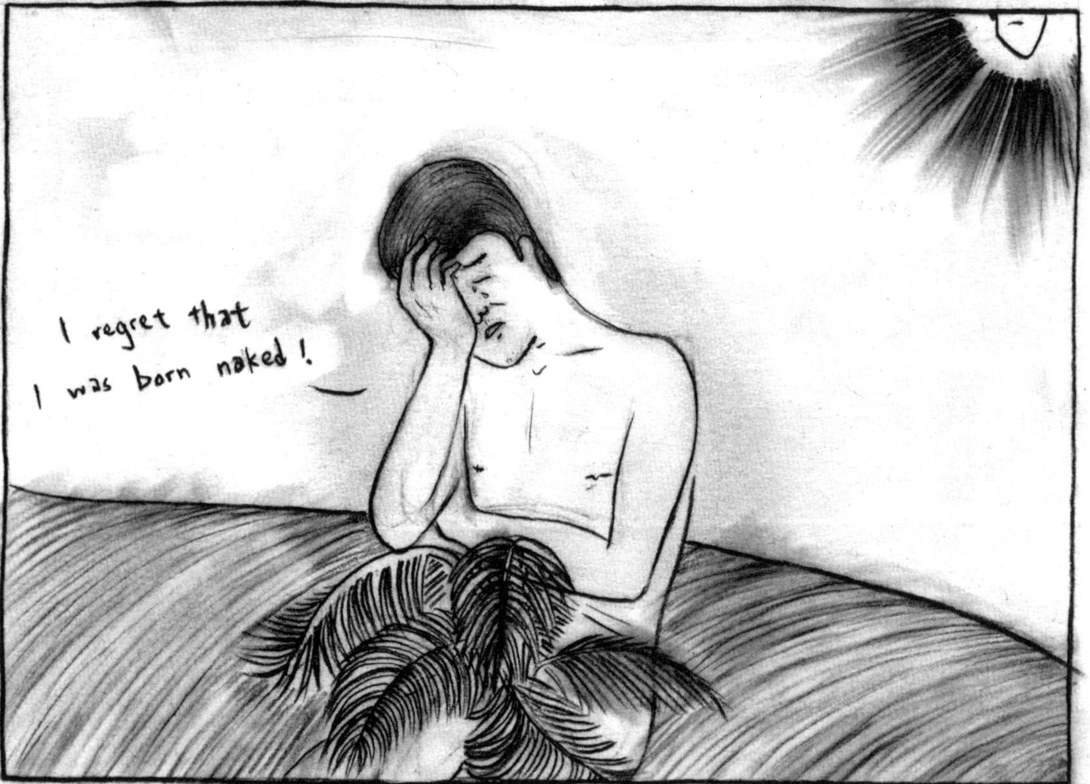
I regret that
I was born naked!

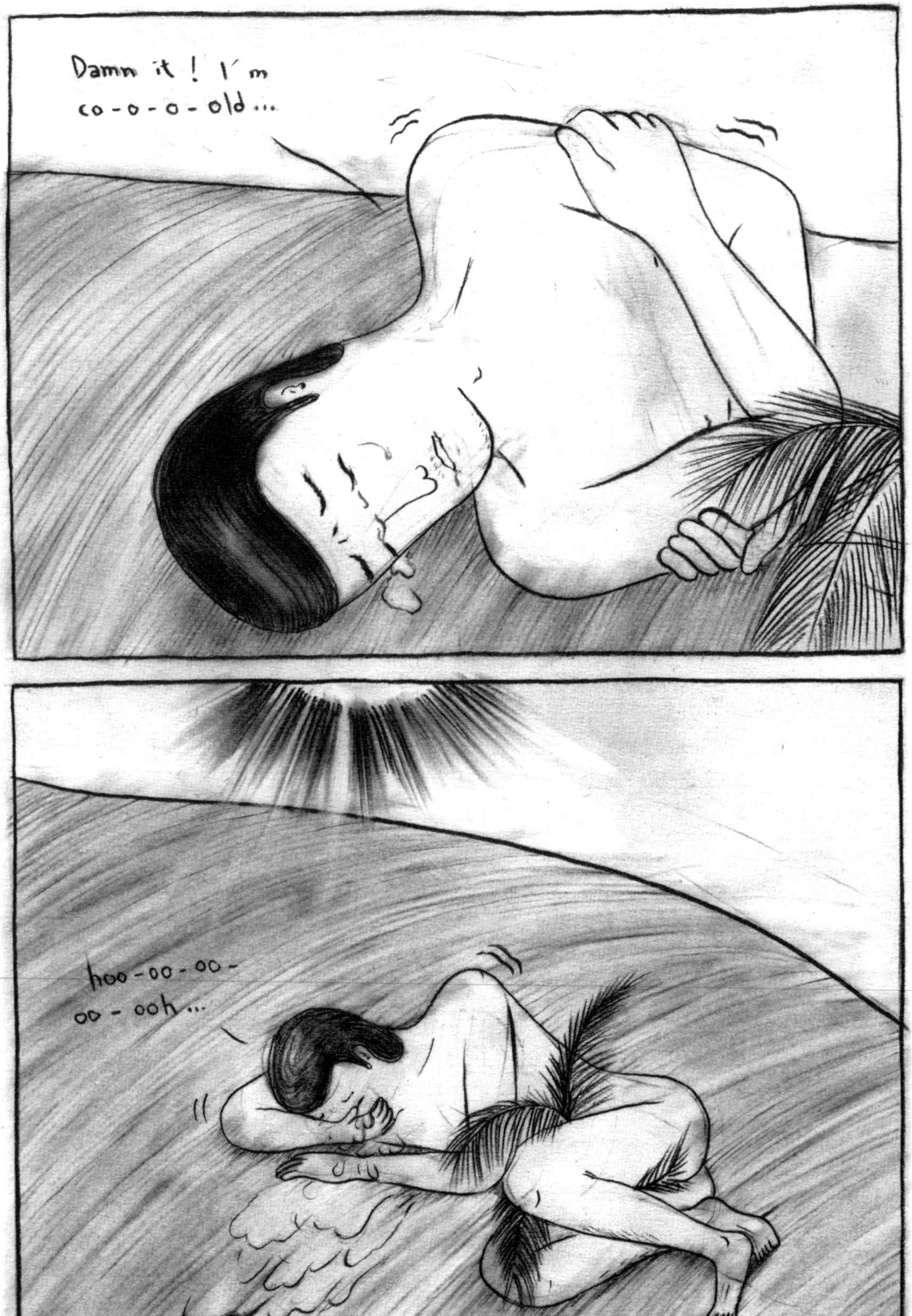
Damn it! I'm co-o-o-old...
hoo-oo-oo-oo-ooh...

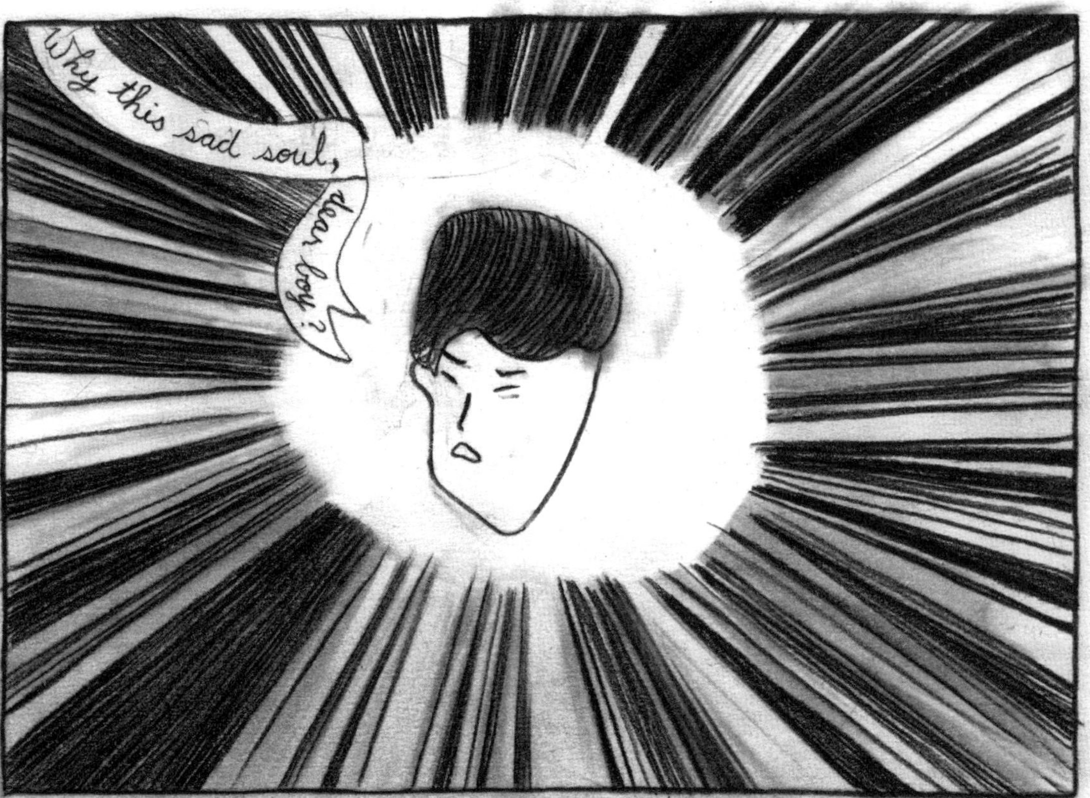
Why this sad soul, dear boy?

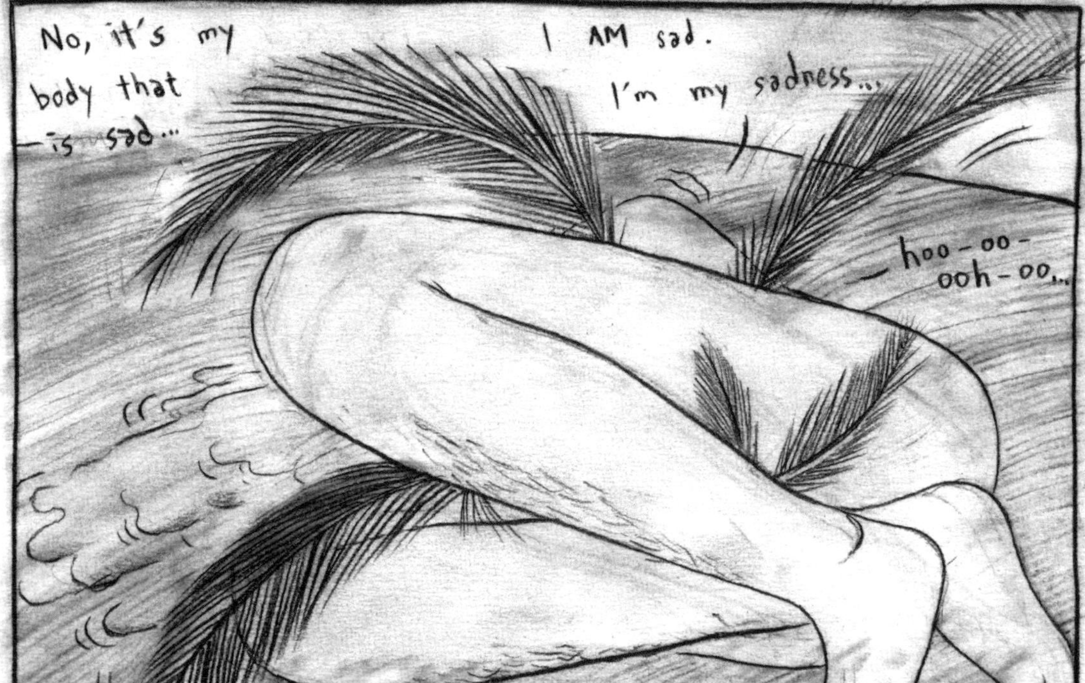
No, it's my body that is sad...
I AM sad.
I'm my sadness...
hoo-oo-ooh-oo...

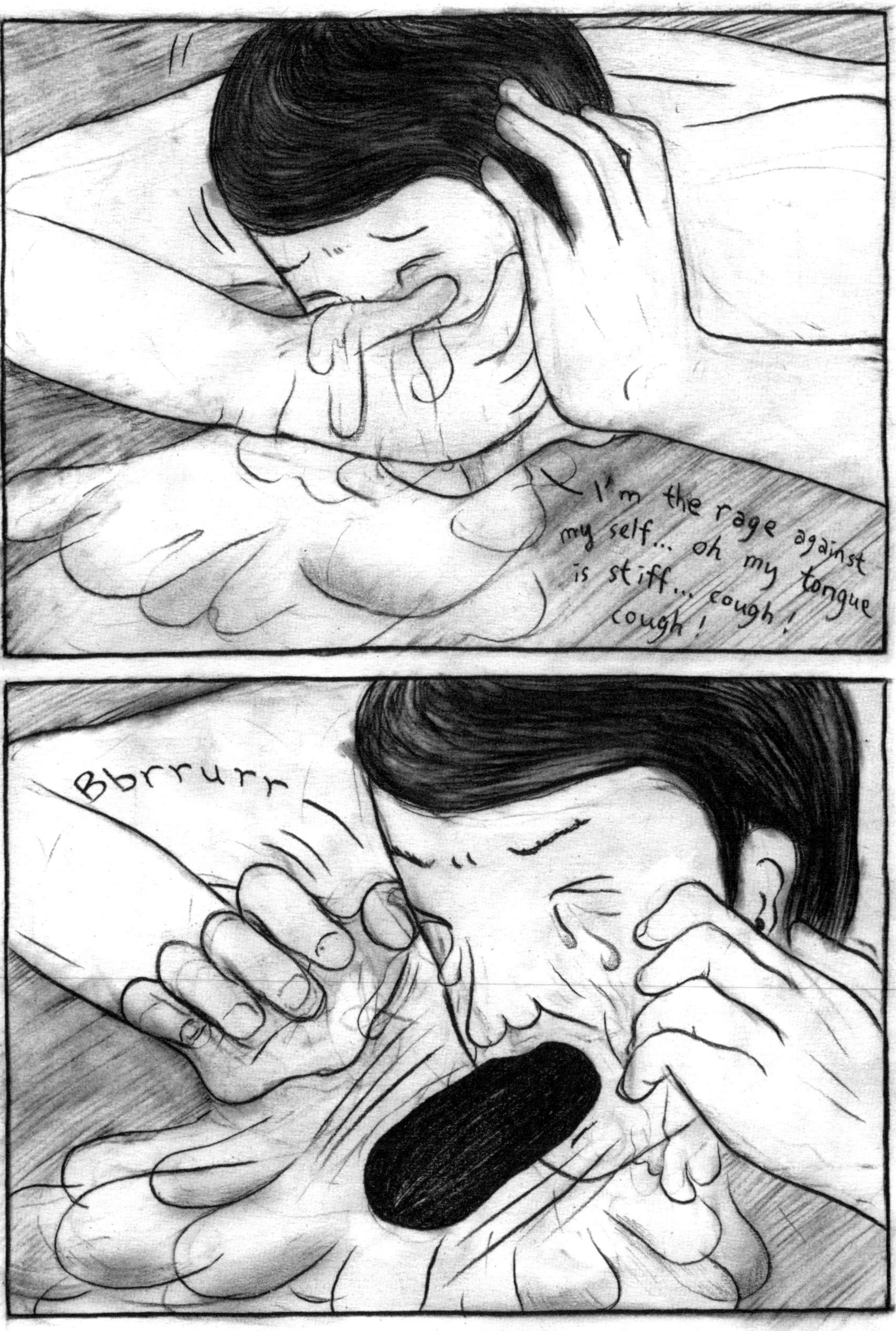
I'm the rage against my self... oh my tongue is stiff... cough! cough!
Bbrrurr

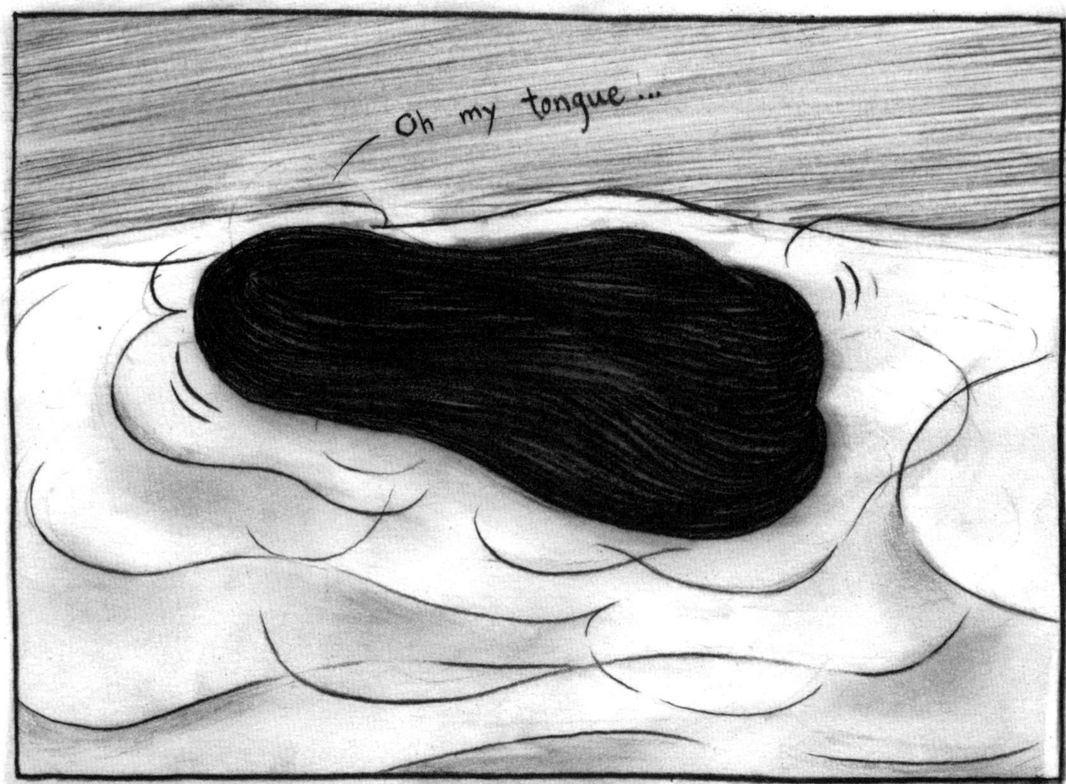
Oh my tongue...

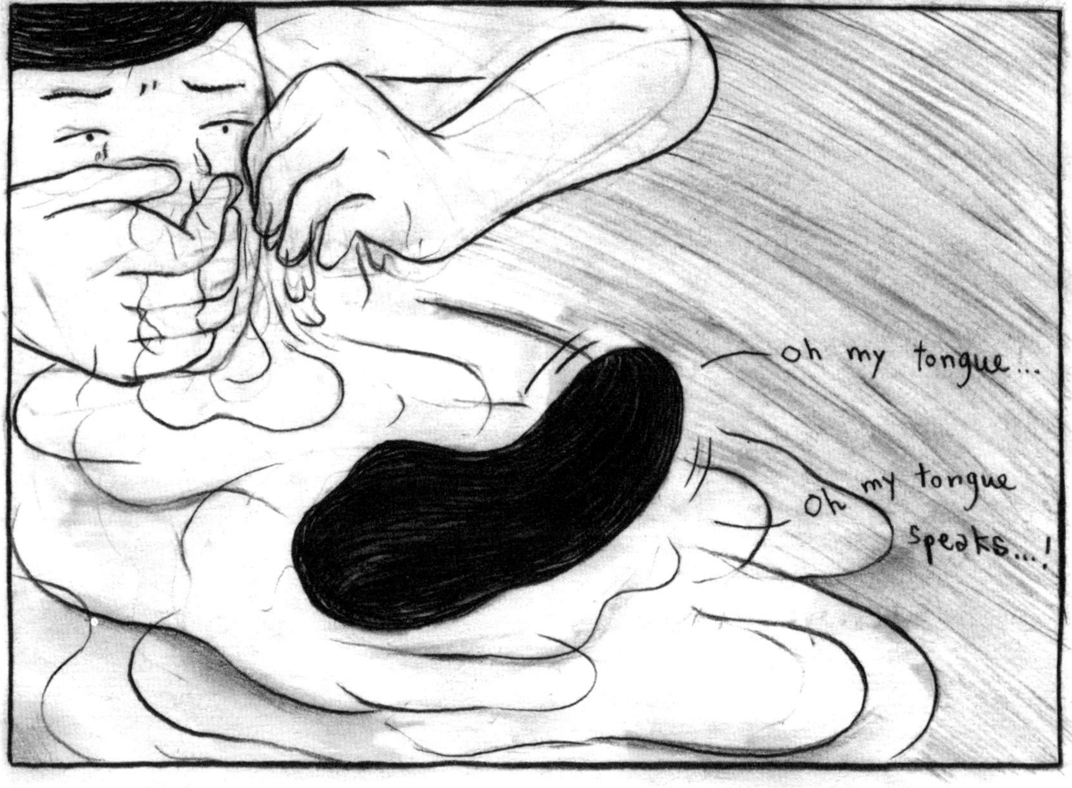
oh my tongue...
Oh my tongue
speaks...!

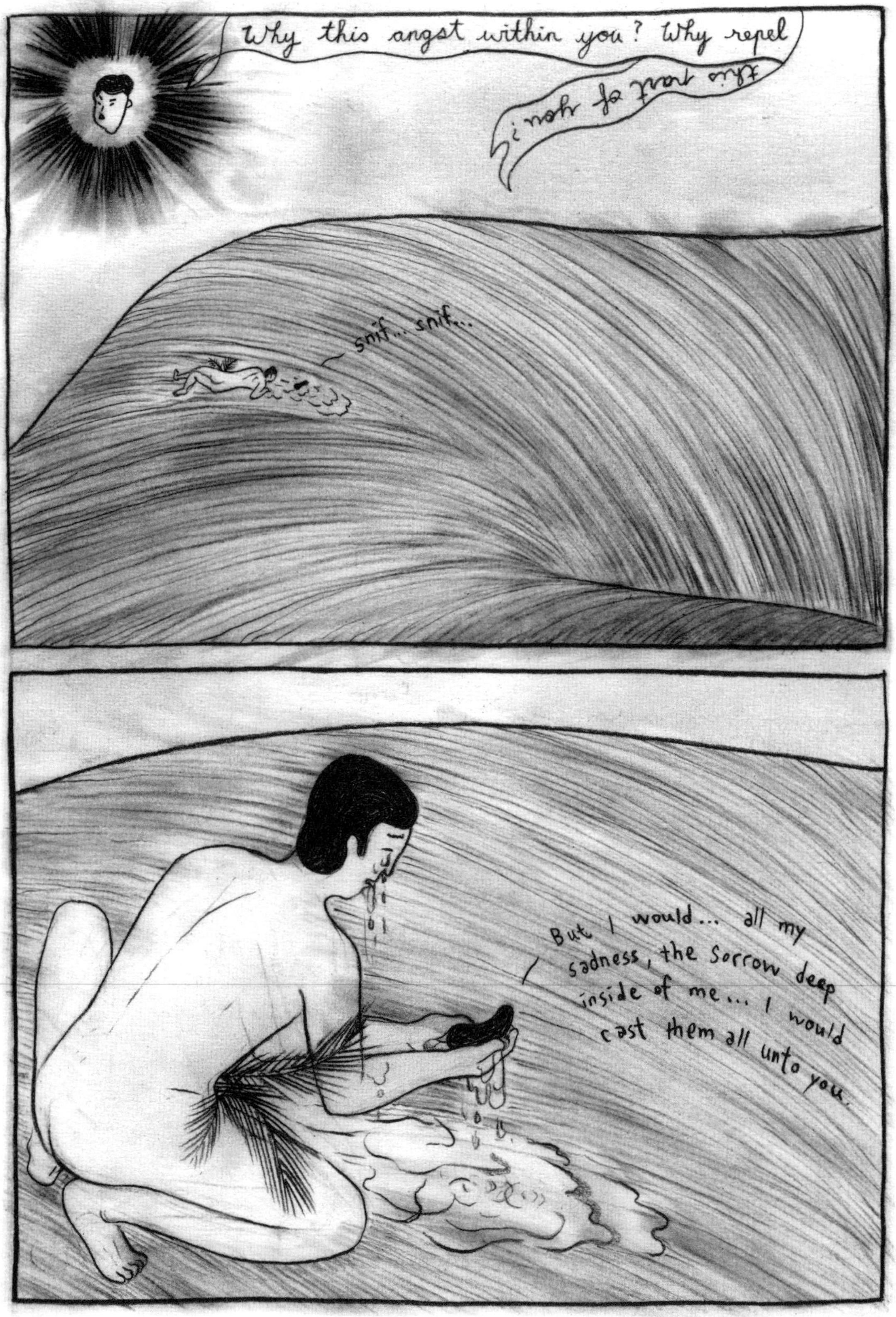
Why this angst within you? Why repel this part of you?
snif... snif...
But I would... all my sadness, the sorrow deep inside of me... I would cast them all unto you.

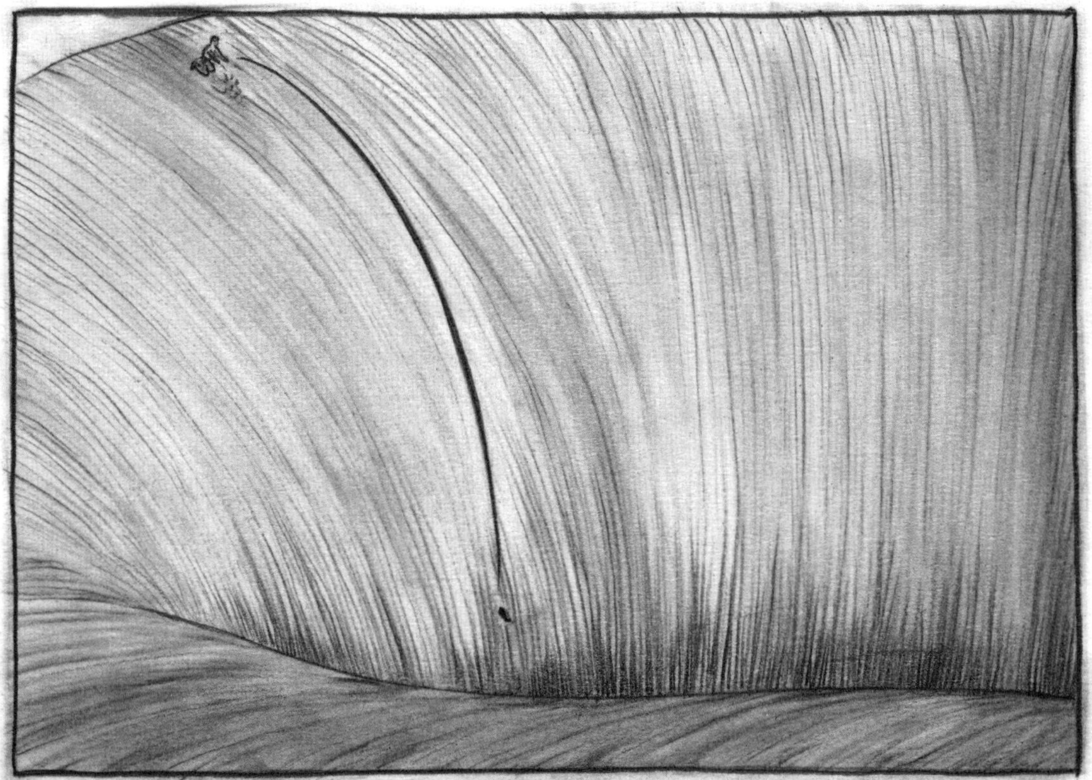

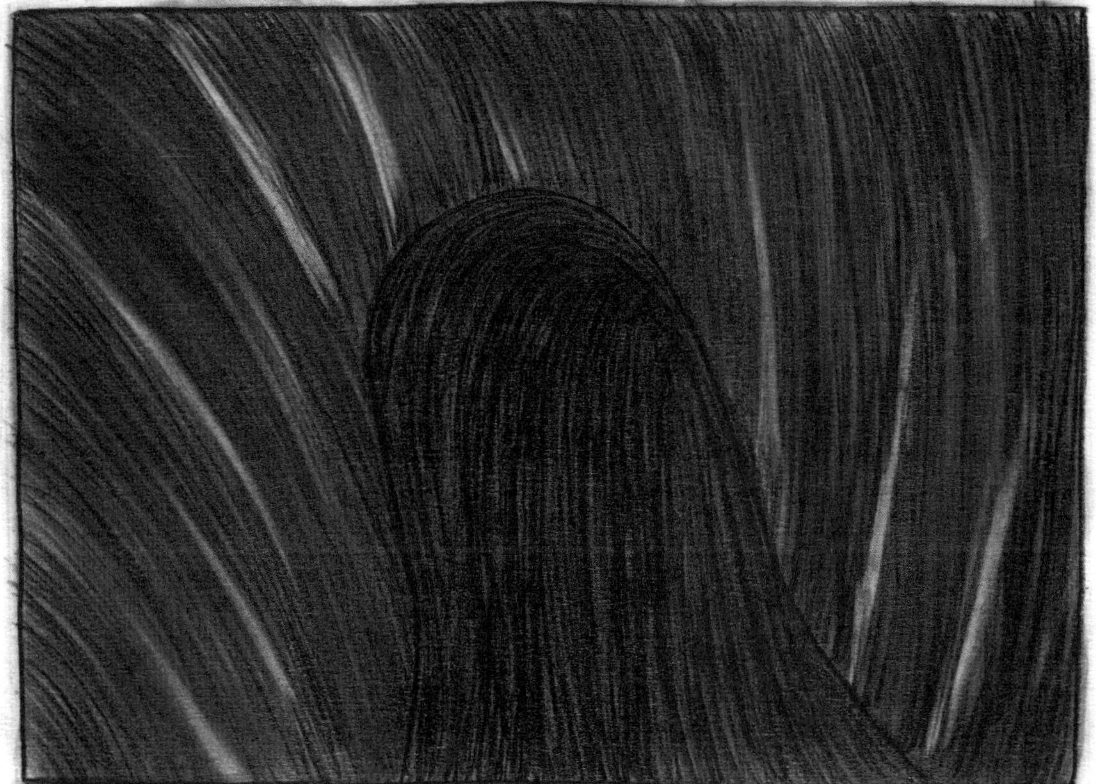

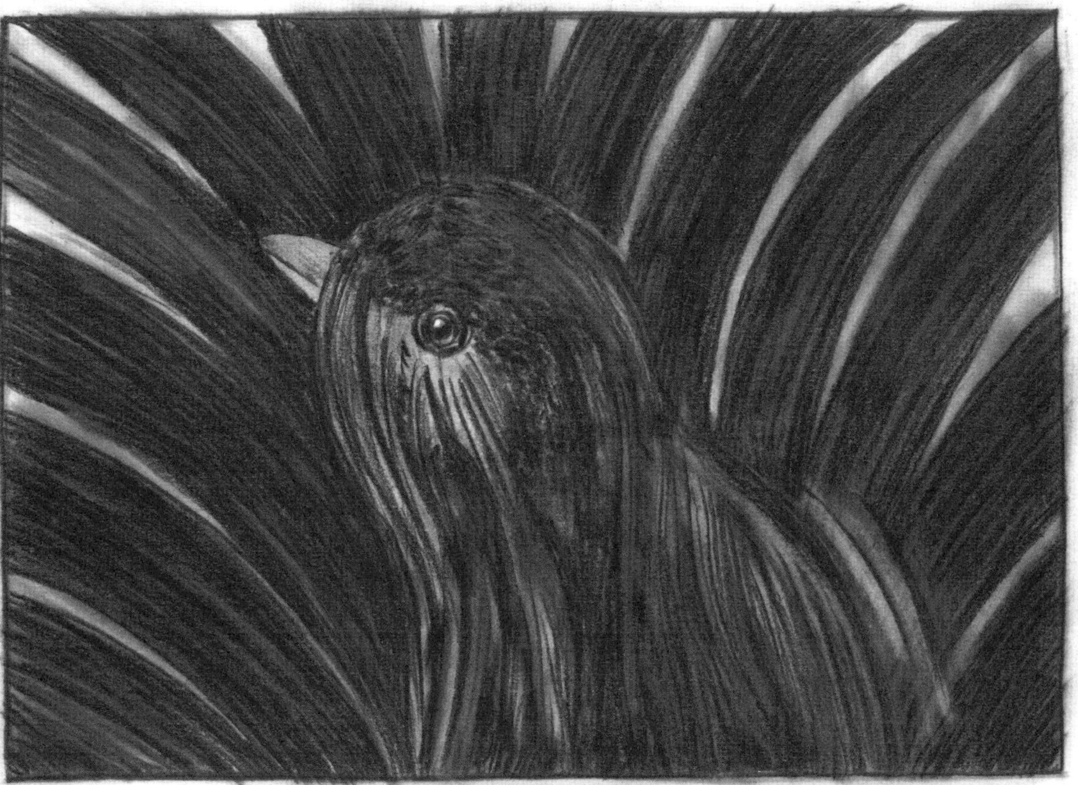

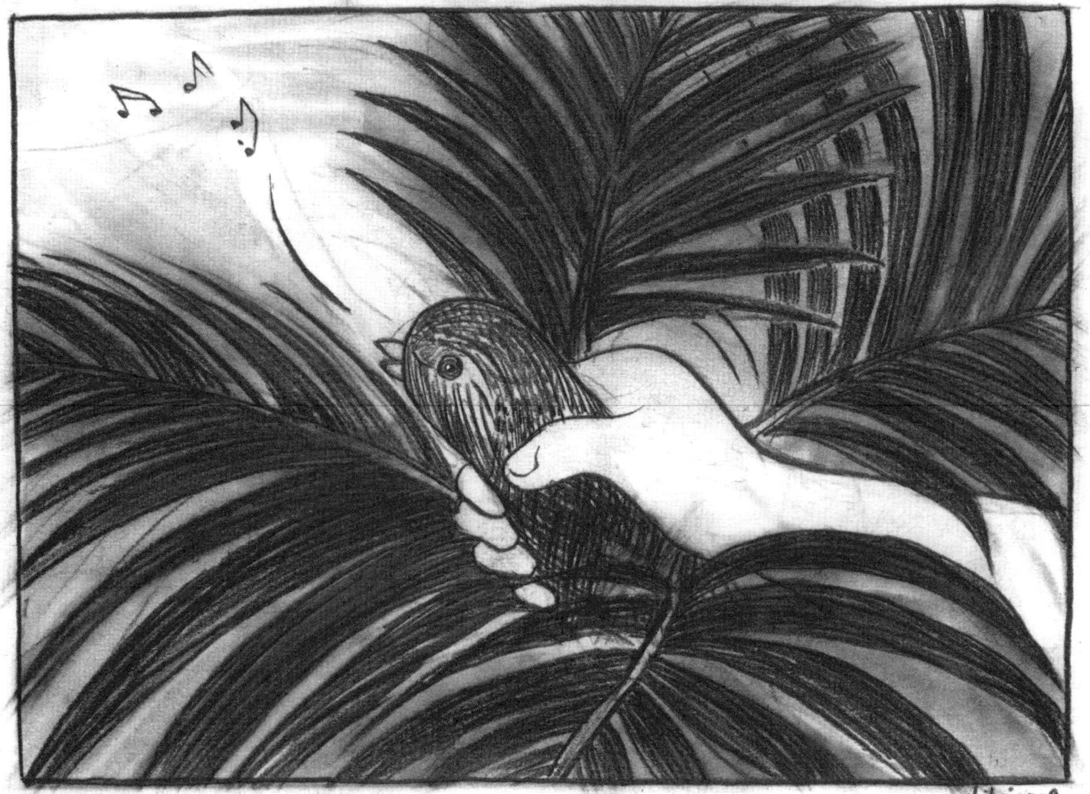

chihoi 2009

# The Library

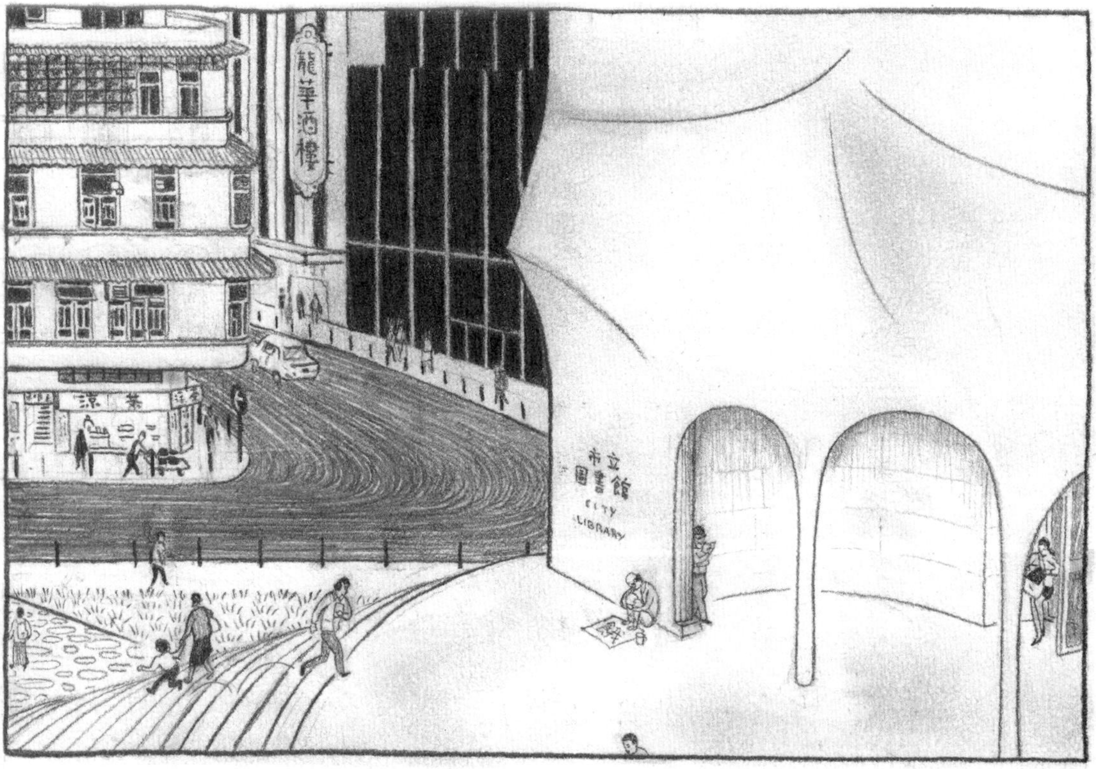
龍華酒樓
市立
圖書館
CITY
LIBRARY

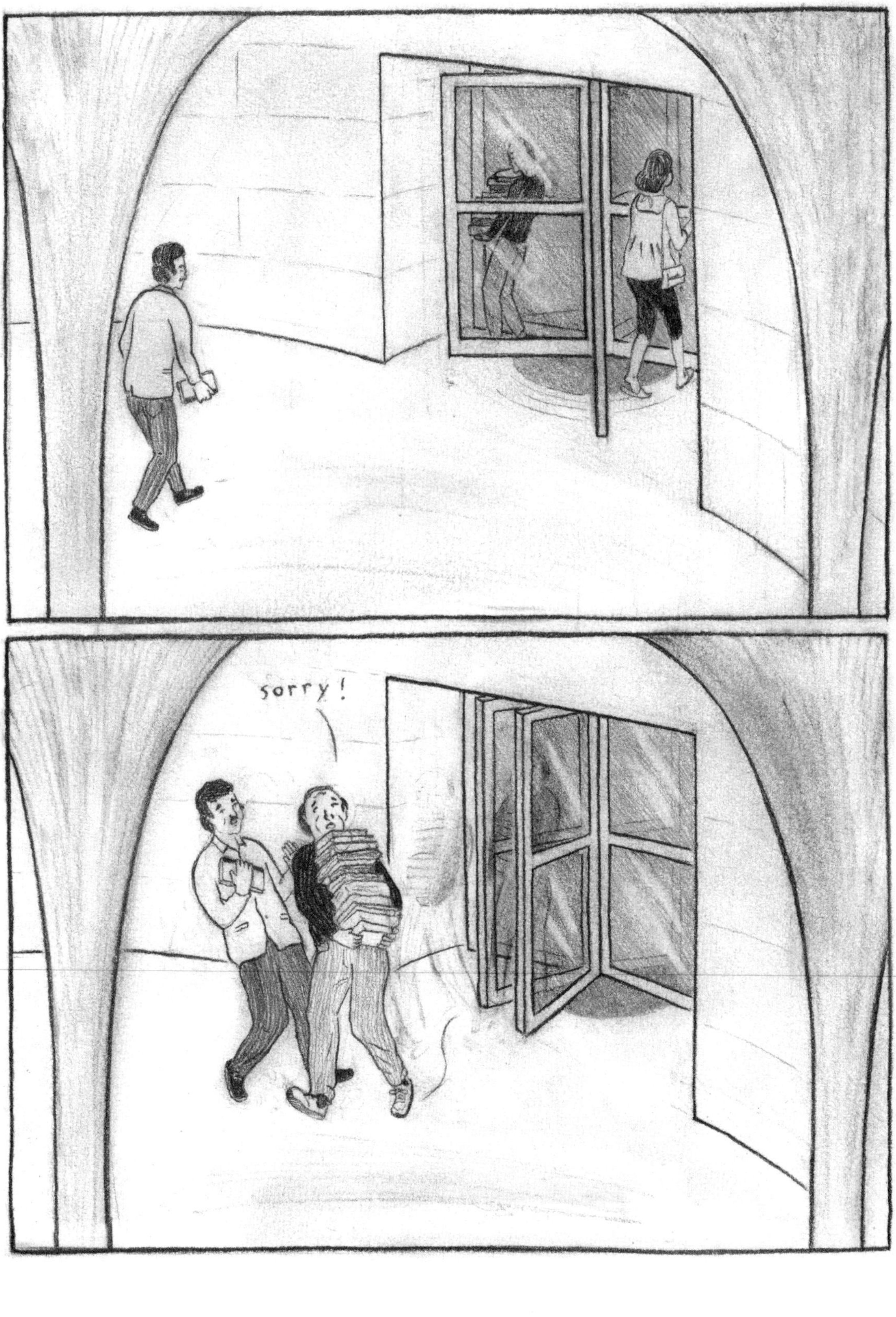
sorry!

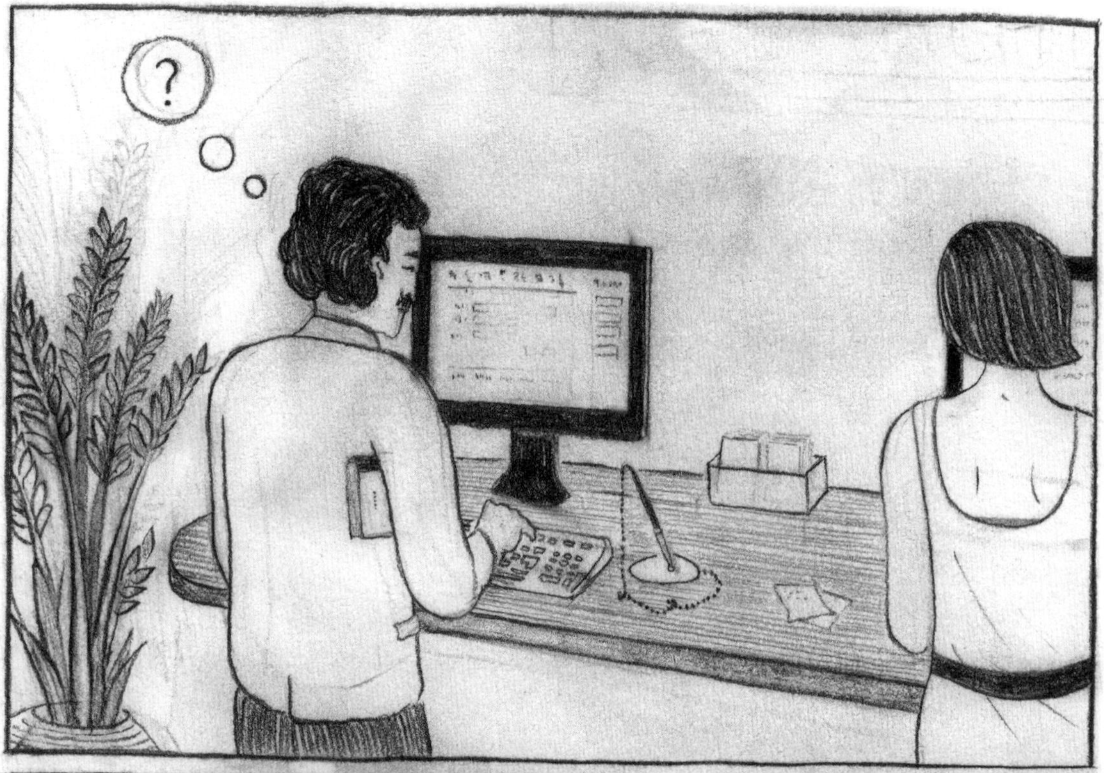
?

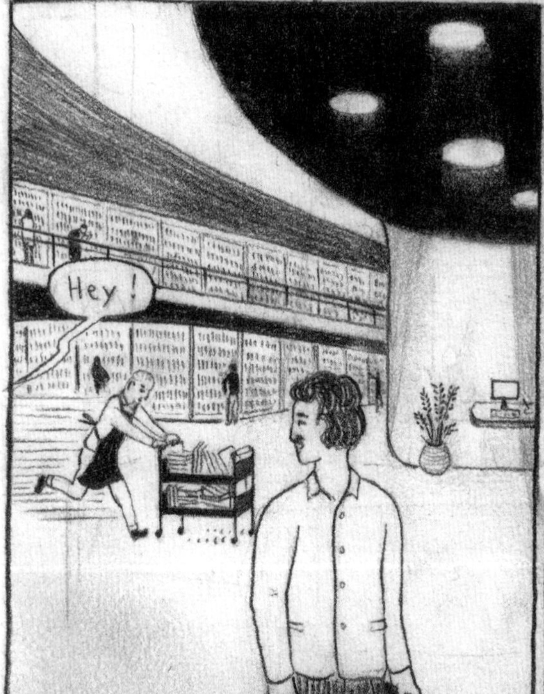
Hey!

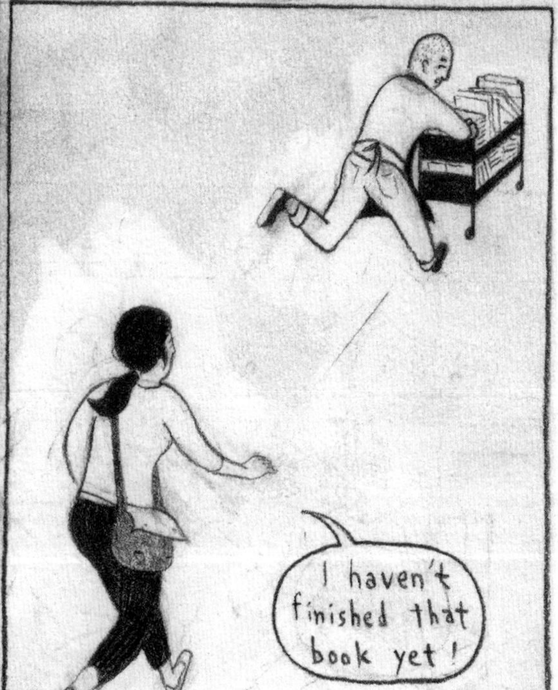
I haven't finished that book yet!

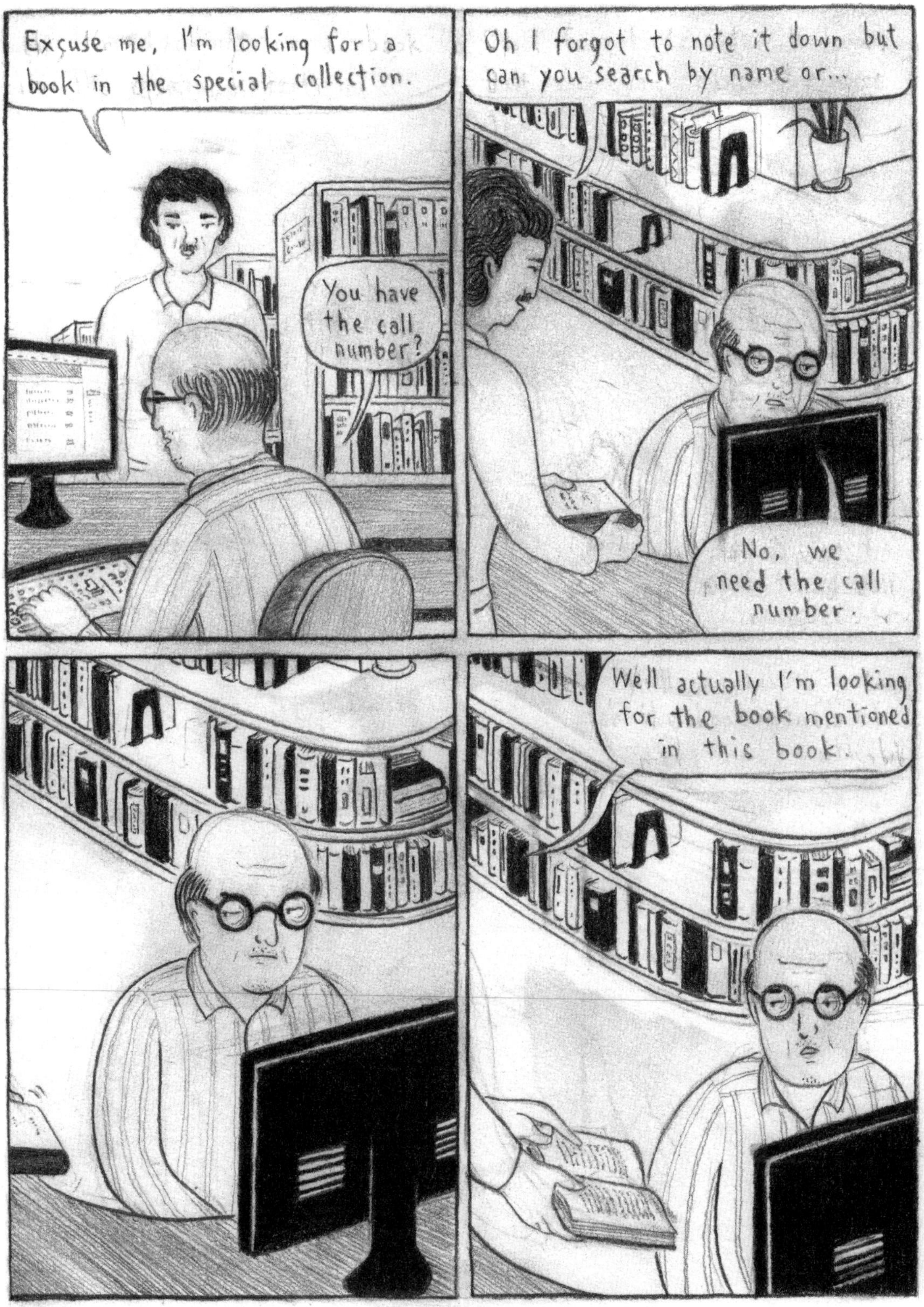
Excuse me, I'm looking for a book in the special collection.
You have the call number?
Oh I forgot to note it down but can you search by name or...
No, we need the call number.
Well actually I'm looking for the book mentioned in this book.

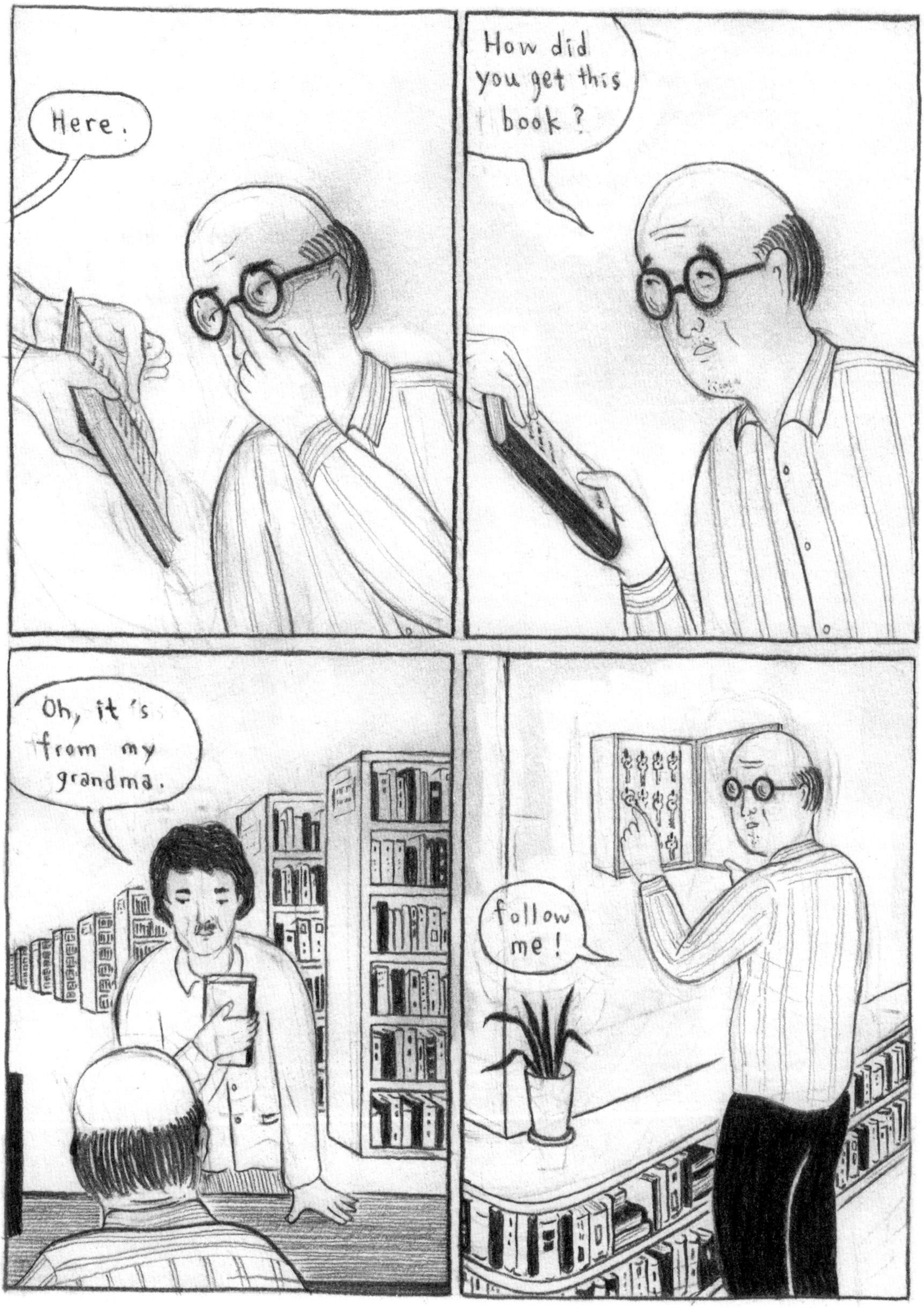
Here.
How did you get this book?
Oh, it's from my grandma.
follow me!

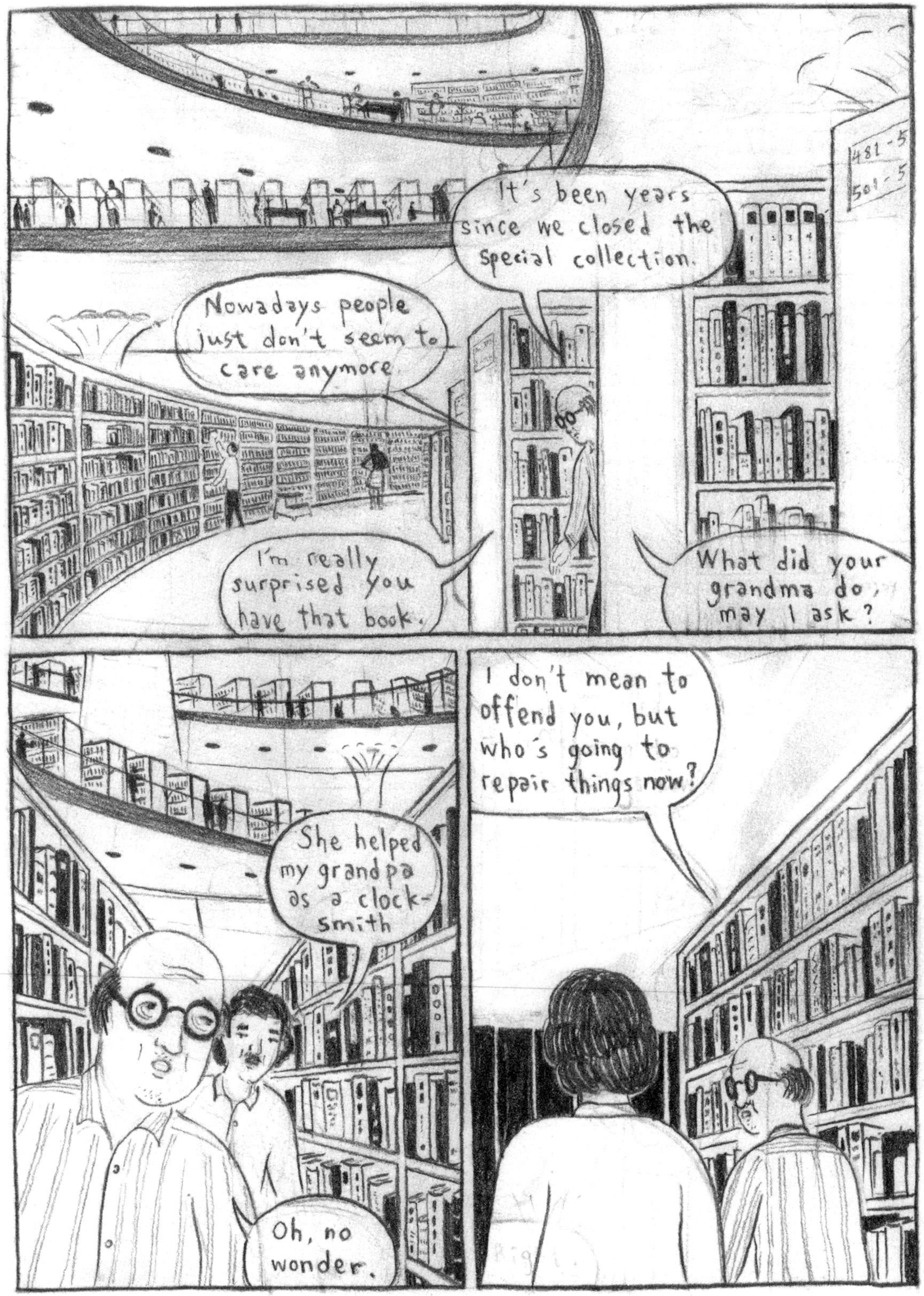
It's been years since we closed the special collection.
Nowadays people just don't seem to care anymore.
I'm really surprised you have that book.
What did your grandma do, may I ask?
She helped my grandpa as a clock-smith
Oh, no wonder.
I don't mean to offend you, but who's going to repair things now?

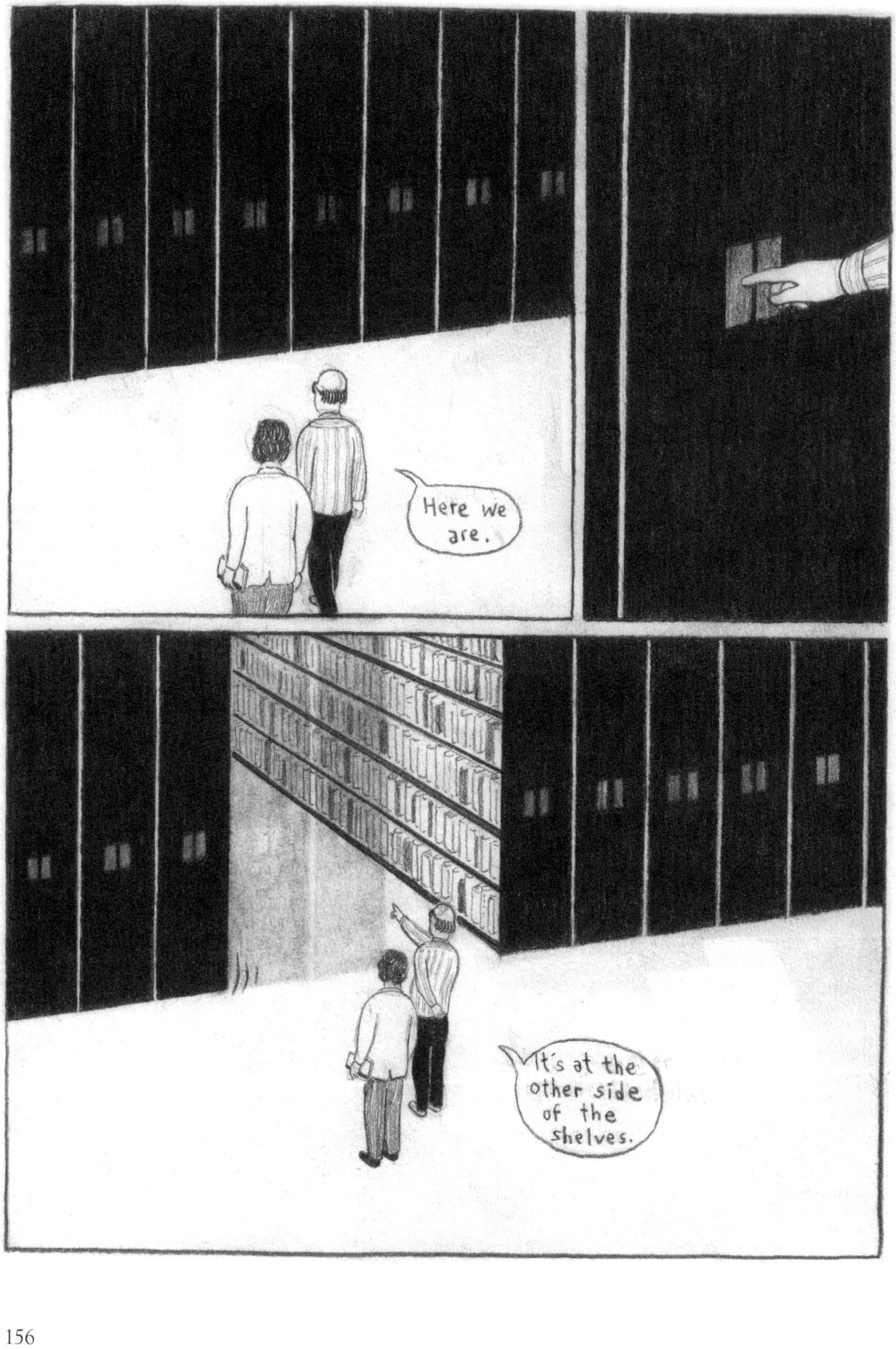
Here we are.
It's at the other side of the shelves.

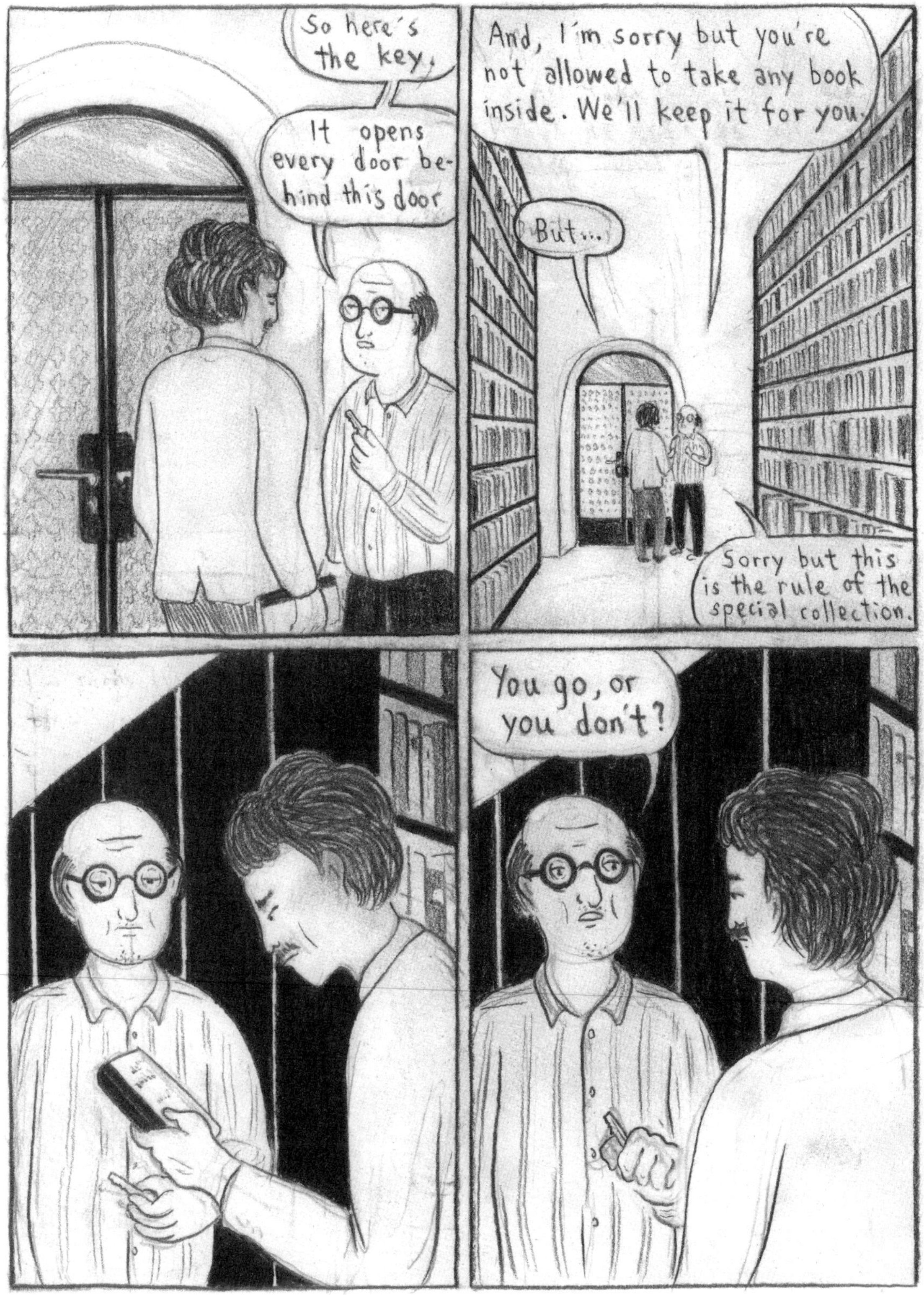
So here's the key.
It opens every door be-hind this door
And, I'm sorry but you're not allowed to take any book inside. We'll keep it for you.
But...
Sorry but this is the rule of the special collection.
You go, or you don't?

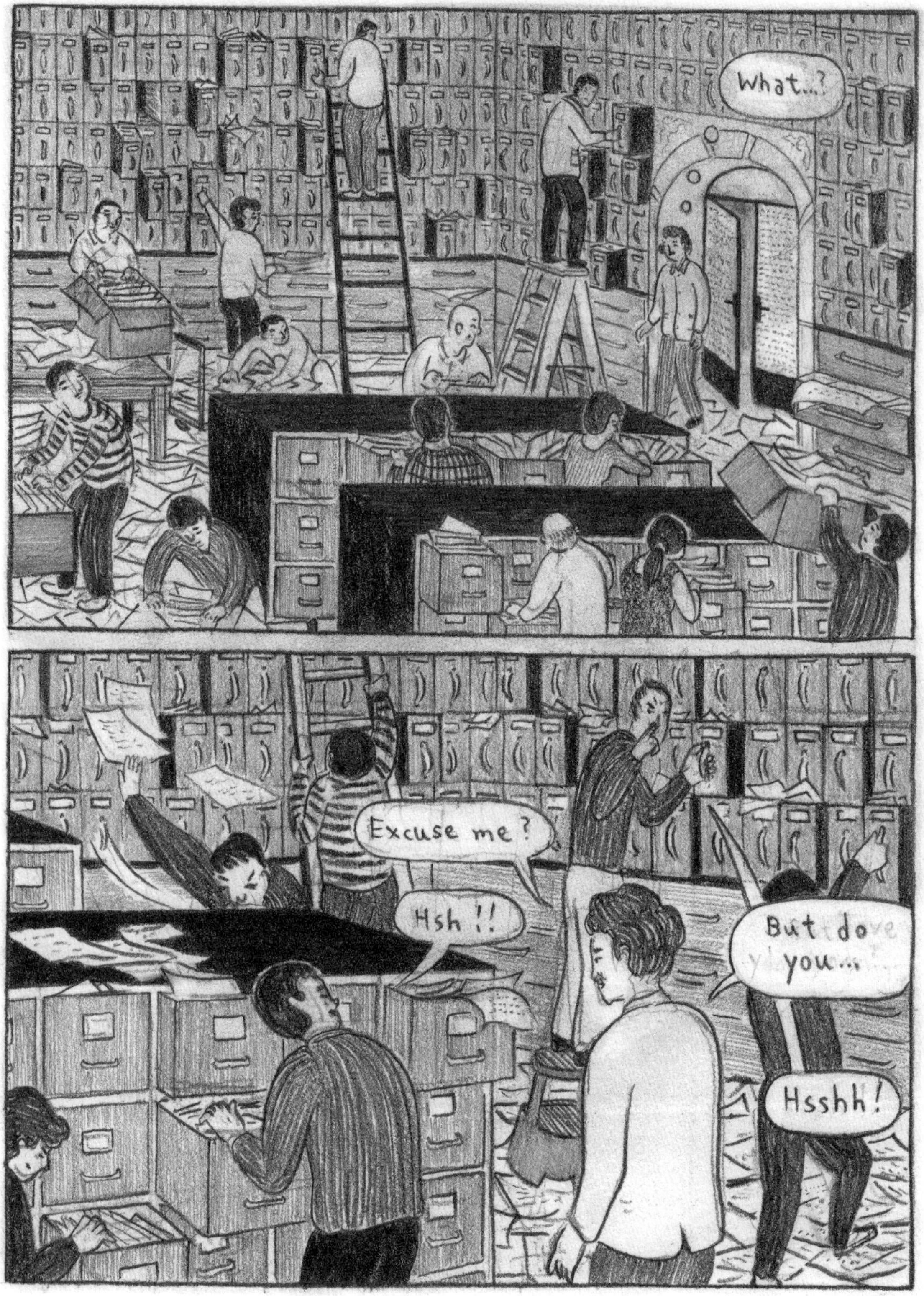
What...?
Excuse me?
Hsh!!
But do
you...
Hsshh!

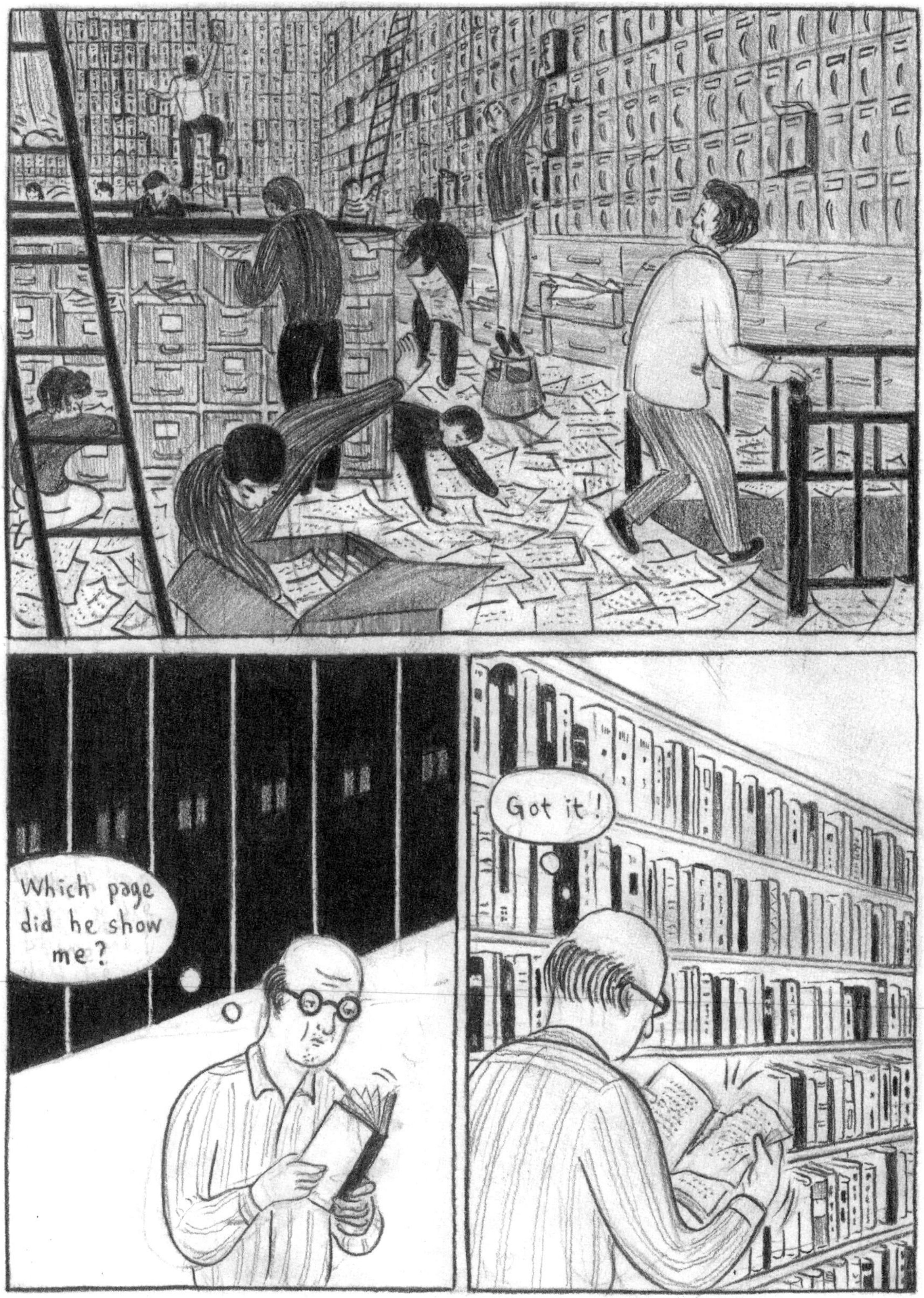
Which page did he show me?
Got it!

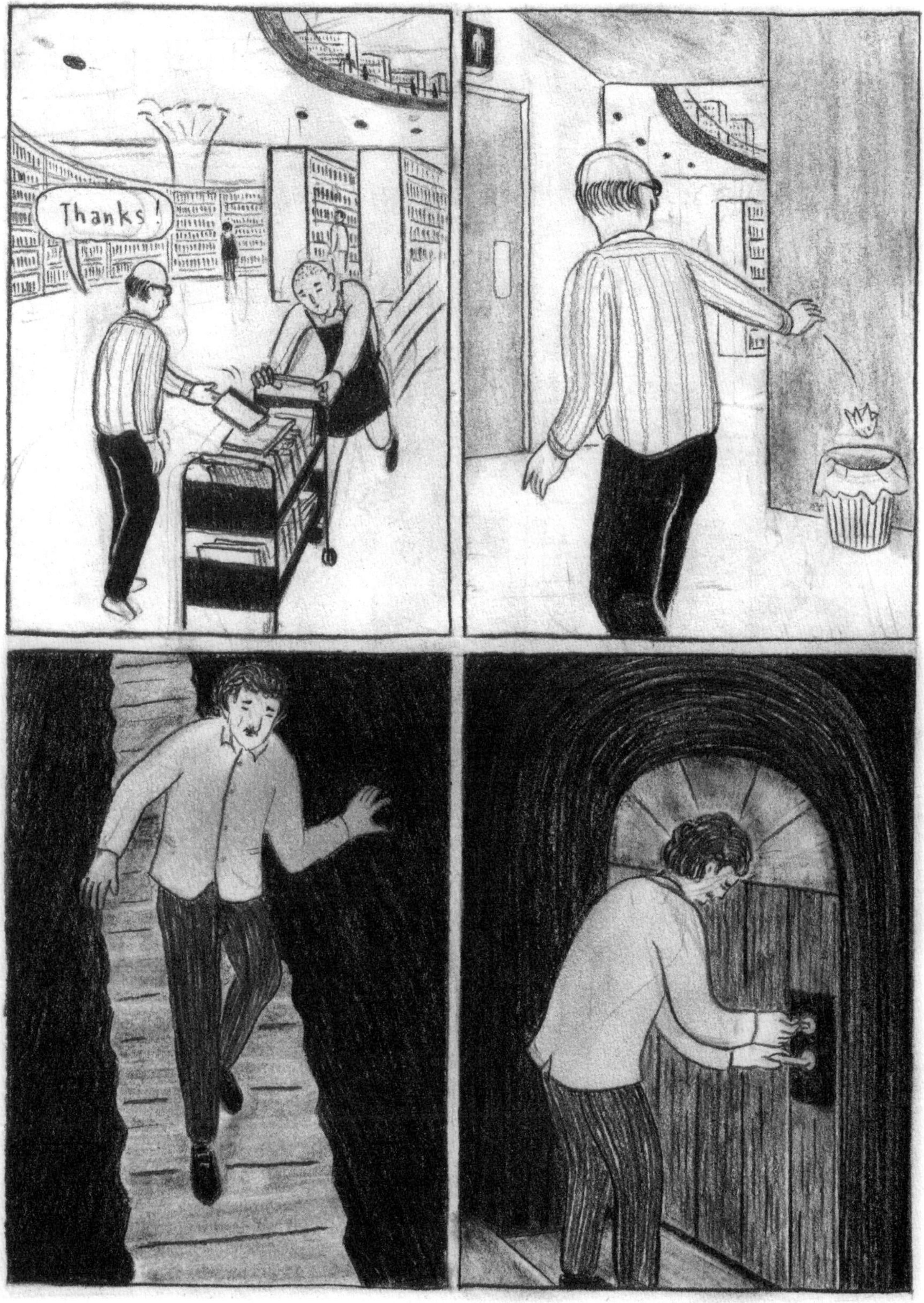
Thanks!

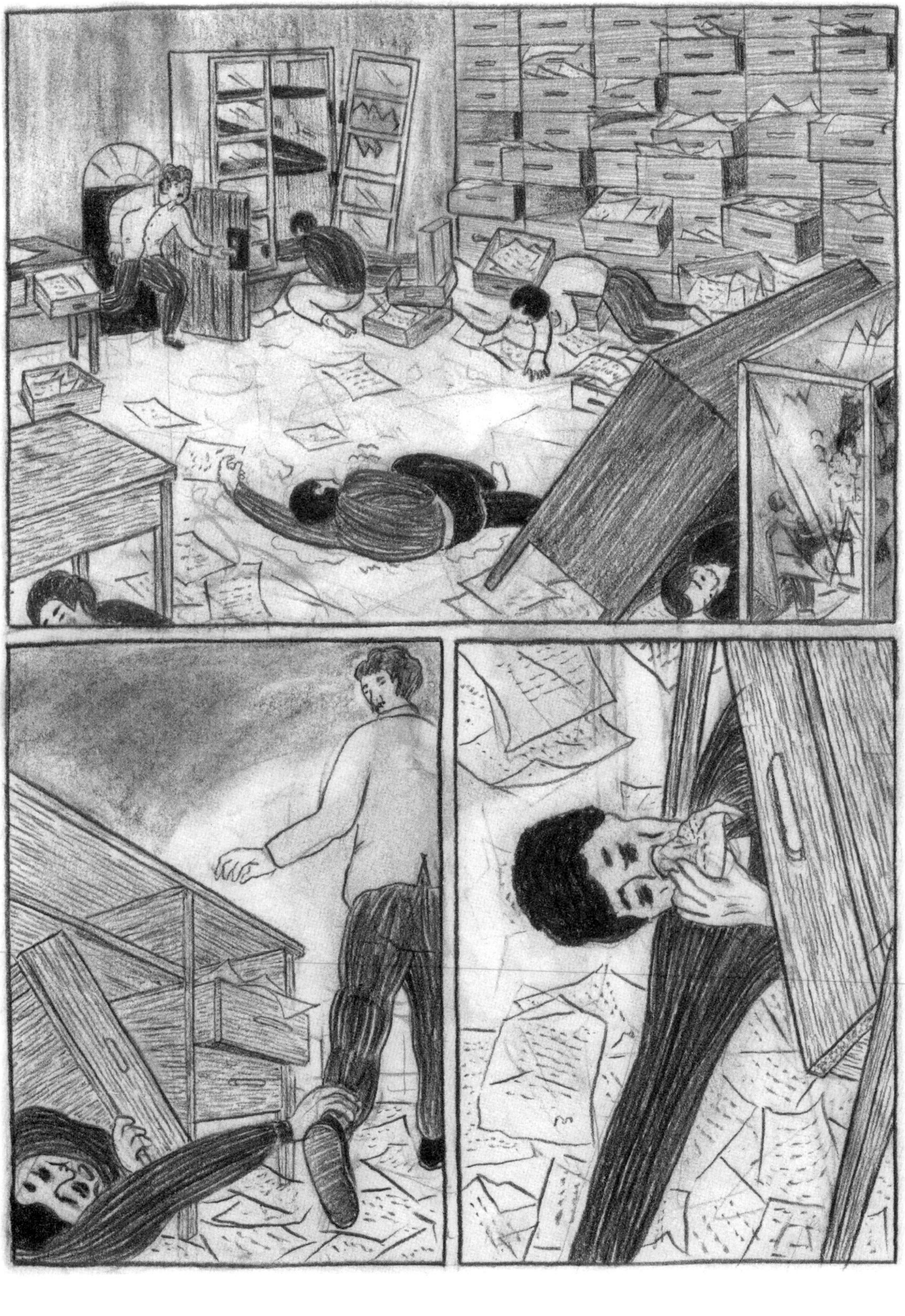

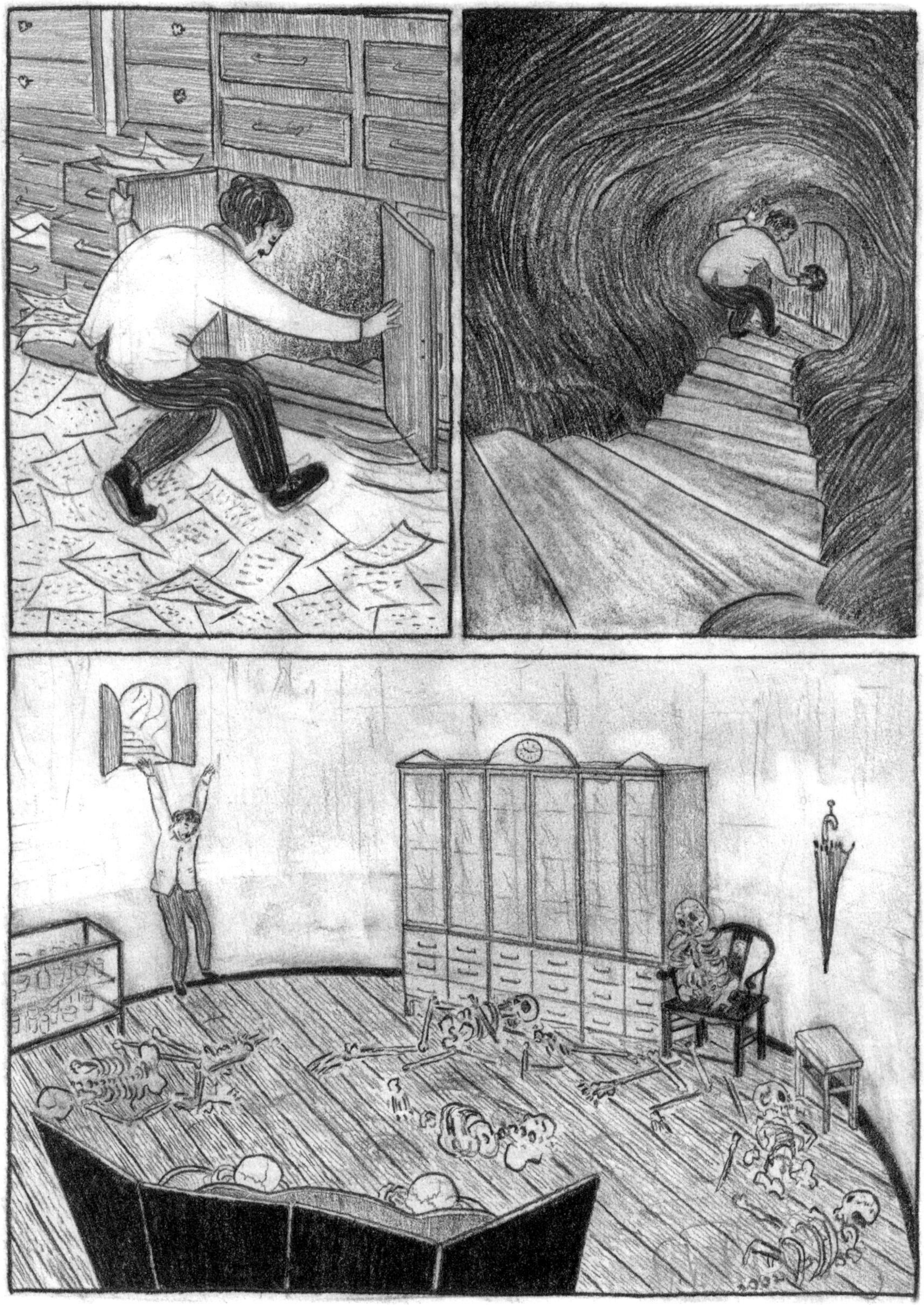

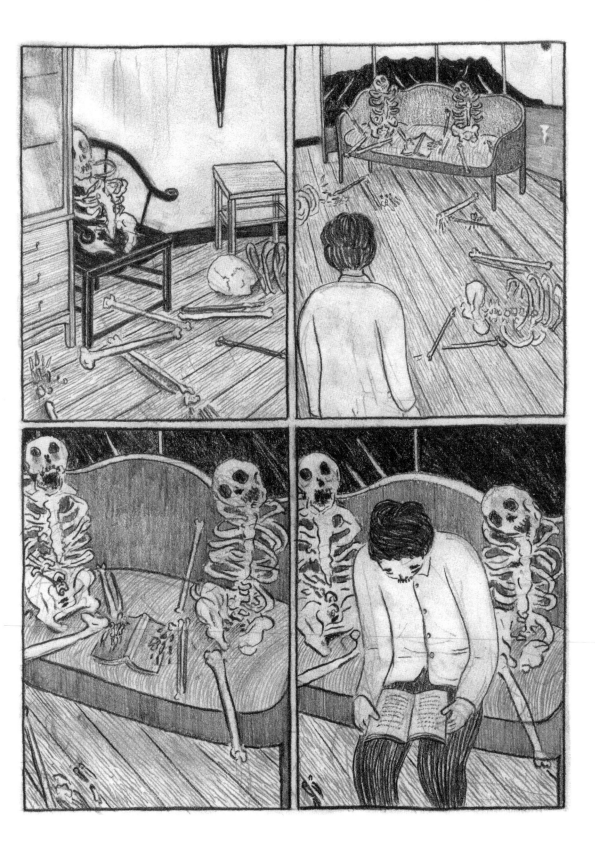

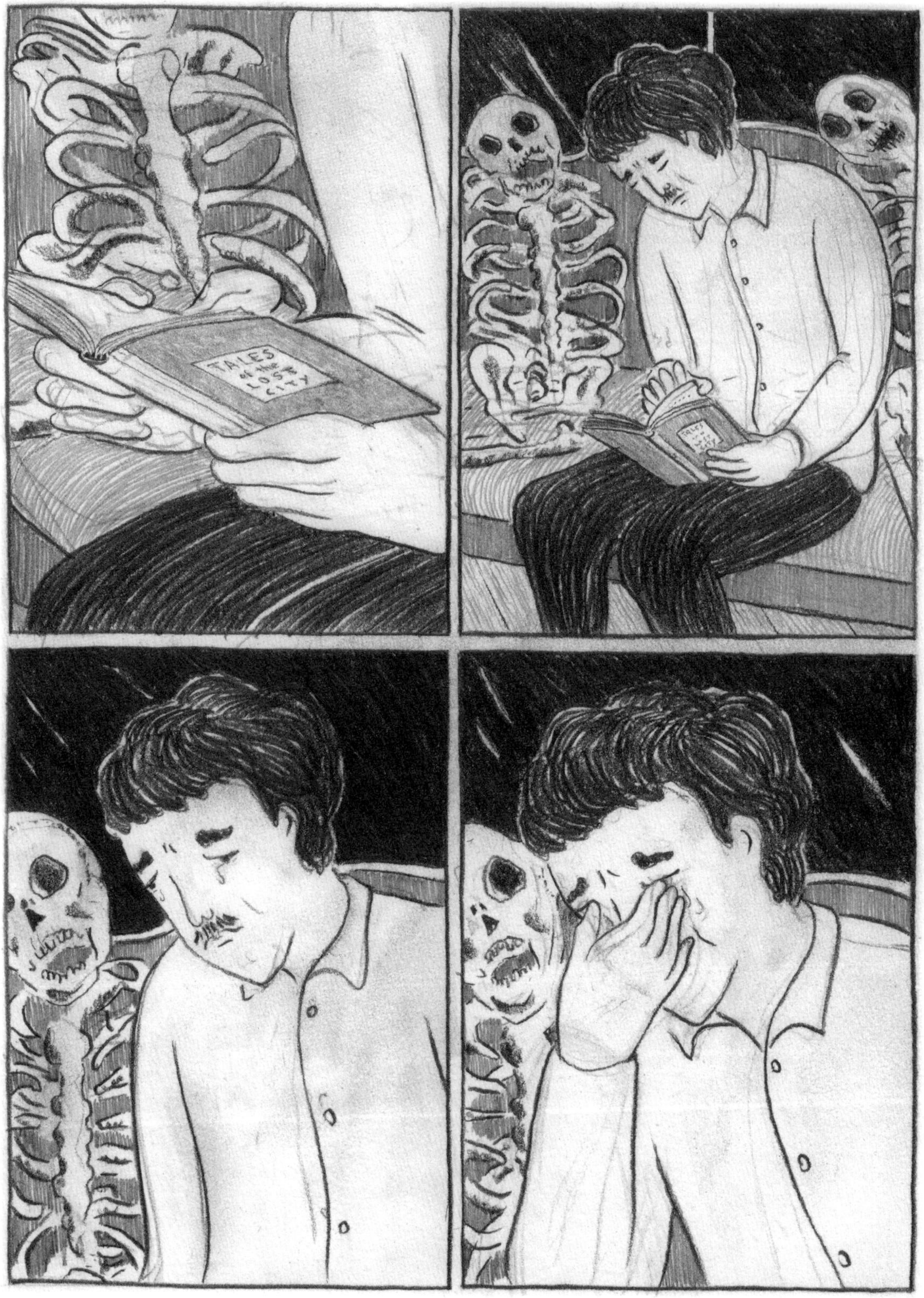
TALES of the LOST CITY

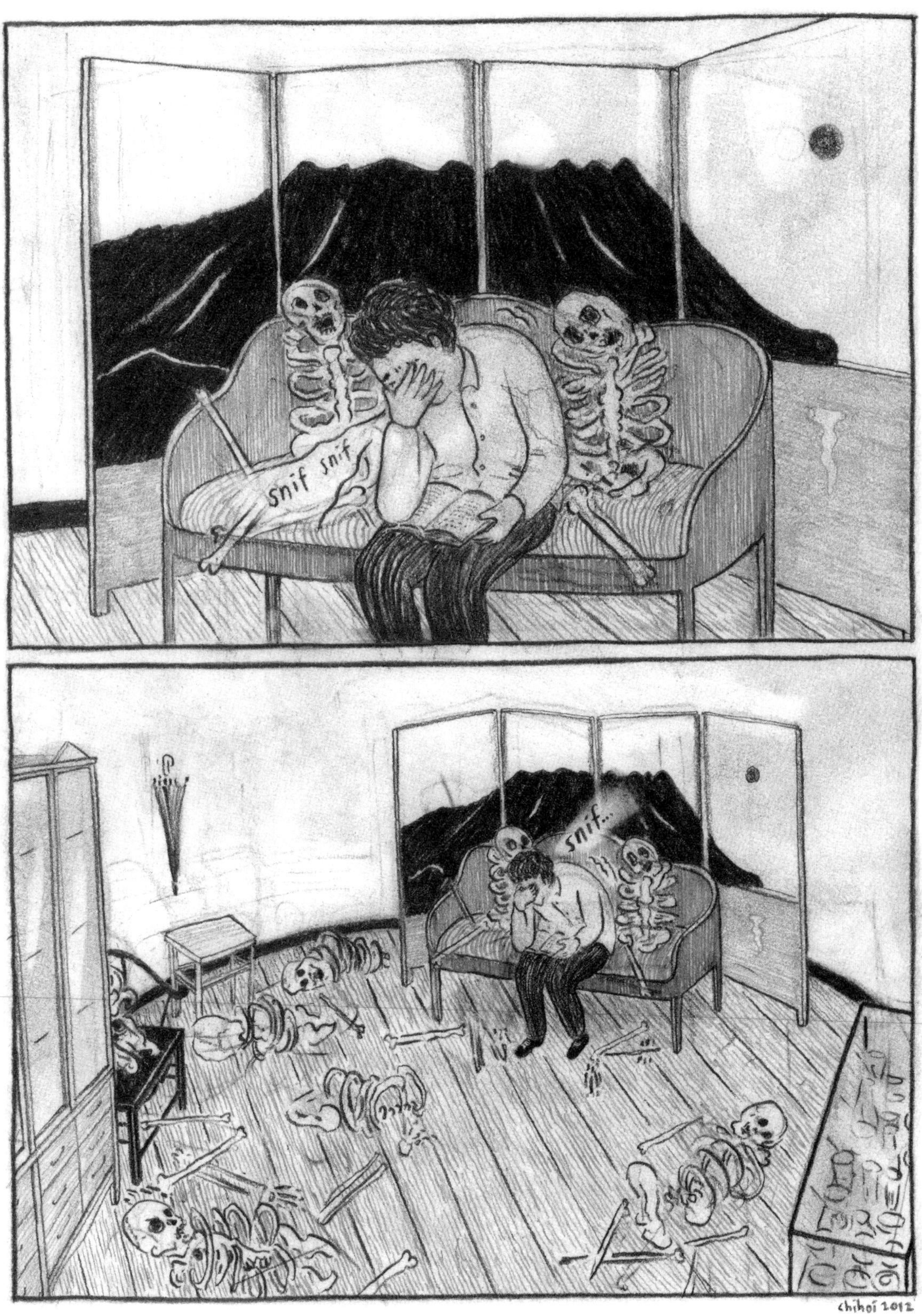
snif snif
snif...
chihoi 2012

# Borrowed Books

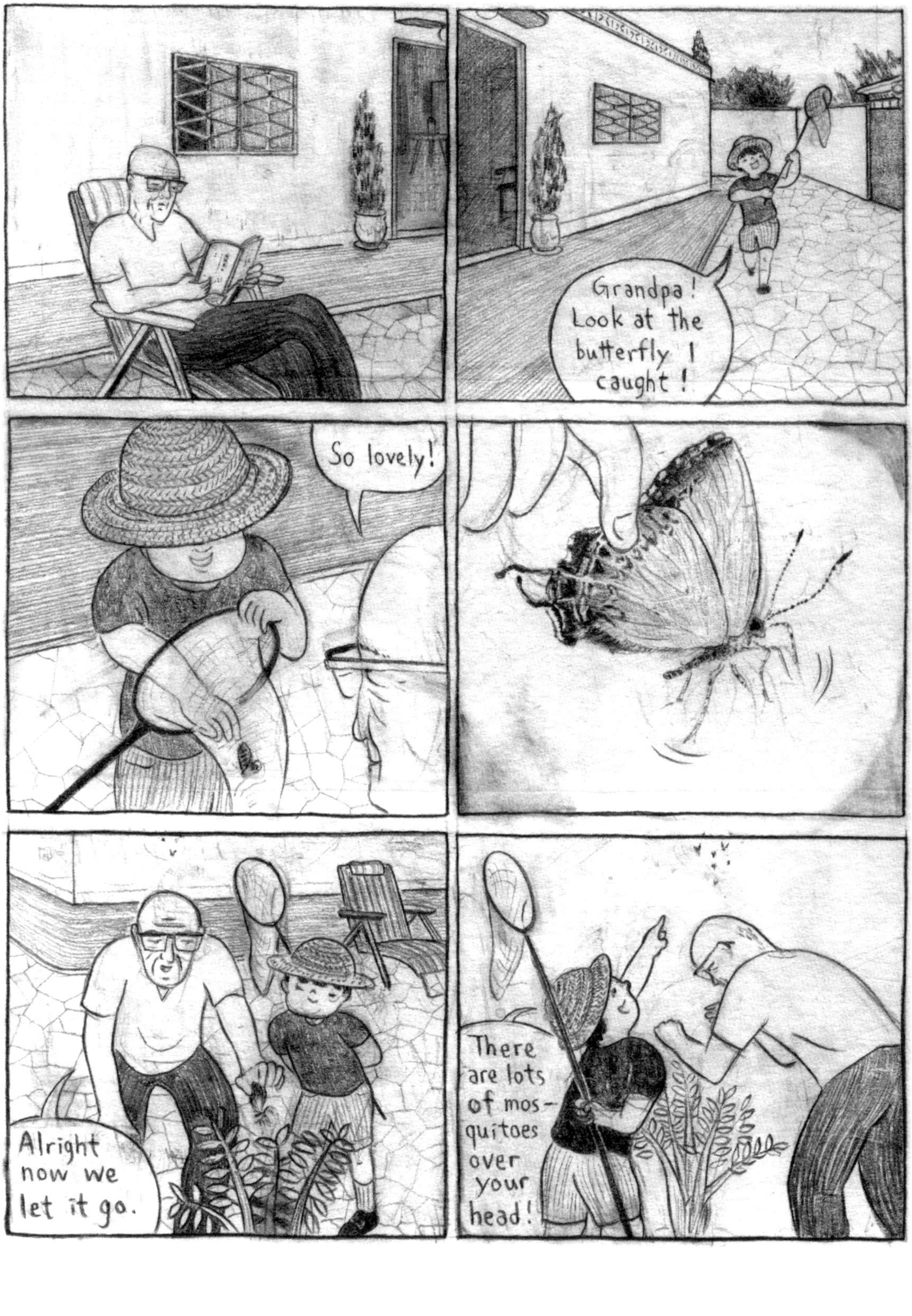
Grandpa! Look at the butterfly I caught!
So lovely!
Alright now we let it go.
There are lots of mos-quitoes over your head!

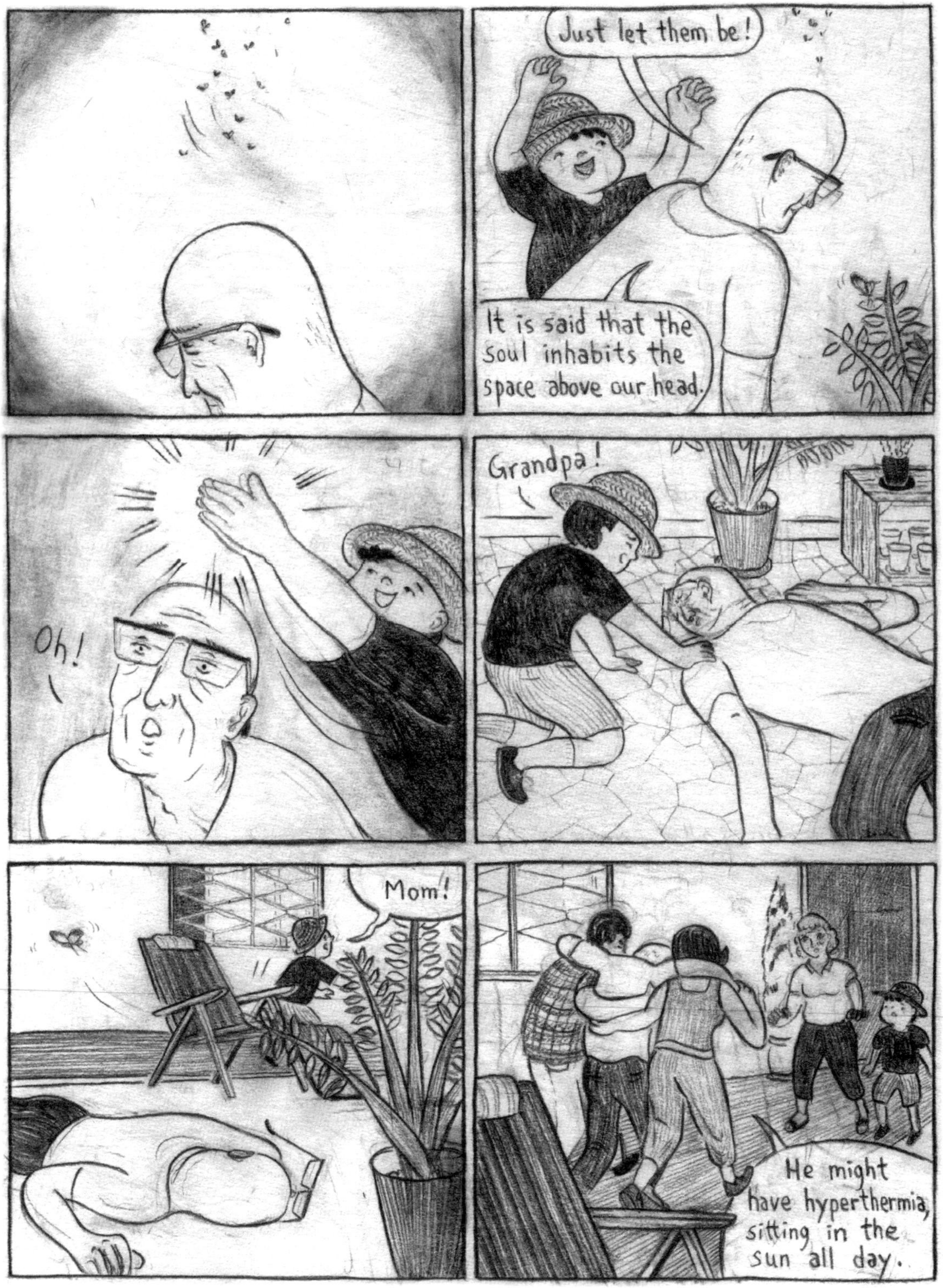
Just let them be!
It is said that the soul inhabits the space above our head.
Oh!
Grandpa!
Mom!
He might have hyperthermia, sitting in the sun all day.

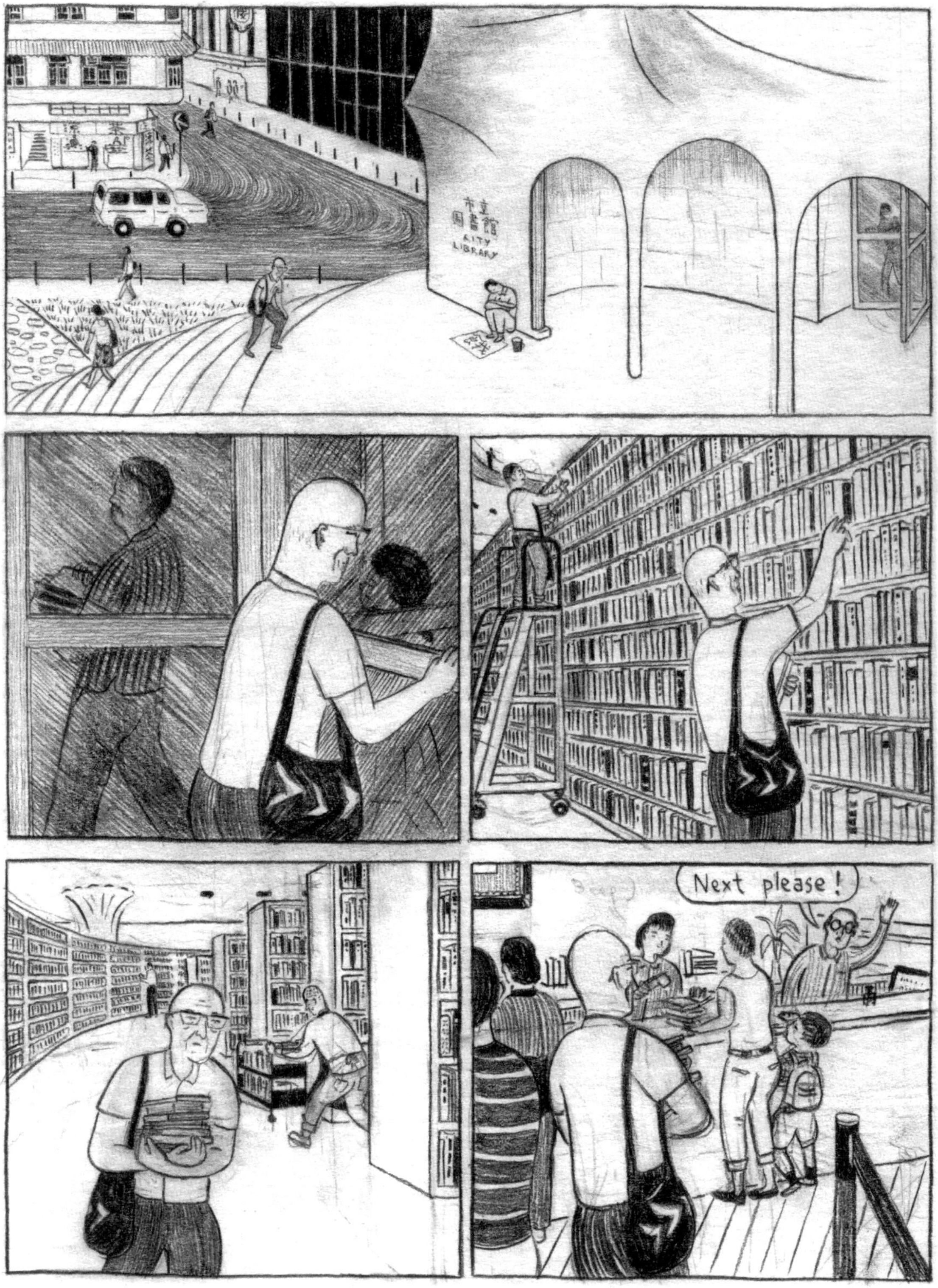
市立
圖書館
CITY
LIBRARY
Next please!

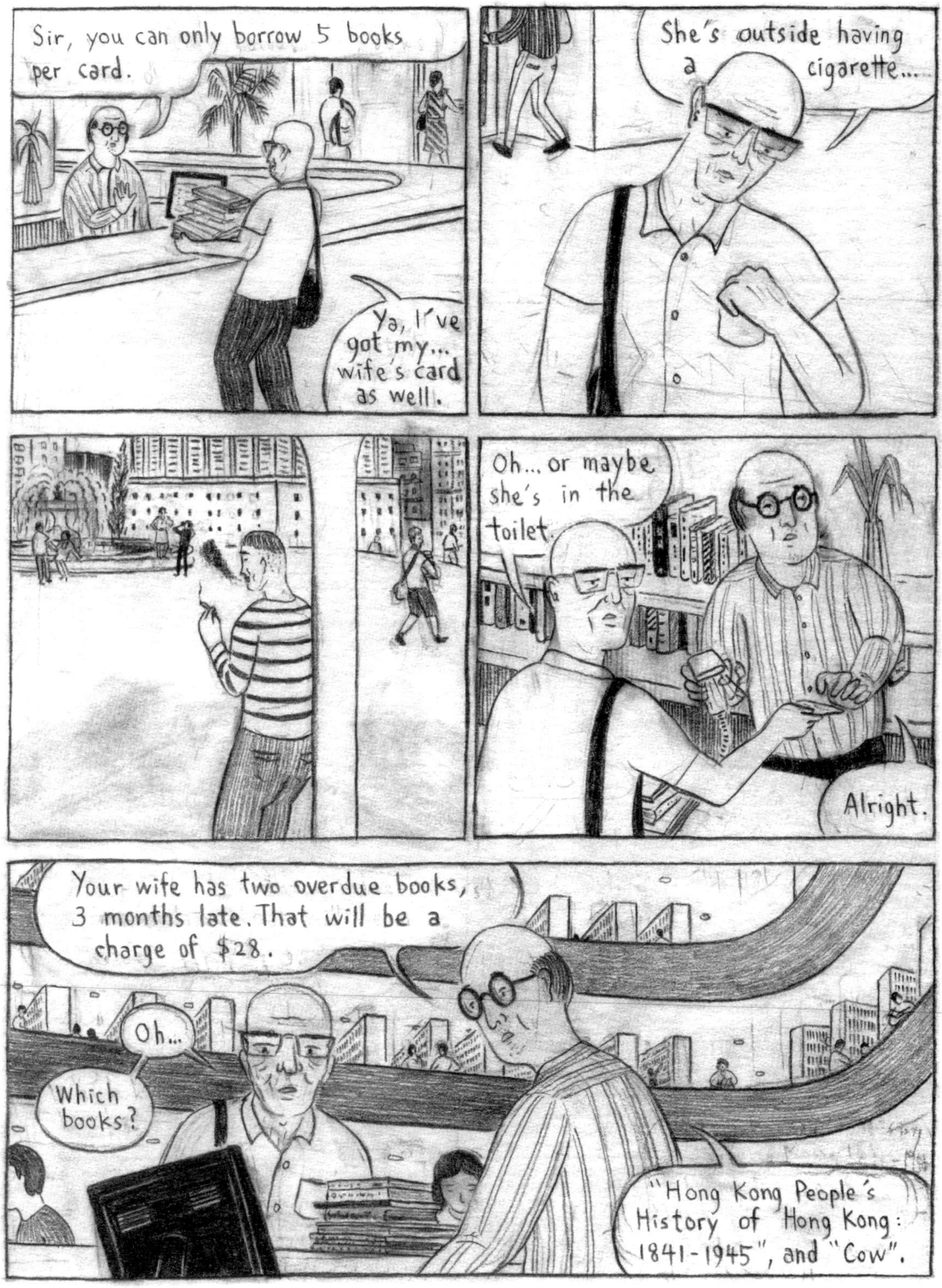
Sir, you can only borrow 5 books per card.
Ya, I've got my... wife's card as well.
She's outside having a cigarette...
Oh... or maybe she's in the toilet.
Alright.
Your wife has two overdue books, 3 months late. That will be a charge of $28.
Oh...
Which books?
"Hong Kong People's History of Hong Kong: 1841-1945", and "Cow".

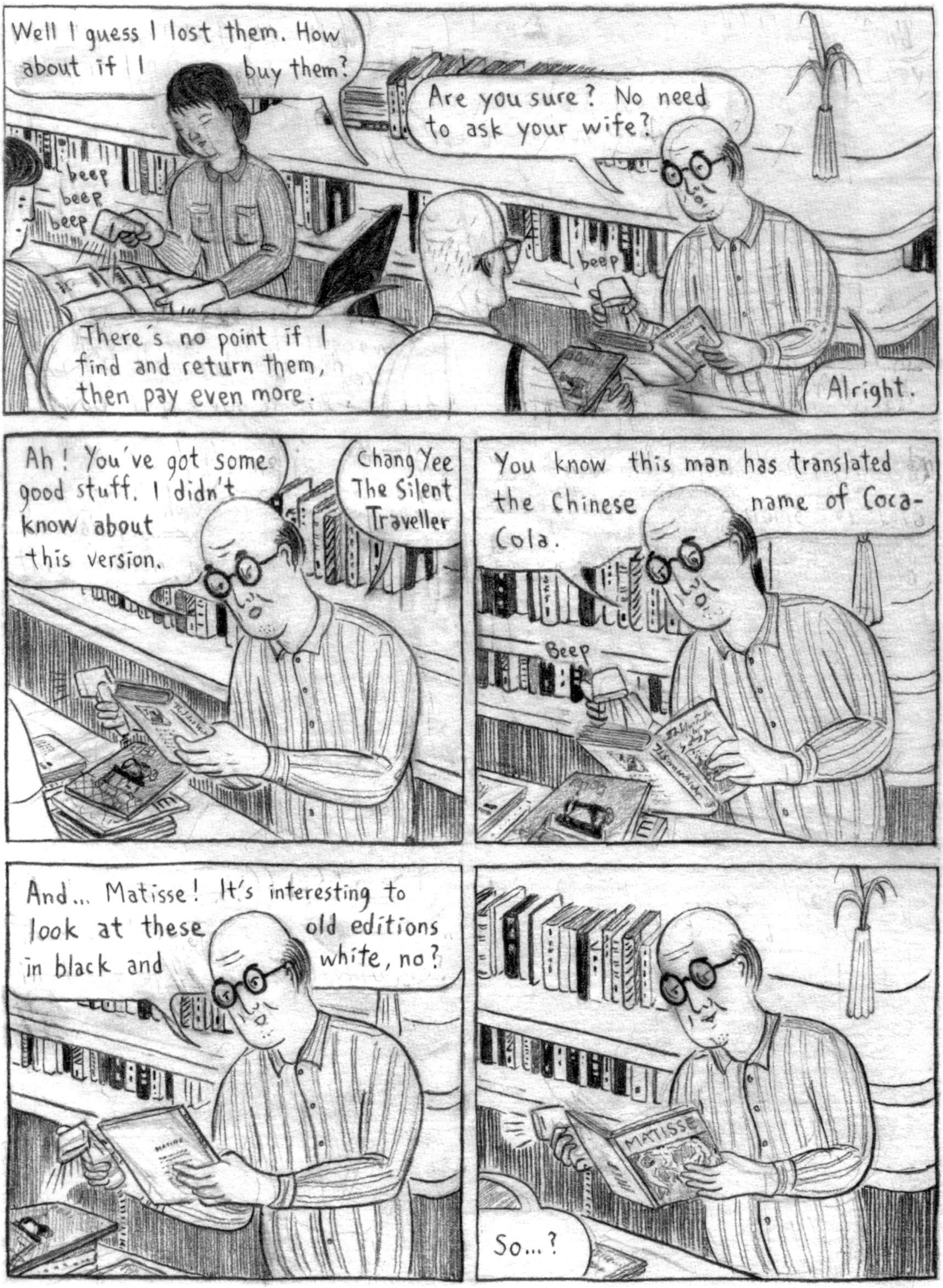
Well I guess I lost them. How about if I buy them?
Are you sure? No need to ask your wife?
beep beep beep
beep
There's no point if I find and return them, then pay even more.
Alright.
Ah! You've got some good stuff. I didn't know about this version.
Chang Yee The Silent Traveller
You know this man has translated the Chinese name of Coca-Cola.
Beep
And... Matisse! It's interesting to look at these old editions in black and white, no?
MATISSE
So...?

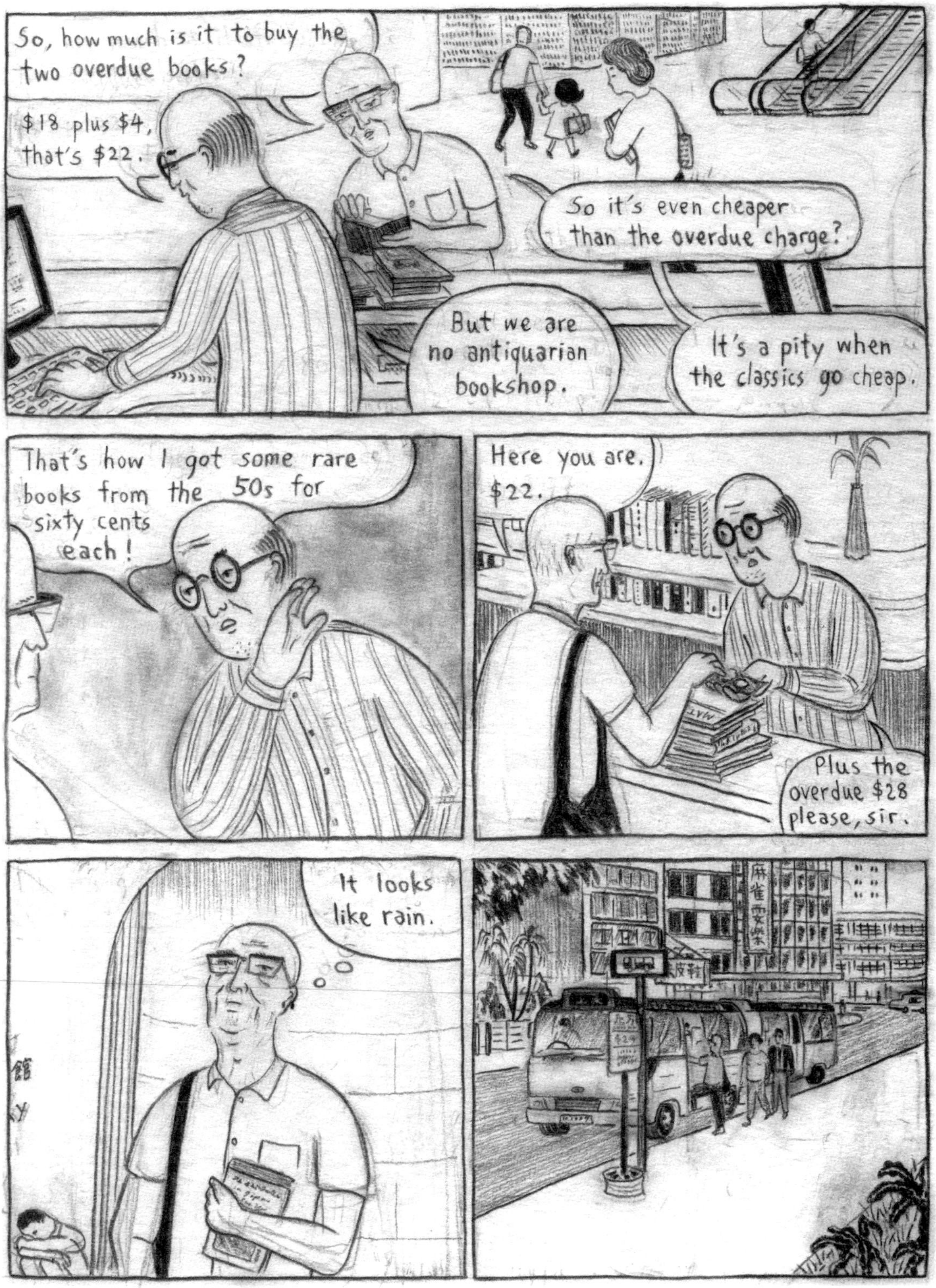
So, how much is it to buy the two overdue books?
$18 plus $4, that's $22.
So it's even cheaper than the overdue charge?
But we are no antiquarian bookshop.
It's a pity when the classics go cheap.
That's how I got some rare books from the 50s for sixty cents each!
Here you are. $22.
Plus the overdue $28 please, sir.
It looks like rain.

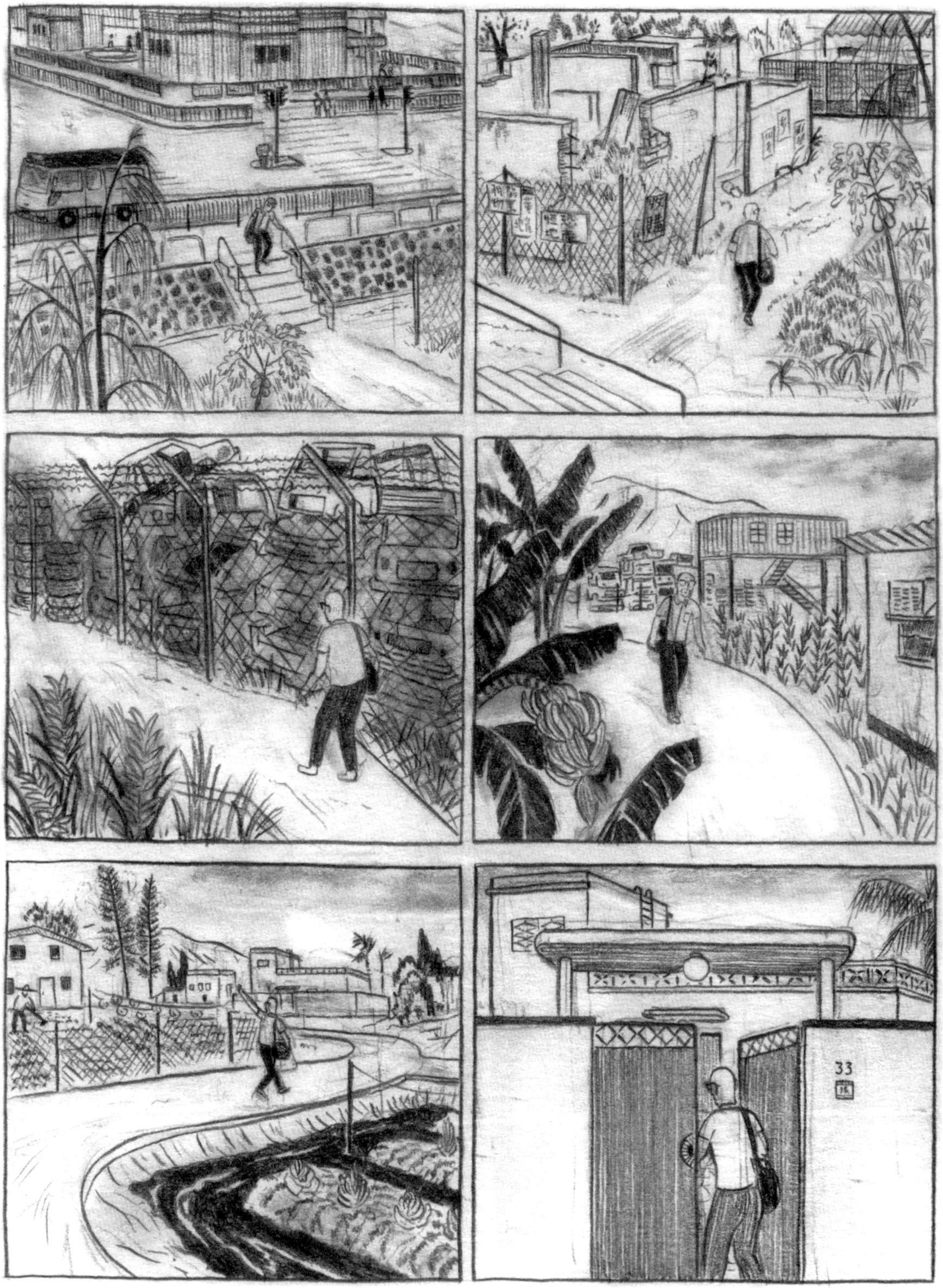
33

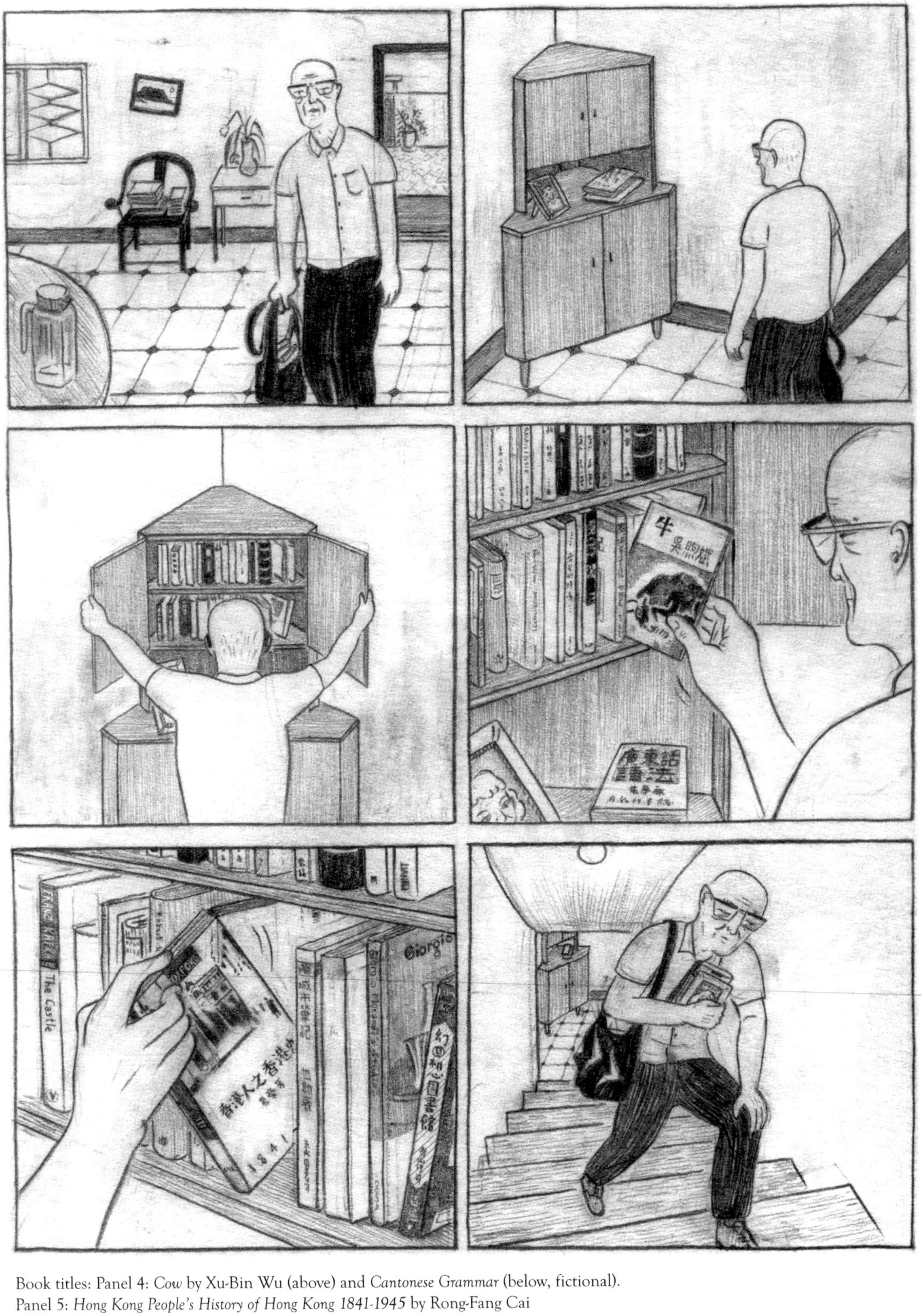
牛
廣東話語法
The Castle
香港人之香港史

Book titles: Panel 4: *Cow* by Xu-Bin Wu (above) and *Cantonese Grammar* (below, fictional).
Panel 5: *Hong Kong People's History of Hong Kong 1841-1945* by Rong-Fang Cai

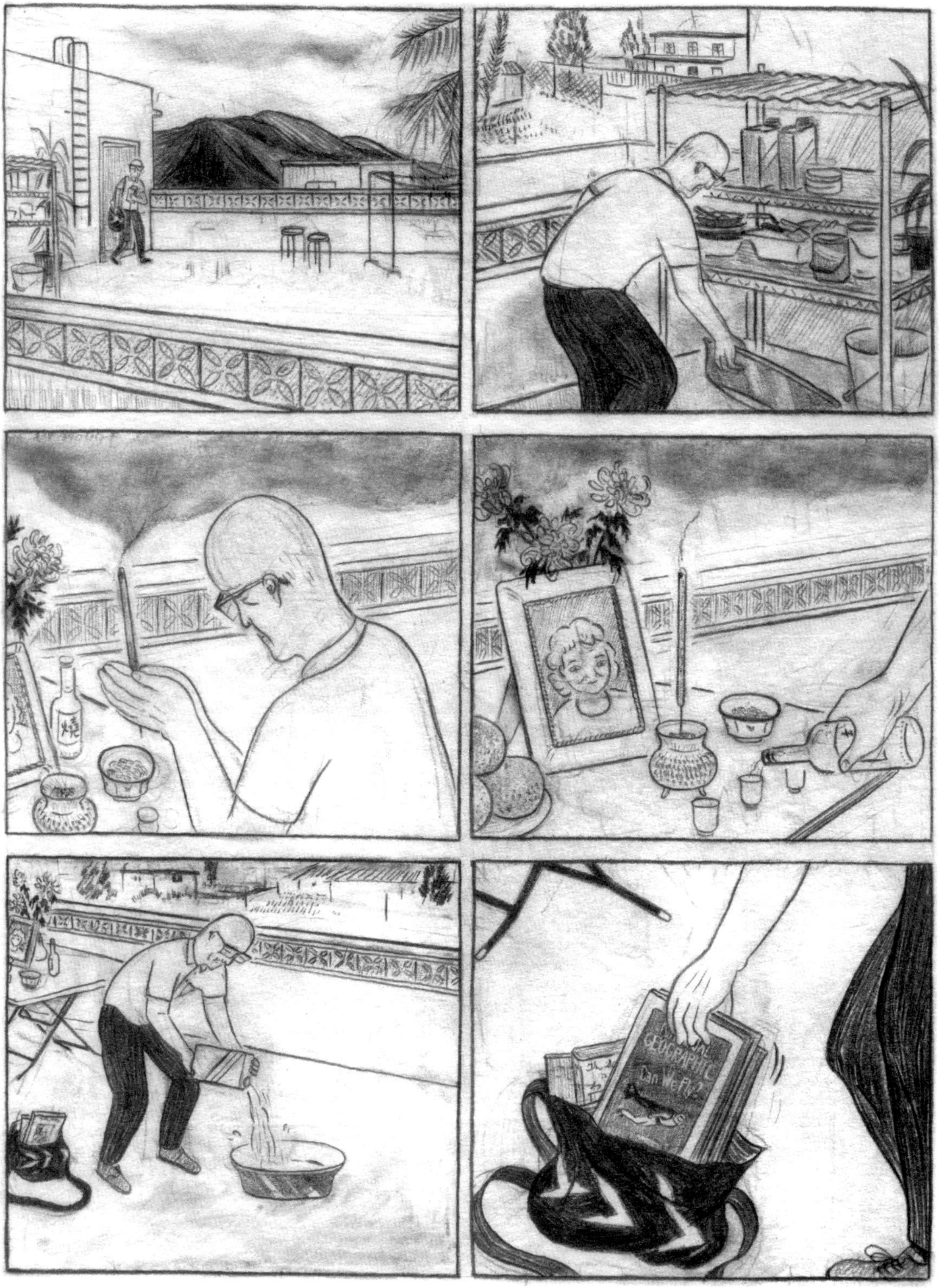
燒
GEOGRAPHIC
Can We Fly?

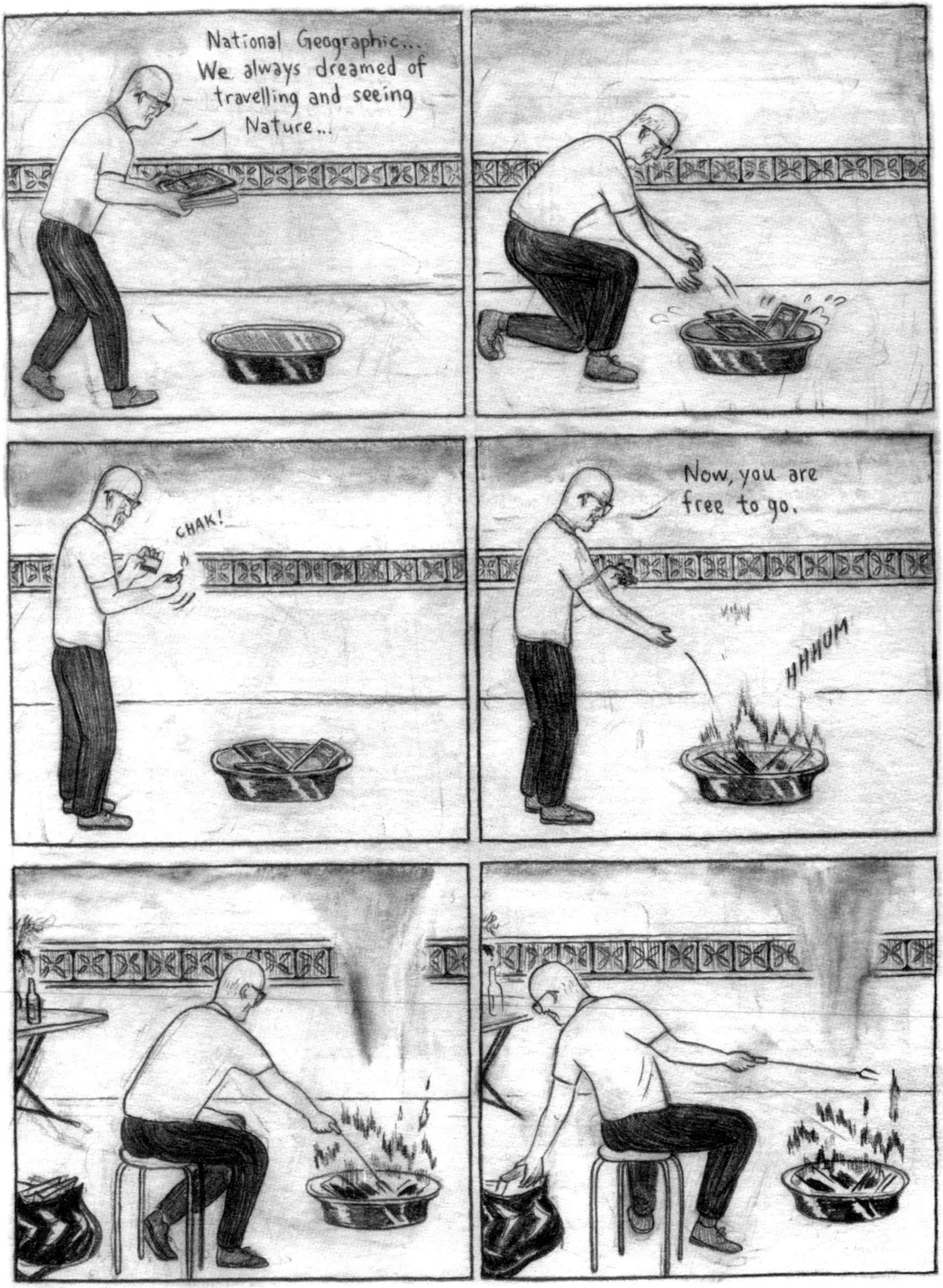
National Geographic... We always dreamed of travelling and seeing Nature...
CHAK!
Now, you are free to go.
HHHUM

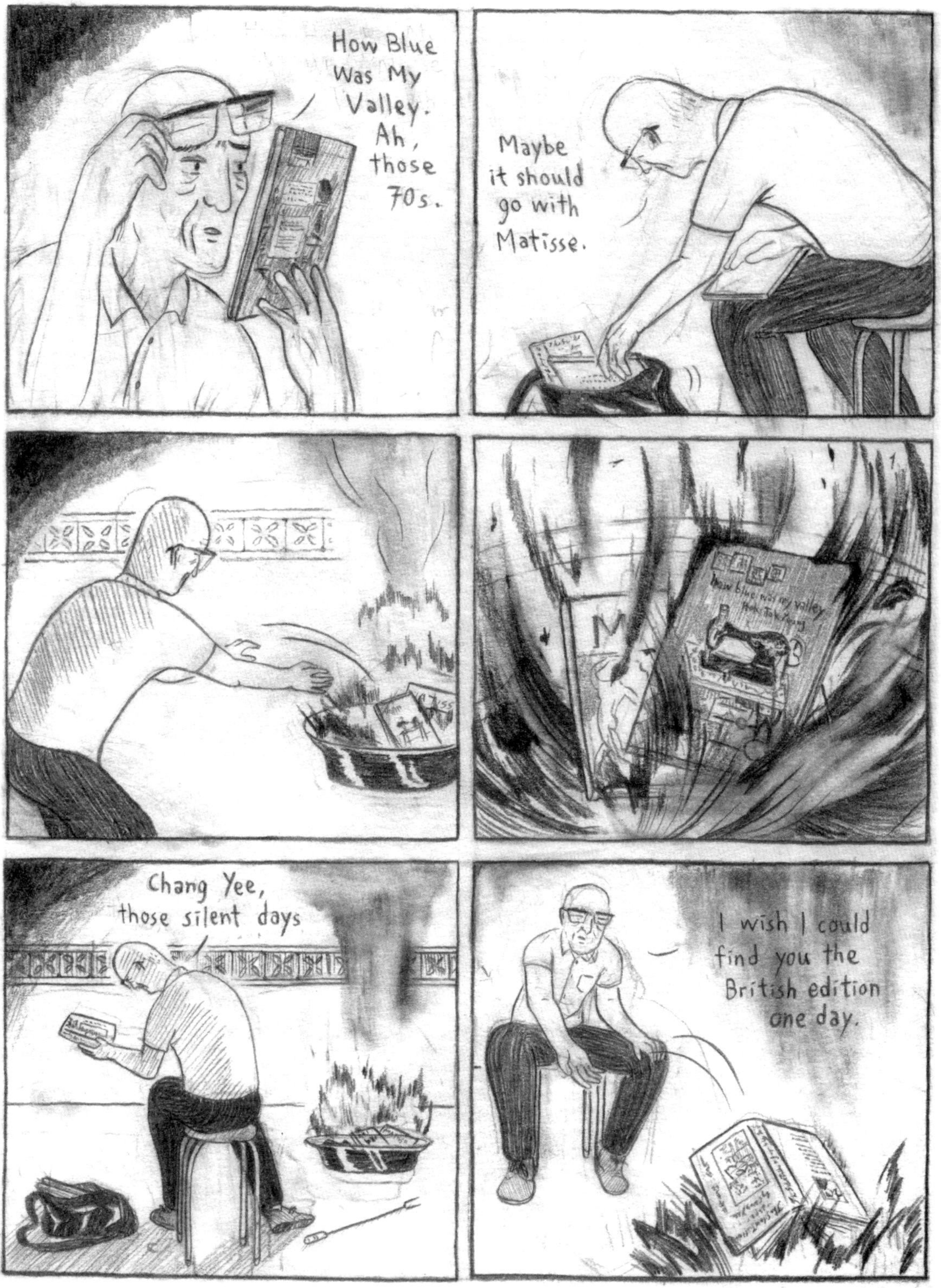
How Blue Was My Valley. Ah, those 70s.
Maybe it should go with Matisse.
Chang Yee, those silent days
I wish I could find you the British edition one day.

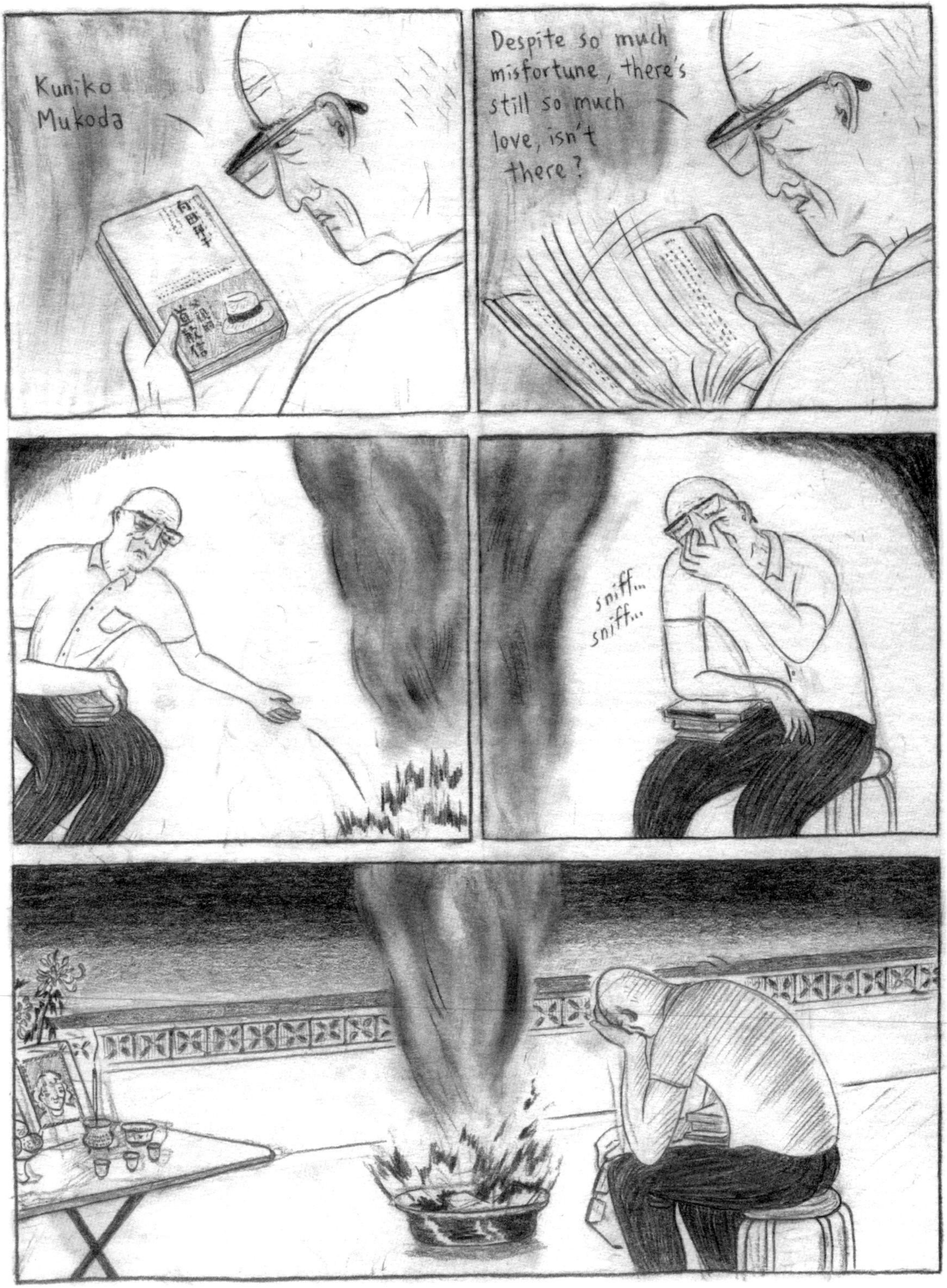
Kuniko Mukoda
Despite so much misfortune, there's still so much love, isn't there?
sniff... sniff...

Book title: Panel 1: *Father's Letter of Apology* by Kuniko Mukoda

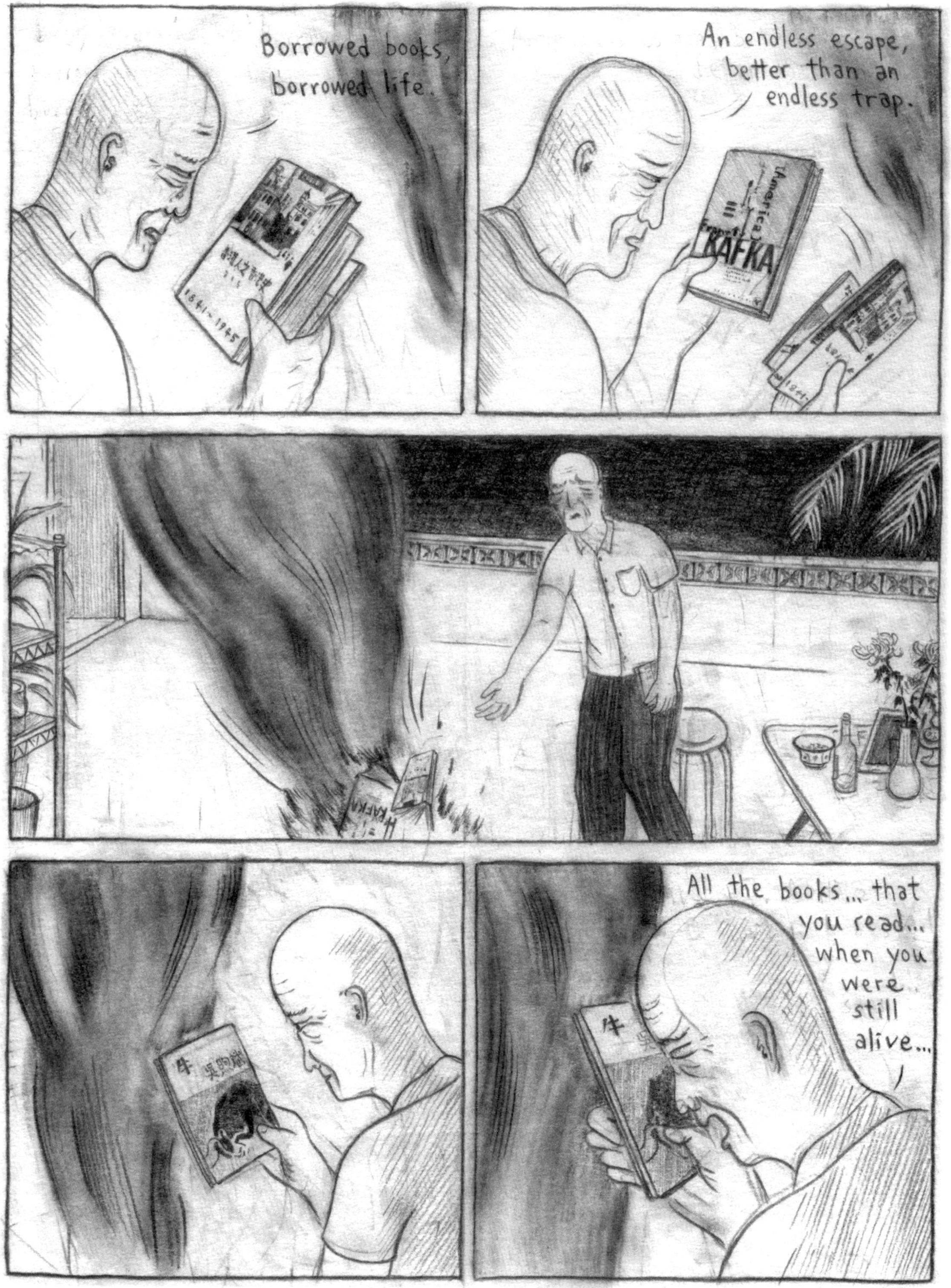
Borrowed books, borrowed life.
An endless escape, better than an endless trap.
All the books... that you read... when you were still alive...

Book titles: Panel 1: *Hong Kong People's History of Hong Kong 1841-1945* by Rong-Fang Cai
Panel 4: *Cow* by Xu-Bin Wu

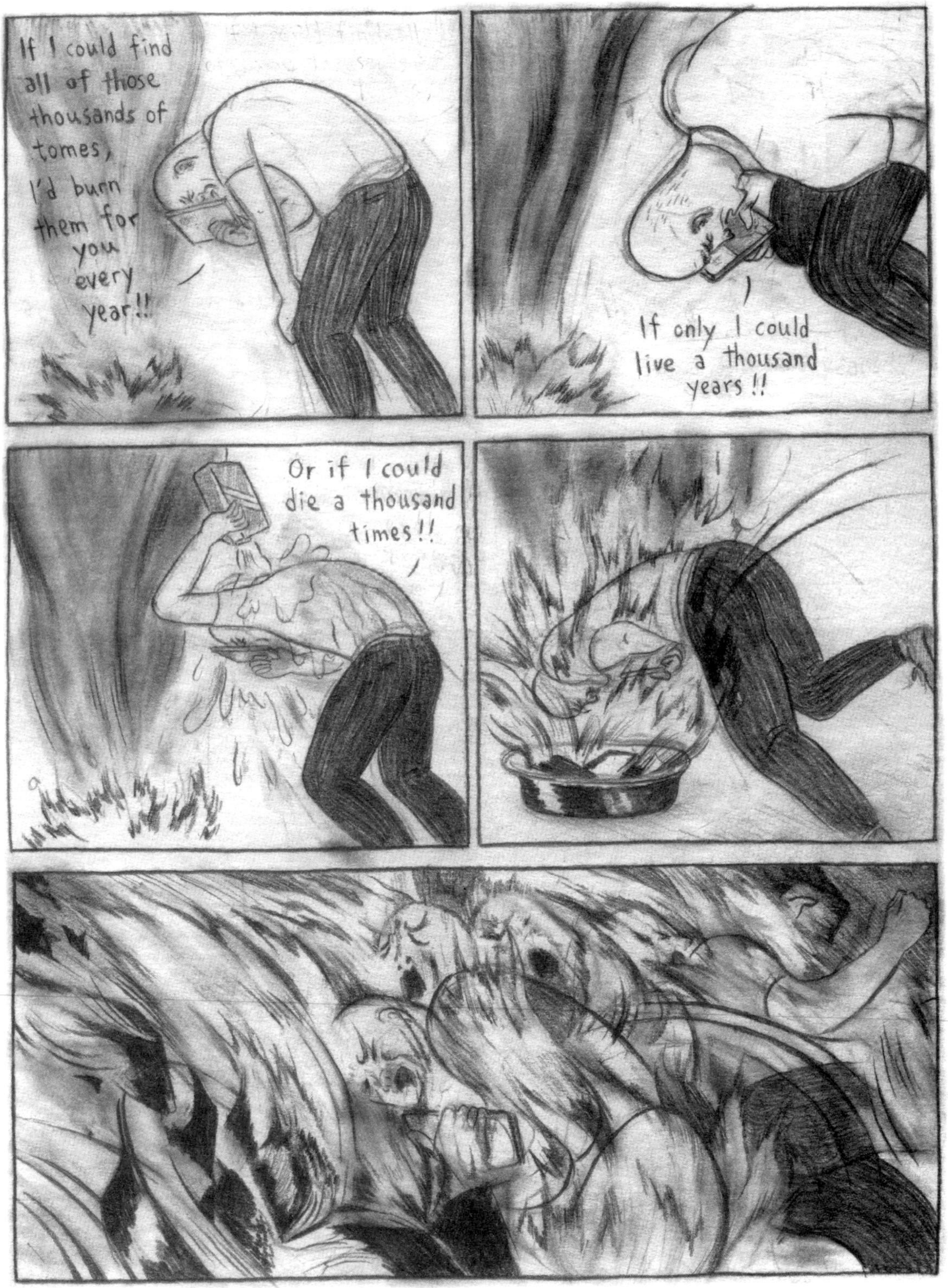
If I could find all of those thousands of tomes, I'd burn them for you every year!!
If only I could live a thousand years!!
Or if I could die a thousand times!!

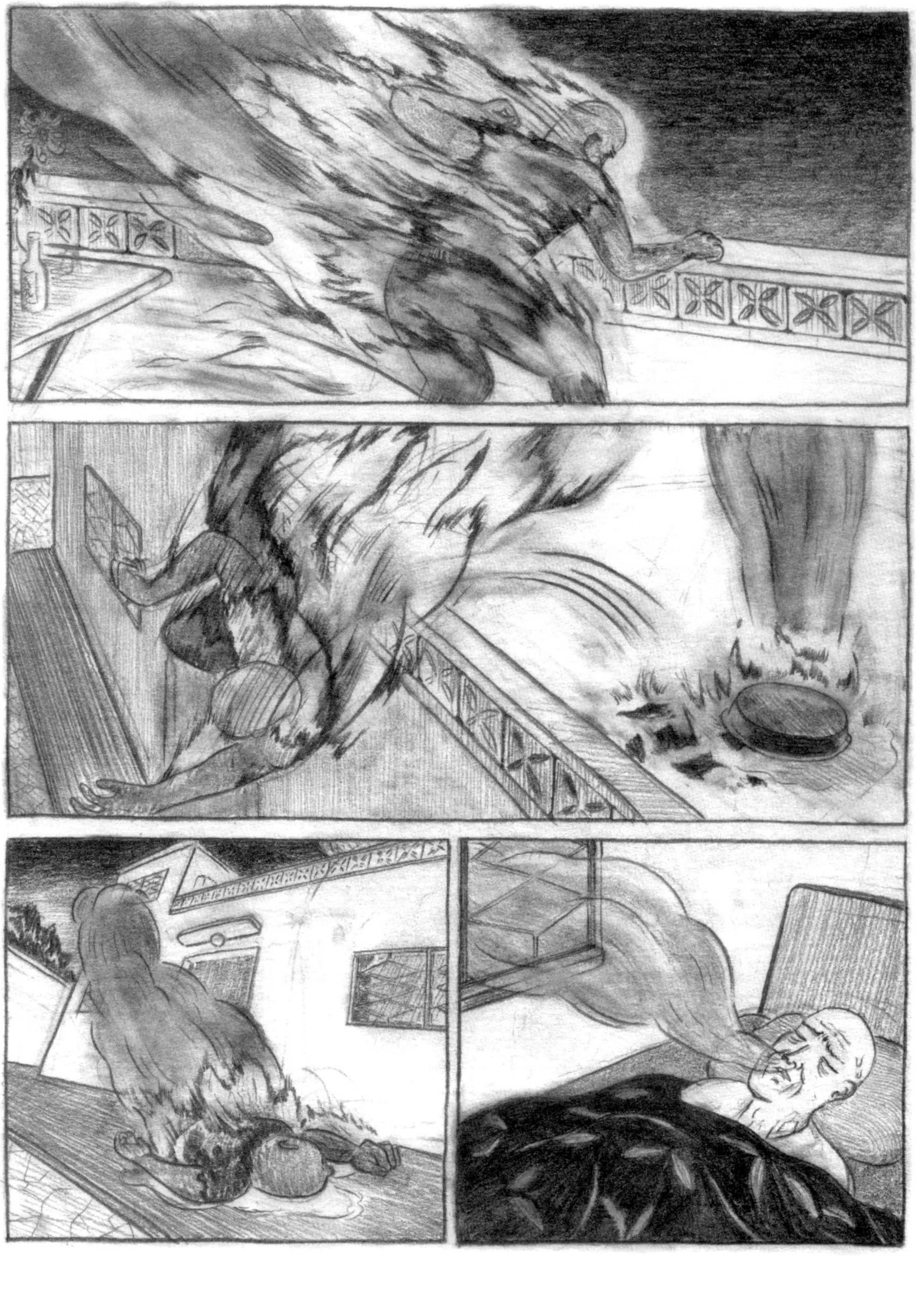

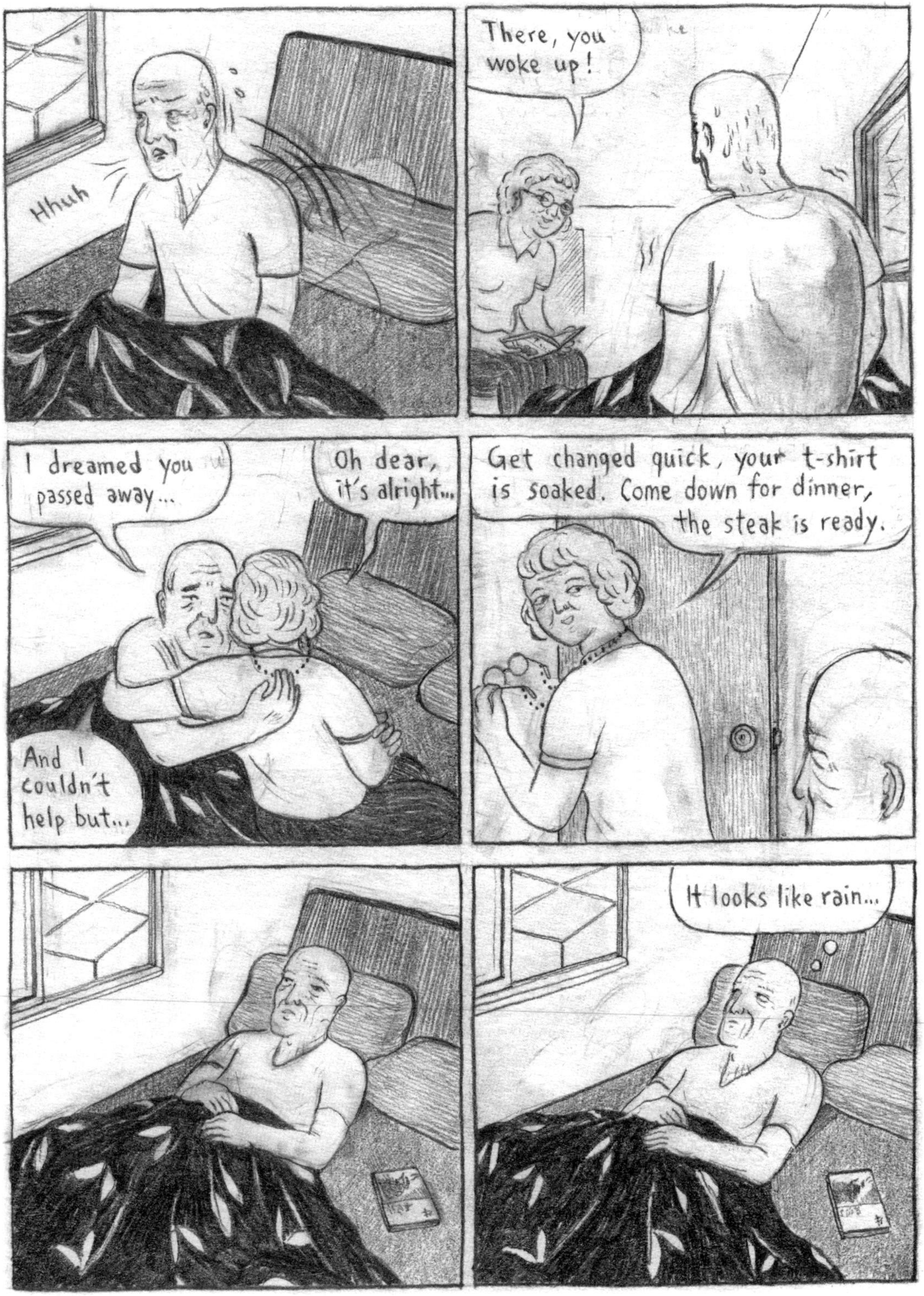
Hhuh
There, you woke up!
I dreamed you passed away...
Oh dear, it's alright...
And I couldn't help but...
Get changed quick, your t-shirt is soaked. Come down for dinner, the steak is ready.
It looks like rain...

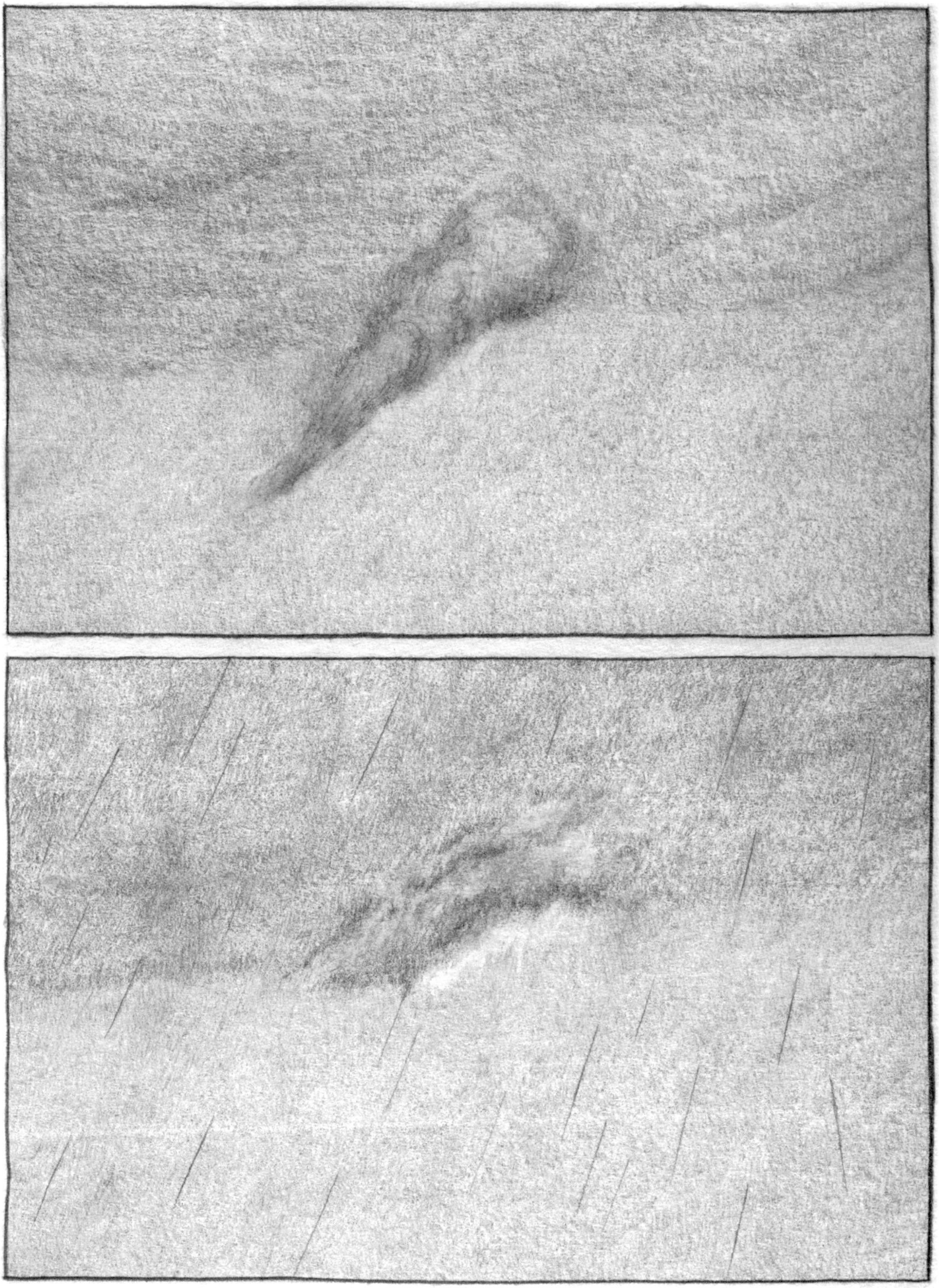
chihoi 2013